CAMBRIDGE UNIVERSITY PRESS.

SUBJECTS FOR CAMBRIDGE LOCAL EXAMINATIONS, 1892.

PITT PRESS SERIES.

De Vigny.—La Canne de Jonc. Edited with Notes by H. W. Eve, M.A. late Fellow of Trinity College, Cambridge, Head Master of University College School, London. *1s. 6d.*

Hauff.—Die Karavane. Edited with Notes by A. Schlottmann, Ph.D., late Assistant Master at Uppingham School. *3s.*

Goethe's Hermann und Dorothea. With an Introduction and Notes. By the late W. Wagner, Ph.D. New Edition. Revised by J. W. Cartmell, M.A., Fellow of Christ's College. *3s. 6d.*

Caesar. De Bello Gallico, Book I. with Maps and English Notes by A. G. Peskett, M.A., Fellow of Magdalene College. *1s. 6d.*

Vergil. Aeneid, Book II., with Notes by A. Sidgwick, M.A., Tutor of Corpus Christi College, Oxford. *1s. 6d.*

Cicero. Pro Murena. With English Introduction and Notes. By W. E. Heitland, M.A., Fellow and Classical Lecturer of St. John's College, Cambridge. *3s.*

Livy. Book XXI., with Notes and Introduction, by M. S. Dimsdale, M.A., Fellow of King's College. *2s. 6d.*

Xenophon. Anabasis, Book II., with English Notes by Alfred Pretor, M.A., Fellow of St. Catharine's College. *2s. 6d.*

Homer. Iliad, Book VI., with Introduction and Notes by G. M. Edwards, M.A., Fellow of Sidney Sussex College. *2s.*

Herodotus. Book IX., Chapters 1-89, with Notes, Introduction and Map, by E. S. Shuckburgh, M.A., late Fellow of Emmanuel College. *3s. 6d.*

Platonis Apologia Socratis. With Introductions, Notes and Appendices by J. Adam, M.A., Fellow and Lecturer of Emmanuel College. *3s. 6d.*

Milton's Paradise Lost. Books XI. and XII. Edited by A. W. Verity, M.A., sometime Scholar of Trinity College. [*Ready in April*

Geography, Elementary Commercial. A Sketch of the Commodities and the Countries of the World. By H. R. Mill, D.Sc., F.R.S.E., Lecturer on Commercial Geography in the Heriot-Watt College, Edinburgh. *1s.*

An Atlas of Commercial Geography. Intended as a Companion to the above. By J. G. Bartholomew, F.R.G.S. With an Introduction by Dr. H. R. Mill. *3s.*

PITT PRESS MATHEMATICAL SERIES.

Arithmetic for Schools. By C. Smith, M.A., Master of Sidney Sussex College, Cambridge. *3s. 6d.*

Elementary Algebra (with Answers to the Examples). By W. W. Rouse Ball, M.A., Fellow and Mathematical Lecturer of Trinity College, Cambridge. *4s. 6d.*

Euclid's Elements of Geometry. Books I and II. Edited by H. M. Taylor, M.A., Fellow and formerly Tutor of Trinity College, Cambridge. *1s. 6d.* Books III. and IV. By the same Editor. *1s. 6d.*

———— Books I.—IV. in one Volume. *3s.*

Elements of Statics and Dynamics. By S. L. Loney, M.A., late Fellow of Sidney Sussex College, Cambridge. *7s. 6d.*

Part I. ELEMENTS OF STATICS. *4s. 6d.*

Part II. ELEMENTS OF DYNAMICS. *3s. 6d.*

COMPLETE CATALOGUES ON APPLICATION.

LONDON: C. J. CLAY AND SONS,
Cambridge University Press Warehouse, Ave Maria Lane.

CAMBRIDGE UNIVERSITY PRESS.

SUBJECTS FOR CAMBRIDGE LOCAL EXAMINATIONS, 1892.

THE CAMBRIDGE BIBLE FOR SCHOOLS AND COLLEGES.

General Editor—THE BISHOP OF WORCESTER.

The Second Book of Kings. By the Rev. Professor LUMBY, D.D With Three Maps. 3*s*. 6*d*.

The Gospel according to St. Luke. By Archdeacon F. W. FARRAR, D.D. With Four Maps. 4*s*. 6*d*.

The same with Greek Text. By the same EDITOR. 6*s*.

The Acts of the Apostles. By the Rev. Professor LUMBY, D.D. With Four Maps. 4*s*. 6*d*.

The Epistle to the Ephesians. By the Rev. H. C. G. Moule, M.A. 2*s*. 6*d*.

The Epistle to the Philippians. By the Rev. H. C. G. MOULE, M.A. 2*s*. 6*d*.

THE SMALLER CAMBRIDGE BIBLE FOR SCHOOLS.

"All that is necessary to be known and learned by pupils in junior and elementary schools is to be found in this series. Indeed, much more is provided than should be required by the examiners. We do not know what more could be done to provide sensible, interesting, and solid Scriptural instruction for boys and girls. The Syndics of the Cambridge University Press are rendering great service both to teachers and to scholars by the publication of such a valuable series of books, in which slipshod work could not have a place."—*Literary World.*

"The notes are brief, but just what young students want, and we earnestly urge head teachers to insist upon their pupil-teachers using such of the books as bear upon their Scriptural syllabus."—*School Journal.*

The Second Book of Kings. By the Rev. Professor LUMBY, D.D. With Map. 1*s*.

The Gospel according to St. Luke. By Archdeacon F. W. FARRAR, D.D. With Map. 1*s*.

The Acts of the Apostles. By the Rev. Professor LUMBY, D.D. With Map. 1*s*.

EXAMINATION PAPERS FOR ENTRANCE AND MINOR SCHOLARSHIPS AND EXHIBITIONS IN THE COLLEGES OF THE UNIVERSITY OF CAMBRIDGE.

MICHAELMAS TERM, 1890.

PART I. **Mathematics and Science.** 2*s*.

PART II. **Classics, Mediæval and Modern Languages and History.** 2*s*.

LENT TERM, 1891.

PART III. **Mathematics and Science.** 2*s*.

PART IV. **Classics, Law, and History.** 2*s*.

COMPLETE CATALOGUES ON APPLICATION.

LONDON: C. J. CLAY AND SONS,
CAMBRIDGE UNIVERSITY PRESS WAREHOUSE, AVE MARIA LANE.

CHAPMAN AND HALL'S

SCIENCE AND ART PUBLICATIONS.

ELEMENTARY PHYSIOGRAPHIC ASTRONOMY. By J. MILLS. Crown 8vo. 1*s.* 6*d.*

ADVANCED PHYSIOGRAPHY. By J. MILLS. Crown 8vo. 4*s.* 6*d.*

ALTERNATIVE ELEMENTARY PHYSICS. By J. MILLS. Crown 8vo. 2*s.* 6*d.*

HANDBOOK OF QUANTITATIVE ANALYSIS. By J. MILLS and B. NORTH. Crown 8vo. 3*s.* 6*d.*

PRACTICAL METALLURGY. By A. R. GOWER, Royal School of Mines. Crown 8vo. 3*s.*

SCIOGRAPHY: or, Parallel and Radial Projection of Shadows. Being a Course of Exercises for the use of Students in Architectural and Engineering Drawing, and for Candidates preparing for the Examinations in this subject and in Third Grade Perspective, conducted by the Science and Art Department. By ROBERT PRATT, Head Master, School of Science and Art, Barrow-in-Furness. With numerous plates. Oblong 4to. 7*s.* 6*d.*

ELEMENTARY PRINCIPLES OF ORNAMENT. By J. WARD, Head Master of the Macclesfield School of Art. 8vo. 5*s.*

WOOD CARVING IN PRACTICE AND THEORY, as applied to Home Arts, with Notes on Design having Special Application to Carved Wood in Different Styles. By F. L. SCHAUERMANN. Preface by WALTER CRANE. With 124 Illustrations. 8vo. 7*s.* 6*d.*

DECORATIVE DESIGN. An Elementary Text-Book of Principles and Practice. By F. G. JACKSON. Fully Illustrated. Second Edition. Large Crown 8vo. 7*s.* 6*d.*

HAND-BOOK OF PERSPECTIVE. By H. A. JAMES, M.A. Cantab. With 75 Diagrams. Crown 8vo. 2*s.* 6*d.*

LONDON: CHAPMAN AND HALL, LIMITED,
AGENTS TO THE SCIENCE AND ART DEPARTMENT.

DIAGRAMS APPROVED BY THE SCIENCE AND ART DEPARTMENT.

METALLURGICAL LECTURE OR WALL DIAGRAMS. By Prof. W. H. GREENWOOD, M.Inst.C.E., Assoc.R.S.M. The Diagrams have been Designed for the use of Teachers and Lecturers upon Engineering, Metallurgy, and Technical Chemistry in Colleges, Technical Schools, and Science Classes; and, although accurate, and made to show considerable detail, they are yet sufficiently clear to admit of being understood by the most elementary student. 22 Sheets, Coloured, 30 inches by 40 inches, £2 10*s*. net.; on Rollers, £4 10*s*. net.

BUILDING CONSTRUCTION. By WILLIAM J. GLENNY. 10 Sheets, 31 in. by 23 in., £1 1*s*.; on Rollers, Varnished, £2 5*s*.

LAXTON'S EXAMPLES OF BUILDING CONSTRUCTION. 32 Imperial Plates, 20*s*.

BUSBRIDGE'S DRAWINGS OF BUILDING CONSTRUCTION. 36 Sheets, 9*s*.; mounted on cardboard, 18*s*.

OF THE STEAM-ENGINE. By Prof. GOODEVE and Prof. SHELLEY. 41 Diagrams, 52½ Sheets, Coloured, 40 in. long by 27 in. wide, £3 net.; on Rollers, £8 5*s*. net.

OF THE MECHANICAL POWERS. By DR. JOHN ANDERSON. Coloured, on Stout Paper, 3 ft. 6 in. by 2 ft. 6 in. 8 Diagrams, £1 net; on Rollers and Varnished, £2 net.

MACHINE DETAILS. Sixteen Coloured Diagrams. By Prof. UNWIN. 31 in. by 23 in., £2 2*s*.; on Rollers and Varnished, £3 14*s*.

ZOOLOGICAL. Illustrating the Classification of Animals. By R. PATERSON. 10 Coloured Diagrams, 42 in. by 31 in., £2; on Rollers, Varnished, £3 10*s*.

BOTANICAL. Illustrating a Practical Method of Teaching Botany. By PROF. HENSLOW. 9 Sheets, Coloured, 42 in. by 31 in., £2; on Rollers and Varnished, £3 3*s*.

LONDON: CHAPMAN AND HALL, LIMITED.
AGENTS TO THE SCIENCE AND ART DEPARTMENT.

b

THE GUARDIAN.

THE GUARDIAN is a Weekly Journal of Politics, Literature, Science, and the Fine Arts, Ecclesiastical, Home, Foreign, and Colonial News. Its promoters are Churchmen; and they endeavour to maintain that character in the treatment of Ecclesiastical subjects, and its Correspondence columns are open to all shades of opinion. Special reports are given of the Meetings of Convocation, Church Congress, and all important matters connected with the Church and Education. Great care is taken with the Parliamentary Intelligence. Special attention is paid to the Foreign and Colonial News, a full digest of which is given every week, illustrated by original correspondence. Every effort is made, in the selection of News, of Works chosen for review, and by the exclusion of all objectionable matter, to render THE GUARDIAN a good Family and Literary Newspaper.

The GUARDIAN is issued every WEDNESDAY AFTERNOON, price 6*d.*; by post, 6½*d.*, and is supplied regularly, post-free, direct from the Office to Subscribers *paying in advance only*, at—

		£	s.	d.
Per Quarter	(13 numbers)..............	0	7	0
„ **Half-Year**	(26 „)..............	0	13	6
„ **Year**	(52 „)..............	1	6	0

To Subscribers abroad—India and the East, £1 12*s.* 6*d.*, elsewhere £1 10*s.* per annum.

Advertisements must reach the Office **before 6 p.m.** on **Monday**, and in any urgent case of a short Advertisement **not later than 11 a.m.** on **Tuesday**, and payment made at the time, on the following scale:—

Three Lines and under		**Four Shillings.**
Every Additional Line		**Ninepence.**
Special Column	**Three Lines and under**	**Twelve Shillings.**
	Every Additional Line	**Two Shillings.**
Leader Page......	**Three Lines and under**	**Sixteen Shillings.**
	Every Additional Line	**Three Shillings.**

On an average three words may be reckoned for the first line, and eight words for each line afterwards, the address counting as part of the Advertisement; but all Advertisements are charged according to space occupied.

Notices of Testimonials, Births, Marriages, and Deaths are inserted at 3*s.* 6*d.* each for two lines, and a Shilling for every additional line.

All letters respecting Advertisements and Subscriptions should be addressed **"The Publisher," Guardian Office, 5, Burleigh Street, Strand, W.C.** Money and Postal Orders, on the Post Office, 369, Strand, should be made payable to JOHN JAMES; Orders and Cheques to be crossed "London and County Bank." Postage stamps can only be received at the rate of thirteen to the shilling. If a receipt is required for a sum under seven shillings a stamped envelope must be enclosed.

5, Burleigh Street, Strand, London, W.C.

"Guardian, London," is all the address necessary for telegrams.

INDEX TO ADVERTISERS.

Colleges, Schools, and Institutions.

Papers.

Publishers, etc.

SCHOLARSHIPS AND EXHIBITIONS, 1892

THE

SCHOOL CALENDAR

AND

HANDBOOK OF EXAMINATIONS

AND

OPEN SCHOLARSHIPS,

1892.

WITH A PREFACE

BY

F. STORR, B.A.,

Chief Modern Master, Merchant Taylors' School

SIXTH YEAR OF ISSUE.

LONDON:

WHITTAKER & CO., 2, WHITE HART STREET,

PATERNOSTER SQUARE, AND

GEORGE BELL & SONS, YORK ST., COVENT GARDEN.

1892.

CHISWICK PRESS:—C. WHITTINGHAM AND CO., TOOKS COURT,
CHANCERY LANE.

PREFACE.

THE chronicler of 1891, as far as secondary education is concerned, has little of importance to record. Among the heads of our great public schools there have been no changes, and in the schools themselves no marked vicissitudes or public scandals. The opening of the new buildings of Bedford Grammar School, erected at a cost of £25,000, marks the extraordinary growth of this popular day school which, under its energetic headmaster, Mr. J. S. Phillpotts, has increased from 250 to 800 pupils. The successes of Merchant Taylors' and St. Paul's Schools in scholarship examinations during the past two years are likewise significant, and lead us to expect an increasing demand for instruction which is at once cheaper and more efficient than that of boarding schools.

The passing of the Free Education Act cannot fail to have grave consequences, not only on primary education, a subject outside our province, but also on intermediate education. It will tend, on the one hand, to extinguish the inferior middle class schools, which since the creation of Board Schools in 1870 have been struggling for existence, and it will also, we can hardly doubt, give a fresh impulse to the agitation for middle-class schools to be subsidised by the rates or taxes. Such institutions are as much needed in England as in Wales, and a Government that has made a present of two millions a year to the working classes can hardly refuse to the class above them a boon that it has granted to the Principality.

The movement for the Registration of Teachers has advanced a stage. Two Bills with this object—one presented by the College of Preceptors, the other by the Teachers' Guild—were introduced in the House of Commons at the beginning of last Session and referred to a Select Committee of the House. The Special Report of this Committee, with the minutes of evidence, was published about the end of August. This is not the place to comment on the contentious matter involved in the rival Bills. One point only, and that by far the most important, can here be noticed. On the necessity of training for teachers, secondary as well as elementary—training of some sort, whether by apprenticeship or in special institutions, or as tested by examination, however acquired—the Committee, from its Chairman, Sir W. Hart Dyke, downwards, were virtually unanimous. This recognition by a Parliamentary Committee of the necessity of professional preparation marks a new departure, and its effect on public opinion is already visible. The headmasters who have hitherto ignored or sneered at the Teaching Diplomas of the University of Cambridge are beginning to send up their assistants for the examinations of the syndicate, or even to enter themselves.

But the matter which has engrossed the attention of the scholastic world and excited the greatest public interest during the past year has been the Greek question. To Mr. Welldon belongs the honour, or, according to Professor Freeman, the disgrace, of setting the ball rolling. His motion before the Headmasters' Conference, that it would be a gain to education if Greek were not a compulsory subject of education, was rejected by the narrow majority of two. Those at Cambridge who sympathised with Mr. Welldon's views, brought forward a grace in the Senate for the appointment of a Committee of Inqiury. This grace, which was virtually a trial of the main issue whether Greek was to be retained as a compulsory subject, was rejected by the overwhelming majority of 525 votes to 185. After so crushing a defeat it is not likely that the agitation will be revived in this generation. Again, without entering on the controversy, we may safely venture to point a moral. The advocates of Greek relied mainly on the argument that compulsory Greek at the Universities was the only guarantee for the retention of the study in schools. But Mr. Welldon's statistics show that in spite of the authority of Oxford and Cambridge, the schools have been drifting away to modern subjects, and that even in those schools which professedly prepare for the Universities, one half of the pupils are not at the present moment learning Greek. This tendency is certain to continue, and the newer Universities will profit by the restrictions which the older Universities have determined for better or for worse to retain. Let us hope that Oxford and Cambridge having taken their stand on Greek, will have the courage of their opinions, and make the study a reality instead of the wretched pretence that has made "Little-Go-Greek" a bye-word.

In the obituary of the year, we have to record the deaths of the Rev. R. H. Quick, sometime Master in Harrow School, and author of "Educational Reformers"; Archdeacon Balston, Headmaster of Eton College from 1862-68; Dr. Carpenter, F.R.S., Assistant-master of Eton; and Mr. W. H. Widgery, Assistant-master of University College School, a philologist of much promise. To these we must add the sudden and premature death of the Rev. W. Grundy, Headmaster of Malvern College.

F. Storr.

TABLE OF CONTENTS.

CALENDAR OF EXAMINATIONS, ETC.

1892.

JANUARY.

N.B.—The dates for returning forms, etc., given in the calendar, are those by which they must be sent in.

Jan. 1-3.—Coll. of Preceptors Diploma Exam. (Dec. 31, 1891 to Jan. 3, 1892).
„ 2.—Lond. Univ. B. Mus. Pass List pubd.
„ 3.—Last day for Notice Law Society's Prel. Feb. Exam.
„ 4-6.—Lond. Univ. Intermed. Laws and LL.B. Exams.
„ 4-9.—Trinity College, London, Higher Examinations for Diplomas and Certificates.
„ 5.—Edinburgh Term begins.
„ 5.—Owens Coll. Manch. Lent Term begins (Med.)
„ 6.—Return forms for King's College Entrance Examination.
„ 7.—Last day for Applications C.S. Exam. for Boy Clerks. 100 vacancies.
„ 7.—Bangor Adm. and Reg. of Students.
„ 8.—Exams. for Cambridge Univ. Schps. and Chancellor Classical Medals begin.
„ 8.—Cambridge Lent Term begins.
„ 9-10.—Liverpool, Univ. Coll. Entrance Exam.
„ 11.—Return forms for Durham 1st year Examination.
„ 11-15.—London University Matriculation Examination.
„ 12.—Applications sent in for R.C.M. Free Schps. Exam.
„ 12.—Pharmaceutical Soc. Preliminary Examination begins.
„ 12.—Adm. and Reg. of Students Bangor Univ. Coll.
„ 12.—Owens Coll. Manchester Term begins.
„ 12-13.—Law Society's Final Exam.
„ 12-14.—Coll. of Organists F.C.O. Exam.
„ 13.—King's College, London, Matriculation.
„ 14.—Oxford Hilary or Lent Term begins.
„ 14.—Law Society's Intermediate Examination.

Jan. 16.—Lond. Univ. Interm. Laws and LL.B. Pass Lists pubd.
„ 18.—London University Prel. Sc. and Int. Med. Exams.com.
„ 19-21.— „ „ Int. Laws, LL.B. Hons. LL.D. Ex.
„ 19.—Durham University Epiphany Term begins.
„ 19-21.—Coll. of Organists A.C.O. Exams.
„ 20.—Durham admission and 1st year in Arts and Theology Examinations begin.
„ 20.—St. David's Coll. Lampeter Matriculation.
„ 20.—Birmingham Mason Science Col. Adm.
„ 20.—C. S. Exam. for Boy Clerks. 100 appointments.
„ 22.—Lond. Univ. Univ. Prel. Sc. (M.B.) Exam. com.
„ 26.—Dublin University Entrance Examination.
„ 26-27.—Surveyors' Institution Preliminary Examination.
„ 29.—Cambridge University Matriculation.
„ 30.—Associated Boards of R.A.M., and R.C.M. Prel. Loc. Exam. Forms of Entry returned to Hon. Local Representative of Centres.

During January.

City and Guilds of London.—Finsbury Technical College (should vacancies occur).
Dublin.—King's and Queen's College of Physicians in Ireland —Membership and other Examinations.
Sheffield.—Firth College—Entrance and Scholarship.

FEBRUARY.

Feb. 1.—Notice to be given and Fee paid for Lond. D. Sc. Exam.
„ 1.—Lond. Univ. Last day for entry for D.Sc. Exam.
„ 1.—Apply for Ex. Papers (to Secy. of the Socy. of Arts) for Elem. Exams. at Instns. in connection with the Soc.
„ 3-4.—Law Society's Prel. Exam.
„ 5.—Lond. Univ. Int. (Med.) Exam. com.
„ 8.—Return Forms C.P. Prof. Prely. Exam.
„ 10.—Lond. Univ. Prelim. Sci. (M.B.) Pass List published.
„ 12.—Last day for Applications to C.S. Comrs. for Army Prel. Exam.
„ 15.—Applications must be made for substitutions under Reg. 17 of the Oxford and Cambridge Schools Exam. for Higher Certificates and under Reg. 19 for Lower Certificates before this date.
„ 16.—Lond. Univ. Int. Med. Pass List published.
„ 17.—Lond. Univ. Classified Matr. List published.
„ 17.—Committees to nominate a custodian of S. and A. Dept. Exam. Papers not later than Feb. 28.

Feb. 18.—Return forms for Apothecaries' Society Arts Exam.
„ 22.—Return forms for Durham Certificate Examination.
„ 23.—Return forms for Oxford Exam. for Women. 2nd Honours, Latin and Greek.
„ 23.—Send in notice and deposit articles for Law Society's Final Exam. Apl.
„ 23-25.—Elem. Exams. by Instns. in union with the Soc. of Arts.
„ 24.—Associated Board of R.A.M. and R.C.M. Prelim. Local Examinations begin.
„ 24.—Return forms and fees for Edinburgh Preliminary Exam. in Arts for Medical and Science Degrees.
„ 26.—Return forms for A.R.C.M. Exam.
„ 28.—Return forms for Irish Inter. Exams. (2*s.* 6*d.* stamps).

DURING FEBRUARY.

Royal College of Music.—Free Scholarships.

MARCH.

March 1.—Victoria University. Dissertations for M.D. degree to be sent in.
„ 1.—Return forms for Oxford and Cambridge Preliminary for Holy Orders.
„ 1-3.—Edinburgh Preliminary Examination in Arts for Medical and Science degrees.
„ 2.—*Ash Wednesday.*
„ 4-5.—Apothecaries' Society Arts Examination.
„ 6.—Apply for forms for Whitworth Schp. and Exhn. Exams. Sc. and Art. Dept., S.K.
„ 7.—Return form and deposit "Articles" for Law Society's Intermediate Apl. Exam.
„ 8.—Committees having Cands. for Exam. by the Society of Arts must apply on or before this date to Secretary of the Society.
„ 8-10.—C.P. Prof. Prely.
„ 9.—Army Prel. Exams. begin.
„ 9.—Return forms for Glasgow University Examination in General Education for Medical Students.
„ 10.—Oxford University Exam. for Women. 2nd Honours in Latin and Greek.
„ 11 (about).—St. Andrews' Prel. Exam. in Medicine and Science begin.
„ 11.—Send in names and addresses together with Subjects offered for Ordinary and Hon. Certificates to the Clerk of Senatus Edinburgh Univ., with fees and proof of having passed the Local Exams.

March 14.—Oxford Univ. Exam. for Women. 2nd Hons. in Nat. Science (Prely.), Physiology, Morphology, and Botany.

„ 14-18.—Surveyors' Institution Associate and Fellowship Exam.

„ 15.—Last day of application to C.S. Comrs. for Engineer Student's Exam. in Apl.

„ 17.—Oxford University Responsions begin.

„ 21.—Durham Epiphany Term ends.

„ 21.—Return forms for Socy. of Arts Genl. Exam.

„ 22.—Durham Certificate Examination begins.

„ 25.—*Lady Day.*

„ 25.—Glasgow University Examination in General Education for Medical Students begins.

„ 26.—Send applications to Local Secretaries for City and Guilds Institute Technological Examinations.

„ 26.—Application by Local Committees for local exam. papers must be made to Science and Art Department, S.K. for Art Examination, and Science Exam.

„ 28.—Cambridge Lent Term ends.

„ 28.—The Associated Board of the R.A.M. and R.M.C. Final Local Exam. is held not earlier than March 28.

„ 29.—Durham Preliminary Arts Exam. for M.B. begins.

„ 29.—Lond. Univ. Last day for applications for Examinerships.

„ 29.—Last day of application for C. S. Exams. for India Civil Service.

„ 30.—Return forms for Pharmaceutical Society Preliminary Examination.

„ 31.—Last day for applications for Examinerships to London University (after announcement of vacancies.)

„ 31.—Return forms for Irish Intermediate Examinations Board, Dublin (with late Stamp, 10*s.*).

„ 31.—Return Forms to Secy. of R. Agricl. for Senior Exam.

„ 31.—Newcastle Coll. of Medicine, Winter Session ends.

„ 31.—Edinburgh Royal College of Physicians and Surgeons Preliminary Examination begins.

APRIL.

April 1.—Return forms for St. Andrews, L.L.A., to Prof. Knight, the University, St. Andrews.

April 1.—Return forms with fees for Oxford Univ. 2nd Exam. (Pass) for Women and for 2nd Exam. (Honours).
„ 1.—Return forms for St. Andrew's Degree of M.A. and L.A. Certificate.
„ 2 (about).—Oxford and Cambridge Boat-race.
„ 4.—Local Secretaries send returns and fees to City and Guilds of Lond. Inst.
„ 4.—Return forms for Edinburgh R. C. of Physicians and Surgeons Preliminary Examination.
„ 4.—Last day for Notice Law Society's Prel. May Exam.
„ 4.—Lond. Univ. Last day for entry for M.B. Exam.
„ 4-7.—Edin. Univ. Ordin. Certif. in Arts Exam. for Women.
„ 4-7.—Society of Arts General Exam. (7 to 10 p.m.)
„ 5.—Prelim. Exam. for Candidates for Holy Orders.
„ 5-6.—Law Society's Final Exam.
„ 7.—Royal College of Music (A.R.C.M.) Examination.
„ 7.—Law Society's Intermediate Exam.
„ 8.—Edin. Univ. Hon. Certif. in Arts Exam. for Women begins.
„ 9.—Oxford Hilary Term ends.
„ 11.—Durham First Exam. for degrees, Medicine and Surgery.
„ 12.—Pharmaceutical Society Preliminary Examination begins.
„ 14.—Mason Science Col. Birmingham, Adm.
„ 15.—*Good Friday.*
„ 15.—Return forms (No. 330) for Whitworth Schp. and Exhn. Exam. to Sc. and Art Dept., S. Kensington.
„ 15.—Candidates for Whitworth Schps. to send in forms before this date.
„ 16.—St Andrews Graduation Ceremonial.
„ 17.—Edinburgh University Graduation Ceremonial.
„ 17.—*Easter Day.*
„ 18.— „ *Monday.*
„ 18.—Durham, Exam. for B. Degree Hygiene, &c. Second Exam. Med. and Surgery.
„ 19.—*Easter Tuesday.*
„ 19.—Cambridge Easter Term begins.
„ 19.—Further Exam. of Officers of Auxly. Forces for Commissions in the Army.
„ 20.—Return forms for Cambridge Higher Local.
„ 20.—Oxford Easter Term begins.
„ 20.—Return forms for King's College, London, Entrance Examination.
„ 20.—St. David's College, Lampeter, Matriculation.
„ 20.—Return forms for Yorkshire College Shps. Exam.

April 20.—Forms for Edin. Local Exams. may be obtained from the Clerk of Senatus Edin. Univ., and must be returned to him filled up by May 12.

„ 20.—Bangor Univ. Coll. Adm.

„ 20.—Return forms for Surveyors' Inst. Special (Members) Exams.

„ 23.—Return forms for Liverpool Univ. Coll. Scholarships and Studentships Exam.

„ 23.—Send in names, etc., for Liverpool, Univ. Coll. Schps. Exam.

„ 23.—Durham, Easter Term begins.

„ 25.—Durham, Final Exams. for Degrees, Med. and Surg. begin.

„ 27.—Return forms for London Uni. M.A., Branch I. and Branch IV.

„ 27.—King's College, London, Entrance Examination.

„ 27.—Lond. Univ. Election of Examiners.

„ 27.—Yorkshire College, Leeds, Scholarship Exam. begins.

„ 28.—Dublin University Entrance Examination.

„ 29.—Glasgow Uni. Graduation Ceremonial.

„ 30.—City and Guilds of London Institute Practical Typography, Weaving and Textiles, Practical Plumbing and Practical Part of Breadmaking Examinations (3 to 7 p.m.).

DURING APRIL.

Civil Service Competitions.—Eng. Stud. (in Navy). Dockyard Apprentices.

Science and Art Department. See pp. 14, 15.

MAY.

May 1.—Return forms with fees for Oxford 1st Examination for Women.

„ 1.—Return forms for Glasgow Local and Higher and Degree Exams.

„ 2.—Send in notice and deposit Articles for Law Society's Final Exam. June.

„ 2.—Royal Academy opens.

„ 2.—Newcastle Coll. of Medicine, Summer Session begins.

„ 2.—Lond. Univ. M.B. Exam. begins (Pass only).

„ 4.—**Return forms, etc., for London University Matriculation June Examination.**

„ 4.—City and Guilds of London Institution Technological Examinations (7 to 10 p.m.).

„ 4-5.—Law Society's Prel. Exam.

„ 5.—Return forms for Lond. Uni. M.A., Exam. Branch II.

„ 6.—Cambridge Univ. Matriculation.

May 7.—Send in notice and fees for Inst. Chartered Accountants Prel. Exam., June 7.

„ 9-14.—Liverpool Univ. Coll. Entrance Schps. and Studentships Exam.

„ 10.—Royal Agricl. Society's Senior Exam. begins.

„ 11.—Returns sent in specifying number and age in each class, and names and ages of Cands. for Certificates, with Fees, for **Oxford and Cambridge Schools Exam.**

„ 12.—Last day on which forms of entry for Oxford Local Exams. can be obtained from Local Secretaries.

„ 12.—C.P. Certificate return forms.

„ 12.—Return forms and pay Fees for Edinburgh Loc. Exam.

„ 12.—Return forms for Lond. M.A., Exam. Branch III.

„ 12.—Durham, send in Names for Final Exam.

„ 12.—**Return forms for Oxford Local Examination to Local Secretaries with Fees.**

„ 13.—London University Presentation Day.

„ 13.—Return forms and fees for St. Andrews Local Exam.

„ 15.—Return forms for Aberdeen Local and Higher Cert. for Women Exams.

„ 15.—Return forms for Royal University of Ireland Matriculation Examination.

„ 16.—Return forms, &c., Oxford 2nd Exam. for Women, Honours (Modern History, Nat. Sci., Final, and Literæ Humaniores).

„ 16—Return Forms, &c., Mathematics (on or before May 16).

„ 16.—Return forms and deposit "Articles" for Law Society's June Intermed. Exam.

„ 18-23.—Return Forms for **Oxford and Cambridge Schools Lower and Commercial Cert. Exam.**

„ 19.—Return forms for Apothecaries Society Arts Exam.

„ 20.—Return forms for Society of Arts (Music) Exam. Vocal and Instrumental.

„ 20.—Return Forms for Cambridge Teachers' Train. Synd.

„ 24.—Return Forms for Trinity College, London, Local (Musical Knowledge) Examination.

„ 26.—*Ascension Day.*

„ 30.—Society of Arts Music Examination (Voc. and Instrl.).

„ 31.—St. Andrews University Local Examination begins.

„ 31.—Glasgow Univ. Local Exams. and Higher and Certif. for Degrees (begin).

DURING MAY.

Yorkshire College, Leeds.—Last day for entering for Exam. about May 15.

Science and Art Department.—See pp. 14, 15.

SCIENCE AND ART DEPARTMENT, SOUTH KENSINGTON.

SCIENCE EXAMINATIONS.

April 30.—I.—Practical Plane and Solid Geometry, 6 to 10.
May 2.—VI*a*.—Theoretical Mechanics, Solids, 7 to 10.
" 3—VI*b*.— ——— Fluids, 7 to 10.
" 4.—XIV.—Animal Physiology, 7 to 10.
" 5.—VII.—Applied Mechanics, 7 to 10.
" 6.—XX.—Navigation, 7 to 10.
XII.—Geology, 7 to 10.
" 7.—II.—Machine Construction and Drawing, 6 to 10.
III.—Building Construction, 6 to 10.
IV.—Naval Architecture, 6 to 10.
" 9.—XXIII.—Physiography, 7 to 10.
" 10.—XVIII.—Principles of Mining, 7 to 10.
V.—Mathematics, Stages 6 and 7, 7 to 10.
XXIV.—Principles of Agriculture, 7 to 10.
" 11.—V.—Mathematics, Stages 1, 2, 3, 7 to 10-30.
" 12.—IX.—Magnetism and Electricity, including Alternative Elementary Physics, 7 to 10.
" 13.—VIII.—Sound, Light, and Heat, Elementary, 7 to 10.
VIII*a*.—Sound, Advanced Stage, and Honours, 7 to 10.
VIII*b*.—Light, Advanced Stage, and Honours, 7 to 10.
VIII*c*.—Heat, Advanced Stage, and Honours, 7 to 10.
" 14.—X*p*.—Practical Inorganic Chemistry, Elementary Stage, 6 to 9-30.
" 18.—V.—Mathematics, Stages 4 and 5, 7 to 10.
XXV.—Hygiene, 7 to 10.
" 19.—XI.—Organic Chemistry, 7 to 10.
XXII.—Steam, 7 to 10.
" 20.—X.—Inorganic Chemistry, including Alternative Elementary Chemistry, 7 to 10.
" 21.—X*p*.—Practical Inorganic Chemistry, Advanced Stage, 6 to 10-30; Honours, 2-30 to 10-30.
" 23.—XIX*p*.—Practical Metallurgy, Elem. Stage, 7 to 10.
" 24.—XIX*p*.—Practical Metallurgy, Advanced Stage, 6 to 10; Honours, 2 to 10.
" 25.—XVI. and XVII.—Biology, 7 to 10.
XIX.—Metallurgy, 7 to 10.
" 26.—XV.—Botany, 7 to 10.
" 27.—XIII.—Mineralogy, 7 to 10.
XXI.—Nautical Astronomy, 7 to 10.

N.B.—In order that the examinations may be held simultaneously in Great Britain and Ireland they will commence in Ireland half-an-hour by Dublin time, earlier than the times given on the Time Tables.

SCIENCE EXAMS.—*continued.*

May 28.—XIp.—Practical Organic Chemistry, Elementary Stage, 6 to 9-30; Advanced Stage, 6 to 10-30; Honours, 2-30 to 10-30.

ART EXAMINATIONS.

Second Grade Examinations.

April 28.—Model Drawing, 7 to 8.
Freehand Drawing, 8-20 to 9-50.
„ 29.—Perspective, 7 to 8-30.

Third Grade Examinations.

„ 29.—Anatomy, 7 to 10.
May 2.—Drawing in Stage 5*a*, 7 to 9-30.
„ 3.—Drawing in Stage 3*b*, 7 to 9-30.
„ 4.—Drawing in Stage 5*b*, 6 to 10.
„ 5.—Sciography, 7 to 10.
Drawing from the Antique, 6 to 10.*
„ 6.—Elementary Principles of Ornament, 7 to 10.
Composition from a given Figure Subject, with or without ornament in some one Historic style (23*d*.), 6 to 10.
„ 7.—Painting from Still Life, 10 a.m. to 4 p.m.†
Perspective, 6 to 10.
„ 9.—Drawing from the Life, 6 to 10.
„ 10.—Architectural Historic Ornament, 7 to 10.
„ 11.—Elementary Architecture, 6 to 10.
Historic Ornament, 7 to 10.
„ 12.—Design Ornament. 23*c*, 6 to 10.
„ 13.—Drawing from Memory one of the following Antique figures, the Standing Discobolus, Germanicus, Antinous, or Dancing Faun, 7 to 8.
Painting Ornament in Monochrome (in oil or tempera only) from a Sketch or Photograph.
„ 14.—Plant Drawing in Outline, Stage 10*a*, 7 to 10.
„ 16-18.—Architectural Design Group 6, 10 a.m. to 4 p.m.†

JUNE.

June 1.—Return forms for Victoria University Prel. Arts, Science and Law and First M.B. Exams.

---

* This examination in Drawing from the Antique will be allowed only at Schools of Art having four whole length figures.

† On the 7th and the 16th to the 18th May, the six hours 10 a.m. to 4 p.m. include half an hour allowed for refreshment.

June 1-2.—St. Andrews University Local Examination (cont.)
„ 1-3.—Glasgow Univ. Local Exams. and Higher and Certif. for Degrees (cont.).
„ 2.—Oxford University Exam. for Women, 2nd Honours, in Mechcs. and Physics and Chemy.
„ 2-4.—Edinburgh University Local Examination.
„ 3.—Oxford Easter Term ends.
„ 3-4—Apothecaries' Society Arts Examination.
„ 4.—Eton Commemoration Day.
„ 4.—Oxford Trinity Term begins.
„ 5.—*Whitsun Day.*
„ 5.—Return forms for C. P. Diploma Examination.
„ 6.—*Monday in Whitsun week.*
„ 6.—London Univ. M.A. Branch I. (Classics) Exam. begins.
„ 6.—Last day of Notice for Law Society's Prel. July Ex.
„ 6.—Oxford University Exam. for Women. 2nd (Honours) Mod. History and Literæ Humaniores.
„ 6.—Cambridge University Previous Exam. Part I. begins. General Exam. begins.
„ 7.—*Tuesday in Whitsun week.*
„ 7-9.—Inst. of Chartered Accountants Prel. Exam.
„ 8.—Durham Classical (Pass) begins.
„ 8.—Army Prel. Exams. begin.
„ 9.—Oxford Univ. 2nd Exam. in Maths (Hons.) for Women.
„ 9.—C.S. Comrs. Exam. for Naval Cadetships.
„ 9.—Cambridge Univ. Prev. Exam. Part II. begins.
„ 10.—Return form 400 for Whitworth Scholarships and Exhibs. to S. and A. Dept. South Kensington, before June 10.
„ 10.—Durham, Final Exam. Science begins.
„ 11.—Durham, Exam. B.A. (Honours and Theol.) and L. Th. (Honours and Pass) begin.
„ 11.—Lond. Univ. M.B. Int., Med. (Pass and Hon.).
„ 11.—St. David's Coll. Lampeter Responsions.
„ 11.—Return forms for Bristol Coll. Ent. Schp. Exam.
„ 11.—Cambridge Univ. Prev. Exam. additional subjects.
„ 11.—Cambridge Univ. Term ends.
„ 12.—*Trinity Sunday.*
„ 13.—Lond. Univ. M.A. Examination Branch II. (Mathematics) begins.
„ 13.—Oxford University Examination for Women, 1st Exam. Also 2nd Exam. (Pass). (*See* p. 38).
„ 13.—Soc. of Accountants Exams. begin.
„ 13.—C.P. Mercantile Certificates Exam.
„ 13-17.—London University Matriculation Examination.
„ 14.—Irish Intermediate Examinations begin.

June 14.—Victoria University, Manchester, Entrance Examination in Arts (Medical) begins.

„ 14-15.—Law Society's Final Exam.

„ 14-15.—Institute Chartered Accountants' Intermediate Examination.

„ 14-16.—Surveyors' Inst. Special (Members) Exam.

„ 14-17.—C. P. Pupils' Certificate Exam.

„ 15.—Return forms for London University Intermediate B.A. and B.Sc., and Preliminary Science M.B.

„ 15.—Return forms for London University Intermediate (M.B.).

„ 15.—Latest date for forms, Aberdeen Local Prel. and Higher Cert. for Women.

„ 15.—Return form No. 396 for Whitworth Schps. and Exhibs. to Sc. and Art Dept., S. Kensington.

„ 16.—Oxford University Responsions begin.

„ 16.—Victoria University Preliminary Examinations begin.

„ 16.—Law Society's Intermediate Exam.

„ 16.—Dublin University Entrance Examination.

„ 18.—Return forms for Trinity College London (Music) Higher Examination.

„ 19.—Cambridge Univ. Commencement Sunday.

„ 20.—London Univ. M.A. (Mental and Moral Science) Branch III. Examination begins.

„ 20.—Accession of Queen Victoria, 1837.

„ 20.—Owen's Coll. Ent. Exam. Medicine.

„ 20-25.—**Cambridge University Higher Local Examination.**

„ 21.—Aberdeen Local and Higher Certif. for Women Examinations begin.

„ 21.—Durham Easter Term ends.

„ 21.—Cambridge Univ., Commencement Tuesday.

„ 21-23.—Inst. Chartered Accountants' Final Exam.

„ 21-23.—St. Andrew's L.L.A. Examination.

„ 22.—The Encænia or Commemoration of Founders and Benefactors at Oxford University.

„ 23.—R.M.A. (Woolwich) further Exam. begins.

„ 23.—Oxford Univ. 2nd Exam. in Mathematics (Hons.) for Women.

„ 24.—Cambridge Easter Term ends. Midsummer Day.

„ 24.—Bristol Univ. Coll. Entr. Schps. Exam.

„ 24.—Trinity College London (Music) Local Examination in Mus. Knowledge begins.

„ 24-25.—Dublin University Entrance Exam.ations (Midsummer).

„ 27.—London University M.A. Languages (B. IV.) Examination begins.

June 27.—Return forms for Edinburgh Royal College of Physicians Preliminary Examination.

„ 28.—Return forms for Pharmaceutical Preliminary July Examination.

„ 29.—R.M.C. Sandhurst Further Exam. begins.

„ 30.—Oxford *v.* Cambridge cricket match at Lords' begins.

DURING JUNE.

Civil Service Competitions.—India, India Forest Service, Naval Assist. Clerks, Cadets, &c.

London University.—D. Sc. (within the first twenty-one days in June).

Royal University of Ireland.—Matriculation (Pass and Honours) and Arts Examinations begin towards the end of June. First University (Early in June). Second University (The end of June).

Teachers' Train. Synd., Cambridge.

Royal College of Science, Dublin.—Sessional Exams. First Week.

Guildhall School of Music.—Students' Certificate of Proficiency (Associate) Examination.

Queen's College School.—Presentation.

Scotch Ed. Dept.—Examination Leaving Certificates for Higher Schools.

Nottingham University College.—Examination Open Scholarships.

Sheffield, Firth College.—Examination Earnshaw's Scholarship.

JULY.

July 1-2.—Edinburgh Royal College of Physicians and Surgeons Preliminary Examination.

„ 5.—C.P. Diploma Exams. begin.

„ 5-8.—C.P. Diploma Examination.

„ 6.—Royal Holloway College, Egham, Exam.

„ 6.—Scotch Ed. Dept. Exam. for Admission to Training Colleges.

„ 6-7.—Law Society's Prel. Exam.

„ 7.—Return forms for Coll. of Organists, A.C.O. and F.C.O. Exam.

„ 8.—Eton *v.* Harrow cricket match at Lords' begins.

„ 9.—Oxford Trinity Term ends.

„ 11.—London University Int. Med. Exam. (Pass and Hons.) begins.

„ 11-16.—Trinity College London (Music) Higher Exams. for Diplomas and Certificates.

„ 11-16.—Oxford Local Examination.

July 11-23.—**Oxford and Cambridge Schools Examination Board's Higher Certificate Examination.**

„ 12.—Pharmaceutical Preliminary Examination begins.

„ 12.—Coll. of Organists F.C.O. Diploma Exam. begins.

„ 18.—London University Prel. Sci. M.B. (Pass and Honours) Int. B.A. and Int. B.Sc. Examinations begin.

„ 18-23.—**Oxford and Cambridge Schools Examination Board's Lower and Commercial Certificate Examination.**

„ 19-21.—Coll. of Organists A.C.O. Exams.

„ 20.—Lond. Matr. Classified List published.

„ 27.—Rugby *v.* Marlboro' cricket match at Lords' begins.

„ 30.—Newcastle Coll. of Medicine, Summer Session ends.

During July.

Royal University of Ireland.—B.A. (Early in July). Engineering (Towards the middle of July).

Froebel Union and Kintergarten Co. Exam. for Certificates.

AUGUST.

Aug. 1.—Bank Holiday. Royal Academy closes.

„ 6.—Return forms for C.P. Prof[l]. Prel. Exam. Sept.

„ 10.—Lond. Univ. Inter. Arts and Prel. Sc. Lists published.

„ 15.—Cambridge Local Forms ready (to Sept. 30).

„ 15.—Return forms for Royal University of Ireland Matriculation Examination (Pass only).

„ 19.—Return forms for Apothecaries' Society Arts Exam.

„ 27.—Return for Durham Cert. of Proficiency.

„ 27.—Return for Durham Prel. Arts Exam.

During August.

Civil Service Competitions.—Cadets for Ceylon, Hongkong, etc.

SEPTEMBER.

Sept. 1.—Return forms for Oxford and Cambridge Preliminary Examination for Holy Orders.

„ 1.—Return forms for the Univ. Colleges of Aberystwith, Bangor and Cardiff Scholarship Examinations.

„ 2-3.—Apothecaries Society Arts Examination begins.

„ 6-8.—C.P. Professional Preliminary Examination begins.

„ 9.—Return forms for Victoria University, Manchester, Preliminary and Entrance Examinations.

„ 12.—Durham, First Exams. for Degrees in Med. and Surg. begin.

„ 14.—Army Prel. Exams. begin.

„ 12.—Return for City and Guilds Central Institute and Technical College.

Sept. 14.—Return forms for London Univ. B. Sc. Exam.
„ 14-20.—Return forms for Glasgow University Examination in General Education (Medical Students); also for B. Sc., and B. L.
„ 15.—Aberystwith and Cardiff University Colleges Schp. Exams. begin.
„ 15-18.—Bangor Univ. College Scholarship Examination.
„ 17.—Return forms for Durham College of Science, Newcastle, Matriculation and Exhibition Examinations.
„ 18 (about).—Victoria Univ., Manchester Entr. in Arts (Med.) begins.
„ 19.—Send in names for St. David's College, Lampeter Scholarship Examination.
„ 19.—Return forms for Scholarship Exam. St. David's College, Lampeter.
„ 19.—Durham, Exam. for B. in Hygiene and 2nd Exam. for Degrees in Medicine and Surgery begin.
„ 19.—Last Day of Notice for Law Society's Oct. Prel. Ex.
„ 21.—Return forms for Lond. Univ. B.A. Exam.
„ 21-24.—City and Guilds Institute, Entrance Exam.
„ 24.—Return forms for King's College London Scholarship Examination (about this date).
„ 25.—Firth Coll. Sheffield. Entrance Exam.
„ 26.—Victoria University, Manchester, Prely. Exam. (Arts, Sc., Medicine and Law) begins.
„ 26.—Return forms for Edin. R. C. of Phys. and Surgs. Prel. Ex.
„ 26.—Owen's Coll. Manchester. Entrance Exam. Medicine.
„ 26.—Durham College of Science (Newcastle-on-Tyne. Matriculation and Exhibition Examinations begin).
„ 27.—Durham Cert. of Proficiency Exam. begins.
„ 27.—St. David's College Lampeter Scholarships Examination (about this date).
„ 27.—Durham Preliminary Arts Exams. for (M.B.) begin.
„ 27.—Return forms for Pharmaceutical Society Preliminary Examination.
„ 28.—Oxford University Responsions begin.
„ 28.—Return forms for Edinburgh Preliminary Examination (Medicine and Science).
„ 29.—Michaelmas Day.
„ 29.—Durham, 1st Exam. for Degrees in Music begins.
„ 29.—Bangor Univ. Coll. N. Wales Adm.
„ 30.—**Return forms for Cambridge Local and Commercial Certif. Examination.**
„ 30.—Glasgow Exam. in General Education for Med. Studs. and Prely. for Degrees in Science.
„ 30.—Dundee Univ. Col. Return forms Exam.

DURING SEPTEMBER.

Royal University of Ireland (Dublin).—Matriculation Exam. (Pass) and First University (Pass) begin end of this month.
Mason College, Birmingham.—Scholarships Exam.
St. David's Coll. Lampeter.—Exam. begins about Sept. 28.
Yorkshire College, Leeds.—Exam. Chem., Physics, Bibl.
Manchester Technical School.—Exam. Entrance Scholarships early in Sept.
Queen's College, Harley Street.—Scholarships Exam.

OCTOBER.

Oct. 1.—Mason Coll. Adm.
„ 1.—Cambridge Michmaelmas Term begins.
„ 1.—Durham 1st Year Exam. Cands. send in their names.
„ 1.—Edinburgh, latest day for return of forms for Ord. Cert. in Arts for Women; also for Honours Cert. in Arts for Women.
„ 1.—Victoria University, First M.B. Exam.
„ 1.—Cambridge University Previous Exam. Additional Subjects begins.
„ 2.—King's Coll. Lond. Matr. Exam.
„ 3.—Cambridge Univ. Previous Exam. Part I.
„ 4.—St David's Coll. Lampeter Matriculation (about this date).
„ 4-7.—Edinburgh Prel. Exam. in Arts for Med. and Science Degrees.
„ 6.—Cambridge Univ. Previous Exam. Part II. begins.
„ 7.—Royal University, Ireland, Scholarship Examinations begin about this date.
„ 9-10.—Dundee Univ. Coll. Scholarships Examination.
„ 10.—Return forms and deposit "articles" for Law Society's Novr. Intermed. Exam.
„ 10.—Durham Michaelmas Term begins.
„ 10.—Oxford Michaelmas Term begins.
„ 10.—Dublin University Entrance Examination.
„ 11.—Prelim. Exam. for Candidates for Holy Orders.
„ 11.—Pharmaceutical Society Preliminary Examination.
„ 11-14.—Edinburgh Ord. Cert. in Arts for Women.
„ 12.—Durham Adm. and first year in Arts Examinations begin.
„ 13.—Return forms for Aberdeen Bursary Examinations.
„ 14.—Durham Final Exam. Theol. B.A.
„ 15.—Aberdeen Arts Bursary Examinations begin (about this date).

Oct. 15.—Send notice of entering for Royal Agricl. Society's Junior Schp. Exam. in November.

„ 17.—Notice of entry and *Musical Exercise* for Lond. Univ. B. Mus. and D. Mus. Exam.

„ 17.—Edinburgh University, Entrance and Bursaries in Arts Examinations, about this date.

„ 17.—London University B.Sc. Examination begins.

„ 18.—Glasgow Univ. Give in names for Bursary Exams. in Arts, on or before this date.

„ 19.—Send in notice for R.A.M. Licentiate Diploma (L.R.A.M.) Exam.

„ 19.—Notice given for London University Examination in Teaching.

„ 19-21.—Law Society's Prel. Exam.

„ 20.—Dublin University Entrance Examination.

„ 21.—Cambridge Univ. Matriculation.

„ 24.—London University B.A. Examination (Pass) begins.

„ 24.—Glasgow Univ. Gen. Exam., Bursaries in Arts begins.

„ 31.—London University M.B. Exam. begins (Pass & Hons.).

„ 31.—Return Forms for Cambridge Higher Local Dec., 1892

During October.

Oxford and Cambridge.—Preliminary Examination for Holy Orders.

Owens College, Manchester. — Scholarship and Exhibition Examinations (beginning of the month).

Queen's College, Birmingham.—Queen's Scholarships Examination begins.

Civil Service Competitions.—Preliminary and Further Exams. for Officers in Auxiliary Forces.

Royal University of Ireland.—M.A. (about the beginning).

Firth College Sheffield.—Entrance Exam.

City Guilds Institute, Finsbury Technical College.—Exams. Entrance and Saddlers' Scholarships.

Edinburgh Royal College of Physicians and Surgeons.—Prely. Exam. begins.

Aberdeen University.—Exams., Medicine and Law.

Dublin University.—Scholarships.

NOVEMBER.

Nov. 1.—*All Saints' Day.*

„ 1.—Return forms with fees for Oxford 1st Examination for Women.

„ 1.—Return forms for Oxford Exam. for Women, 2nd Honours Nat. Sci. Prely.

„ 1.—Dublin University Entr. Exam.

„ 1.—Return forms for C.P. Cert. Exam.

Nov. 5.—Return Forms for Cam. Teachers' Train. Synd.
,, 6.—Ret. Forms for Inst. Chartered Accts. Prel. Exam.
,, 6.—Camb. Univ. Commemoration of Benefactors.
,, 7.—Certs. sent in for Lond. Univ., M. S., and M.D. Exams.
,, 8-9.—Law Society's Final Exam.
,, 8-9.—Royal Agri. Society's Junior Scholarship's Exam.
,,10-11.—Glasgow Univ. Gen. Exams. for Theol. Bursaries.
,, 10.—Law Society's Intermed. Exam.
,, 10.—Durham, send in Names for Final Exams.
,, 11.—Return forms for Trinity College, London, Local Musical Knowledge Exam.
,, 18.—Return forms, &c., Oxford 2nd Exam. for Women, Honours (Mathematics), on or before Nov. 18.
,, 18.—Return forms for Apothecaries Arts Examination.
,, 19.—London Univer. B.A. and B. Sc. Pass Lists published.
,,21-23.—Lond. Univ. B.A. Exam. (Honours).
,, 24.—Certs. sent in of Lon. Univ. B. S.
,, 24.—Oxford University Exam. for Women, 2nd Honours in Mechs., Physics, Chemy. (Final in June only).
,, 27.—*First Sunday in Advent.*
,,29-30.—London Univ. Scriptural Exams.
,, 30.—Send notice and deposit articles for Law Society's Final Exam., Jan. 1892.
,, 30.—Surveyors' Inst. Return forms for Prelim. Associate and Fellowship Exams.

During November.

Civil Service Competitions.—Assistant Clerks in Navy; Excise Assistants (Probably); Naval Cadets.
R. M. A. (*Woolwich*).—Further Examination.
R. M. C. Sandhurst.—Further Examination.
Aberdeen University.—Divinity Examination.

DECEMBER.

Dec. 2-3.—Apothecaries' Society Arts Examination.
,, 3.—Durham, Exams., B.A. (Honours and Theol.) and L. Th. (Hons. and Pass) begin.
,, 5.—Lond. Univ. M.S. and M.D. Exam.
,, 5.—C.P. Mercantile Certificates Exam.
,, 5.—Cambridge Univ. Previous Exam. Part I. begins.
,, 5.—Soc. Accountants, Exams. begin.
,, 6.—Lond. Univ. D. Lit. Exam.
,, 6.—Lond. Univ. B.S. Exam. (Pass).
,, 6.—Oxford Univ. Exam. for Women 2nd Hons. Nat. Sc. (Prely.) Physiology, Morphology and Botany.
,, 6-8.—Inst. of Chartered Accountants Prel. Exam.
,, 6-9.—C.P. Pupils' Exam.

Dec. 7.—Return Forms for London Matriculation Exam.
„ 7.—Certificates sent in for Lond. Univ. Int. Laws and LL.B. Exam.
„ 8.—Cambridge Previous Exam. Part II. begins.
„ 8.—Oxford University Responsions begin.
„ 11 (about).—Trinity College, London (Music), Local Exam. in Mus. Knowledge begin.
„ 12.—Return Forms for Trin. Coll. Lond. (Music) Higher Exams.
„ 12.—Lond. Univ. Int. B. Mus. and Int. D. Mus. Exam. begins.
„ 12-17.—**Cambridge Local Examinations (begin 2 p.m. on 12th).**
„ 12-17.—Cambridge Higher Local in Languages and Mathematics (Groups B and C), open to all persons qualified to enter in June, 1892.
„ 13.—Oxford University 1st Examination for Women.
„ 13.—Lond. Univ. Exam. in Teaching.
„ 13.—Durham Michaelmas Term ends.
„ 13-14.—Inst. Chartered Accountants Intermed. Exam.
„ 14.—Army Prely. Exams. begin.
„ 14.—Send in notice and deposit articles for Law Society's Intermed. Exam.
„ 15.—Oxford Univ. 2nd Exam. in Mathcs. (Hons.) for Women.
„ 15.—Lond. Univ. B.S. Exam. (Honours).
„ 15.—Notice sent in for London LL.D. Exam.
„ 17.—Oxford Michaelmas Term ends.
„ 19.—Cambridge Michaelmas Term ends.
„ 19.—Lond. Univ. B. Mus. and D. Mus. Exam. begins.
„ 20-22.—Inst. Chartered Accountants Final Exam.
„ 21.—Return Forms and Certificate of Birth sent in for Lond. Univ. Matric. (Jan. 1893).
„ 21.—Notice to be sent in for Lond. Univ. Prel. Sci. M.B. (Jan. 1893).
„ 25.—*Christmas Day.*
„ 28.—Return Forms for Pharmaceutical Prelim. Exam.
„ 31.—Return forms for Coll. of Organists Exams.

During December.

Scotch Ed. Dept.—Exam. Teachers' Certificate of Merit.
Royal Academy of Music.—Metropolitan Exam. for Licentiate Diploma (L.R.A.M.).
Trinity College London (Music).—Local Exam. in Musical Knowledge.
Teachers' Train. Synd.—Cambridge.

LOCAL, PRELIMINARY, AND ENTRANCE EXAMINATIONS

OF

UNIVERSITIES, COLLEGES, AND PROFESSIONAL EXAMINING BODIES

DURING THE YEAR 1892.

ALPHABETICALLY ARRANGED.

Giving the Dates, Fees, Limits of Age, &c.

FOR SCHOLARSHIPS AND EXHIBITIONS

CONNECTED WITH THE ABOVE,

See pages 42, 105, *et sq.*

LOCAL AND OTHER EXAMINATIONS, 1892.

University, Local, &c.	*Examinations.*	*Dates.*	*Latest date for returning forms.*	*Fees.*	*Age Limit.*
Aberystwith.					
University College of Wales.	Entrunce Scholarship.	Sept. 15 ...	Sept. 1 ...	No fee	16 (above).
Principal.—Prof. T. F. Roberts, M.A.					
Registr. and Librar., E. P. Jones, Esq., M.A., B.D.					
Aberdeen.					
The University ...	Local Preliminary	June 21 ...	May 15 ...	7*s.* 6*d.*	No limit specified.
Assist.-Sec., Charles Michie, Esq., M.A.,	,, Junior ...			12*s.* 6*d.*	
Marischal Col. Lib.	,, Senior ...			20*s.*	
	Higher Certificate for Women.	June 21 ...	May 15 ...	21*s.* per subject.	
Bangor.					
University College of North Wales.	Adm. and Reg. of Students (no examination).	Jan. 12, Apr. 20, Sept. 29.	... ...	£1 1*s.* ...	16 and over.
Sec. and Registrar, W. C. Davies, Esq.	Entrance Scholarship.	Sept. 15-18 ...	Sept. 1... ...	No fee. ...	

N.B.—Unless otherwise specified, the age given in the last column is that which may not be exceeded.

Birmingham. Mason Science College. Sec., G. H. Morley.	Adm. of Students (no examination).	Jan. 20. April 14, Oct. 1.			
	Entrance Scholarships, and for Students if under 16.	September ...	10 days prev. ...	... ...	18.
Bristol. University College. Sec., Jas. Rafter, Esq.	Scholarships	June 24 ...	June 11 ...	No fee	16 and over.
Cambridge. The University ... Sec.—Professor G. F. Browne, B.D., Syndicate Buildings, Cambridge. Assistant Secs.— For Exams.—J. N. Keynes, M.A. For Lectures.—S. M. Leathes, M.A.	Local	Dec. 12 to 17...	Aug. 15 to Sept. 30.	£1, local fee 5*s.* to 10*s.*	*Jun. 16. *Sen. 19.
	Commercial Certificates	Monday, Dec. 12	Sept. 30 ...	£1, and local fee ...	None, but suitable for students of 17 years of age
*Under certain conditions Juniors are admitted above the age of 16, Seniors above the age of 19, and Higher local Cands. under the age of 17½.	Higher Local ...	June 20 to 25 ...	April 20 ..	£2 first time, £1 afterwards.	*17½ and over
		Dec. 12 to 17, Groups B. (Langs. Anct. and Mod.) and C. (Mathcs.).	Oct. 31		

University, Local, &c.	*Examinations.*	*Dates.*	*Latest date for returning forms.*	*Fees.*	*Age Limit.*
Cambridge—*cont.*					
	Teachers' Train. Synd.	June	May 20, Nov. 5.	£2 10*s*.	20.
	Prel. for Holy Orders.	April 5-8 and October 11-14	March 1 and Sept. 1.	25*s*.	
Cardiff. University College of South Wales and Monmouthsh. Registrar.— Ivor James, Esq.	Entrance Scholarship.	Sept. 20 ...	Sept. 1. ...	... ...	16
Dublin. The University. Trinity College. Registrar.—G. F. Shaw, LL.D.	Entrance Days	Jan. 26, Apl. 28, June 24, 25 (Midsr.), June 16, Oct. 10, 11. Oct. 20, & Nov. 1.		£15 Entrance. Every subsequent half-year £8 8*s*.	N.B. — There are no age limits except for pecuniary prizes.
	Principal Entrance Scholarships, &c. ...	June and Octr. October.			
Royal University of Ireland, Earlsfort Terrace. Secretaries.— J.C. Meredith, Esq., D. B. Dunne, Esq.	*ARTS.* *Matriculation	June, the end. (Pass and Hon.) Sept., the end. (Pass only.)	May 15 / August 15	£1.†	
	First University	June, early. (Pass and Hon.) Sept., the end. (Pass only.)	At least 1 month previous.	£1.	
All Degrees, Honours,					

Exhibitions, Prizes, and Scholarships in this University, are open to Students of either sex.

The Examinations for Women will be held apart from those for Men, but upon the same days.

*Candidates for any degree in this University must have passed the Matriculation Examination. Students from other Universities and Colleges are included in this rule.

Second University ...	June, the end ...	,,	£1.	
B.A.	July, early ...	,,	£1.	Upon adm. to Degree, £2.
M.A.	October (about the beginning)	,,	£2.	
D. Lit....	... ...	,,	£2.	Upon adm. to Degree, £3
D. Sc.	... ...	,,	£2.	
ENGINEERING.				
First Professional ...	July, towards the middle.	,,	£1.	
Second Professional ...	,,	,,	£1.	
B.E.	,,	,,	£1.	Upon adm. to Degree, £2.
M.E.	,,	,,	£2.	
MUSIC.				
First Exam. in Music...	... .	1 month prev.	£1.	
B. Mus.	... ...	,,	£1.	,, ,,

†N.B.—The attention of Candidates is specially directed to the fact that with the year 1888 the regulation expired under which Candidates who failed at an Examination, were exempted from a second payment of the same fee upon presenting themselves for the same Examination.

Certificates.

Senate has directed that the following charges shall be made henceforward for Certificates in connexion minations:—

For Examinations passed in 1887, 1888, and 1889.

Certificate of having passed an Examination, One Shilling.

C... of having obtained Honours at an Undergraduate Examination, Two Shillings and Sixpence.

...ertificates of Honours at any Degree Examination, Five Shillings.

For Examinations passed subsequent to 1889.

...having passed an Examination, either with or without Honours, One Shilling and Sixpence.

...ertificate of Honours at any Degree Examination, Five Shillings.

University, Local, &c.	Examinations.	Dates.	Latest date for returning forms.	Fees.	Age Limit.
Dublin—*continued.* No Candidates for any of the Degrees of this University, save those in the Faculty of Medicine, are required to pursue their studies at any special places of education. They are only required to pass the prescribed examinations of the University.	D. Mus.	... .	,,	£2. Upon adm. to Degree, £3.	
	LAW.				
	LL.B.	... ...	,,	£1. Upon adm. to Degree, £3.	
	LL.D.	... ...	,,	£2. Upon adm. to Degree, £3.	
Intermediate Education Board.	Preliminary	June 14.	... ...	... ...	Prel. 14.
Communications should be addressed: The Assistant-Commissioners, 1, Hume St., Dublin.	Junior Grade	,,	Feb. 29, or, with late fee, up to March 31 ...	2*s.* 6*d.* each grade. Late fee, 7*s.* 6*d.*	Jun. 16.
	Middle ,, ...	... ,, ...	... ...	2*s.* 6*d.* each grade. Late fee, 7*s.* 6*d.*	Middle 17.
	Senior ,, ...	... ,, ...	... ...	2*s.* 6*d.* each grade. Late fee, 7*s.* 6*d.*	Sen. 18.
Royal College of Physicians of Ireland. Fellow & Registrar: J. W. Moore, M.D.	Licentiate	1st Mon. after 1st Friday in February, May, and November.	Four days before 1st Friday in mo. of Exam.		
	Member.	Quarterly— ... Jany., April, July, and Oct.			
	Diploma in State Med.	Feb. May, Nov.			

Dundee. University College. Sec., G. W. Alexander, Esq., M.A.	Entrance and Scholarship.	Oct. 9 and 10...	Sept. 30.		
Durham. The University. ... Registrar.—W. K. Hilton, Esq., M.A.	Adm. and 1st year in Arts and Theology	Jan. 20 ... Oct. 12 ...	Jan. 11. Oct. 1.		
	Cert. for Prof. in Gen. Education	March 22 ... September 27 ...	A month prev. "	£1.	None.
	Prely. Arts (M.B.)	March 29 ... Sept. 27. ...			
Coll. of Science, and Coll. of Med.—*See Newcastle-on-Tyne.*					
[illegible]burgh. [illegible]e University ... [illegible]retaries.— [illegible]alderwood [illegible]rie. [illegible] [illegible]ith,	Local	June 2, 3, and 4.	May 12 ...	Juniors, 20*s*. Seniors, 30*s*. or 20*s*.	None.
	Ordinary Cert. in Arts for Women.	April 4, 5, 6. and 7. Oct. 11 to 14.	March 13 and Oct. 1.	£2 2*s*.	
	Honours Cert. in Arts for Women.	April 8 and following days.	"		
	Preliminary Exam. in Arts for Med. and Sc. Degrees.	March 1, 2, 3, and 4, and Oct. 4, 5, 6, and 7.	Feb. 24 and Sept. 28.	10*s*.	

University, Local, &c.	*Examinations.*	*Dates.*	*Latest date for returning forms.*	*Fees.*	*Age Limit.*
Edinburgh—*cont.* Royal College of Physicians and Surgeons.	Preliminary	Mar. 31 April 1, 2 June 30 July 1, 2 Oct.	March 28. June 27. Sept. 26.	£1.	
Glasgow. The University ...	Prely. Exam. in Arts, and Exam. for Bursaries.	Oct. 25 to 28.	Oct. 18 ...	... ...	
	Medical Prely. in Gen. Education.	March 23 to 26 & Sept. 28 to Oct. 1	March 9 ... Sept. 5.	10*s.*	
* Certificates granted by the Board are of four grades, viz.:— Secretary.— James Coutts, Esq., M.A.	* Local... ... ... I. Jun., II. Sen. } For both boys and girls. III. Higher, IV. Certif in Degree Subjects, } For women.	May 31 ... June 1, 2, 3	May 1 ...	Jun., 20*s.*; Sen., 30*s.* Higher, £3 3*s.*	Boys' limit 18
Irish Intermediate Board. *See Dublin.*					
Lampeter. St. David's College.	Matriculation ...	Jan. 20.	... ...	£1. (on joining the	

V. Prin.: Rev. W. H. Davey, M.A.		April 20. Oct. 4 (about).		College).	.
	Scholarship	Sept. 27 (about)	Sept. 19 ...	None.	
	Responsions	June 11 ... Nov. 28 (about).	... .	£1 1*s.* and £2 2*s.*	
Leeds. The Yorkshire College, (Affiliated to Victoria University, Manchester. Registrar: W. F. Husband, Esq., LL.B.	Scholarship	April 27 ...	April 20 ...	... .	18.
Liverpool. University College. (Affiliated to Victoria University, Manchester. *See* Owens College, &c. Registrar: Chevalier E. Londini, D.C.L.	Scholarship	May 9, 10, 11, 12, 13 and 14.	April 23 ...	... ...	Not more than 18 on Oct. 1, 1892.
London. The University ...	* Matriculation ...	Jan. 11 to 15. June 13 to 17.	4 weeks prev. ,,	£2	16 (above).
Registrar.—Arthur Milman, Esq., M.A.	*ARTS.* Intermediate	July 18 to 21 (Pass). July 18 to 28 (Honours).	,,	£5.	
* This exam. must be passed before proceeding to any other at the University. No exemptions from this rule.	B.A.	Oct. 24 to Oct. 29 (Pass).	,,	£5.	
	,, ...	Nov. 21 to 23 (Honours).			

University, Local, &c.	*Examinations.*	*Dates.*	*Latest date for returning forms.*	*Fees.*	*Age Limit.*
London—*continued.* The University. (*contd.*)	*ARTS.*—(*cont.*)				
	M. A. Branch I. (Clscs.)	June 6 to 9.	4 weeks prev.	£10, an additional £5 for each branch other than the one taken up for the title of M.A.	20 (above).
	,, II. (Mathcs. and N. Phily.)	June 13 to 16.	,,		
	,, III. (Mtl. and Mor. Sc.)	June 20 to 23.	,,		
	Branch IV. (Langs.)	June 27.	8 weeks prev.		
	D. Lit.	Tues., Dec. 6.	Before Sept. 30	£10.	
	Scriptural Exams. ...	Tues., Nov. 29, 30.	14 days' notice.		
	SCIENCE.				
	Int. B.Sc.	July 18 to Aug. 4 (Pass and Hon.)	4 weeks prev.	£5	16 (above).
	B.Sc.	Oct. 17 to Nov. 2 (Pass). Nov. 21 to Dec. 10 (Honours).	,,	£5.	
	D.Sc.	During first 3 weeks of June.	Feb. 1.	£10.	
	MEDICINE.				
	Prel. Scientific (M.B.)	Jan. 18 to 28 (Pass only).			
		July 18 to Aug. 4 (Pass and Hon.)	4 weeks prev.	£5.	

Int., Med.	Mon., Jan. 18, (Pass only) Printed Papers, — July 11 to 13, (Pass and Hon.) Printed Papers, — Vivâ-voce and Practical, in July and Aug. (Pass and Hon.)	4 weeks prev.	£5	19 (over).
M.B.	Mon., May 2 (Pass only). Mon., Oct. 31 (Pass and Hon.)	,,	£5.	
B.S.	Tues., Dec. 6.	14 days.	£5.	
M.S. and M.D. ...	Mon., ,, 5 ...	4 weeks prev.	£5.	
LAW.				
Int. and LL.B. ...	Mon., Jan. 4.	,,	£5 each.	
D. Laws	Tues., ,, 19.	Dec. 15.	£10.	
MUSIC.				
Int. B. Mus.	Mon., Dec. 12.	8 weeks prev.	£5.	
B. Mus.	,, ,, 19.	,,	£5.	
Int. D. Mus.	,, ,, 12.	,,	£5.	
D. Mus.	,, ,, 19.	,,	£5.	
Art of Teaching ..	Tues., Dec. 13.	9 weeks prev.	£5.	

University, Local, &c.	*Examinations.*	*Dates.*	*Latest date for returning forms.*	*Fees.*	*Age Limit.*
London—*continued.*					
Civil Service. Army Exams. London. Edinburgh. Dublin. Chief Centres.	R.M.C. (Sandhurst) Preliminary	Mar. 9, June 8, Sept. 14, Dec. 14.	Feb. 12, May 12. Aug. 12, Nov. 12.	£1	17 to 20, Uny. Students 17 to 21, Graduates 17 to 22.
	Further ...	June 29 and ... Nov. ...	May 15 Oct.		
	R.M.A. (Woolwich) Preliminary	Mch. 9, Jun. 14, Sep. 14, Dec. 14.	Feb. 12, May 12. Aug. 12, Nov. 12.	£1 ..	16-18.
For further information on Civil Service Exams. generally see pp. 40-41.	Further ...	June 23 and ... Nov. ...	May 15 Oct. 15	£1 ...	
	Army Commissions for Offrs. of Auxly. Forces Preliminary... ...	Mch. 9, June 14, Sept. 14, Dec. 14.	Feb. 12, May 12, Aug. 12, Nov. 12.	£1	24-28.
	Further	Apl. 19, Oct. ...	Feb. 15, Aug.		
King's College ... Sec.: J. W. Cunningham, Esq.	Matriculation... ...	Jan. 13, Ap. 27, Oct. 2	1 week prev.	£4 15*s.* 6*d.*	16.
	Scholarship	Sept., end, and Oct., begin.	1 week prev.		
College of Preceptors Dean.—H. W. Eve, M.A. Sec.—C. R. Hodgson, B. A., Bloomsbury Sq., W.C.	Teachers' Diplomas ...	About July 5-8, and Jan. 2-5, 1893.	1 month prev.	£1 1*s.*	
	Pupils' Certificate ...	June 14-17, and Dec. 6-9.	May 10, Nov. 17.	10*s.* (Not including Local Fee) ...	None.
	Mercantile Certificates	June 13, Dec. 5.	5 weeks prev.	15*s.*	None.

	Professional Prelim. ...	March 8-10, and Sept. 6-8.	30 days ...	25*s*.	
City and Guilds of London Institute.	Central Institn. Entr.	Sept. 19-22.	Sept. 10 ...	£1	C. I. above 16.
	Technical College Entr.	Sept. 27.	Sept. 10 ...	... ...	T. C. above 14.
Hon. Sec., J. Watney, Esq.; Assist. Sec.: A. L. Soper, Esq., Head Office, Gresham Coll., E.C.	Technological Exams.	*April 30, 3 to 7 p.m. †May 4, 7 to 10, p.m. ‡May 7, 3 to 7.30, p.m. [a]May 11, 6 to 10 p.m. [b]May 27 and 28. [c]May, about end of.	Applicn. to be made not later than Mar. 26. Returns & Fees to be sent in by Local Secs. by April 4.	1*s*. (Plumbing 2*s*. 6*d*. extra; Honours, Mine Surveying, 10*s*.)	None.
Society of Arts ... Sec.: Sir H. Trueman Wood, M.A., John St., Adelphi, London, W.C.	Arth., Ger., Port., Russian, Danish, Chinese, Japan.	M. April 4, 7 to 10 p.m.	March 21 ...	2*s*. 6*d*. for each subject.	No limit.
	Bkkpg., Ital., Span., D. Econ.	T. April 5, 7 to 10 p.m.	.. ..	〃	〃
	Eng., Fr., Commcl. Geogra., Theory of Music, Typewriting.	W. April 6, 7 to 10 p.m., Type writing, 7.30 to 10 p.m.	... ...	〃	〃
	Shorthand	Th. April 7, 7.30 to 10 p.m.	... ...	2*s*. 6*d*.	〃
	Practice of Music ...	May 30 ...	... ...	Honours, 10*s*., and 5*s*. ex. for 1st or 2nd Cl., or if with Vocal and Instrumental, 7*s*. 6*d*.	

... examination in the Weaving Section of the five branches of Textile

† Examination in other subjects.

‡ Bread-making, Photography, Plumbing, Typography.

[a] Goldsmiths' Work. [b] Mine Surveying. [c] Boot and Shoe-making.

LONDON (*continued.*)—Science and Art Department, South Kensington.

Grade.	*Examinations.*	*Dates.*	*Examinations.*	*Date.*
	Art:—(See also under Nat. Art Training Sch. p. 35.) see p. 35		Science:—	
2nd Grade Ex.	Model Drawing.	April 28, 7 to 8 p.m.	I. Practical Plane and Solid Geometry.	April 30, 6 to 10 p.m.
"	Freehand Drawing.	April 28, 8.20 to 9.50 p.m.	VI. Theoretical Mechanics, VI*a*. Solids, VI*b*. Fluids.	May 2 and 3, 7 to 10 p.m.
"	Perspective.	April 29, 7 to 8.30 p.m.	XIV. Animal Physiology.	May 4, 7 to 10 p.m.†
3rd Grade Ex.	Anatomy.	April 29, 7 to 10 p.m.	VII. Applied Mechanics.	May 5, 7 to 10 p.m.
"	Drawing in Stage 5*a*. ...	May 2, 7 to 9.30 p.m.	XX. Navigation.	May 6, 7 to 10 p.m.
"	Drawing in Stage 3*b*. ...	May 3, 7 to 9.30 p.m.	XII. Geology.	May 6, 7 to 10 p.m.
"	Drawing in Stage 5*b*.	May 4, 6 to 10 p.m.	II. Machine Construction and Drawing.	May 7, 6 to 10 p.m.†
"	Sciography.	May 5, 7 to 10 p.m.	III. Building Construction.	May 7, 6 to 10 p.m.†
"	Drawing from the Antique. §	May 5, 6 to 10 p.m.	IV. Naval Architecture.	May 7, 6 to 10 p.m †
"	Element. Principls. of Ornament.	May 6, 7 to 10 p.m.	XXIII. Physiography.	May 9, 7 to 10 p.m.
"	Composition from a given Figure Subject, with or without ornament in some one Historic style. (23*d.*)	May 6, 6 to 10 p.m.	XVIII. Principles of Mining.	May 10, 7 to 10 p.m.

”	Painting from Still Life. ...	May 7, 10 a.m. to 4 p.m. (See *Note* below.)	V. Mathematics, Stages 6 and 7.	May 10, 7 to 10 p.m.
			XXIV. Principles of Agriculture.	May 10, 7 to 10 p.m.
”	Perspective.	May 7, 6 to 10 p.m.	V. Mathematics, Stages 1, 2, 3.	May 11, 7 to 10.30 p.m.
”	Drawing from the Life.	May 9, 6 to 10 p.m.	IX. Magnetism and Electricity, including alternative Elementary Physics.	May 12, 7 to 10 p.m.
”	Architect. Historic ornament.	May 10, 7 to 10 p.m.		
”	Elementary Architecture. ...	May 11, 6 to 10 p.m.	VIII and VIII*a*. Sound, Light and Heat.	May 13, 7 to 10 p.m.
”	Historic ornament.	May 11, 7 to 10 p.m.	Xp. Pract. Inorganic Chemistry, Elementary Stage.	May 14, 6 to 9.30 p.m.*
”	Design, Ornament. (23*c*.) ...	May 12, 6 to 10 p.m.	VIII*b*. Light, Advanced Stage and Honours.	May 16, 7 to 10, p.m.
”	Drawing from Memory one of the following Antique figures: the Standing Discobolus, Germanicus, Antinous, or Dancing Faun.	May 13, 7 to 8 p.m.	VIII*c*. Heat, Advanced Stage and Honours.	May 17, 7 to 10 p.m.
			V. Mathcs., Stages 4 and 5.	May 18, 7 to 10 p.m.
			XXV. Hygiene.	May 18, 7 to 10 p.m.
”	Painting Ornament in Monochrome (in oil or tempera only) from a Sketch or Photograph.	May 13, 6 to 10 p.m.	XI. Organic Chemistry. ...	May 19, 7 to 10 p.m.
			XXII. Steam.	May 19, 7 to 10 p.m.
			X. Inorganic Chemist., including alternat. Element. Chemistry.	May 20, 7 to 10 p.m.

Note.—On the 7th, and the 16th to 18th May, the six hours, 10 a.m. to 4 p.m., include half an hour allowed for refreshment.

* See p. 33. † *Ib.* § *Ib.*

LONDON (*continued*).—SCIENCE AND ART DEPARTMENT, SOUTH KENSINGTON (*continued.*)

Grade.	*Examinations.*	*Dates.*	*Examinations.*	*Dates.*
	ART—*continued.*		SCIENCE (*continued*)—	
3rd Grade Ex.	Plant Drawing in Outline, Stage 10*a.*	May 14, 7 to 10 p.m.	Xp. Prac. Inorganic Chemistry. Advanced Stage	May 21, 6 to 10.30 p.m.
			Honours	May 21, 2.30 to 10.30 p.m.
"	Architectural Design, Group 6.	May 16 to 18, 10 a.m. to 4 p.m. (See *Note* below.)	XIXp. Practical Metallurgy, Elementary Stage.	May 23, 7 to 10 p.m.*
"	Modelling from Life.	May 19, 20 and 21, 10 a.m. to 4 p.m. (See *Note* below.)	XIXp. Practical Metallurgy. Advanced Stage	May 24, 6 to 10 p.m.*
			Honours	May 24, 2 to 10 p.m.*
"	Modelling from the Antique; and casting from Waste Moulds, each day from 10 a.m.‡	May 23 and 24, 10 a.m. to 4 p.m. (See *Note* below.)	XVI. & XVII. Biology.	May 25, 7 to 10 p.m.
			XIX. Metallurgy.	May 25, 7 to 10 p.m.
"	Modelling, Design, Ornament. (23*e.*)‡	May 25, 10 a.m. to 4 p.m. (See *Note* below.)	XV. Botany.	May 26, 7 to 10 p.m.
			XIII. Mineralogy.	May 27, 7 to 10 p.m.
"	Modelling. Design. Figure Sub-	May 25, 10 a.m.		

	ject, with or without ornament in some one Historic style. (23 *f.*) ‡	to 4 p.m. (See *Note* below.)	XXI. Nautical Astronomy.	May 27, 7 to 10 p.m.
..	Casting from Waste Moulds.	May 26, 10 a.m. to 4 p.m.	XIp. Pract. Organic Chemistry, Elementary Stage	May 28, 6 to 9.30 p.m.*
			Advanced Stage	May 28, 6 to 10.30 p.m.
			Honours	May 28, 2.30 to 10.30 p.m.*

Note.—The six hours on each of the above days, 19th to 26th May, 10 a.m. to 4 p.m., include half an hour allowed for refreshment.

* See p. 33. ‡ *Ib.*

LONDON (*continued*).—
Science and Art Department, South Kensington.

NOTES TO PAGES 31 AND 32.

N.B.—It must be understood that all articles to be used by the candidate at the examination, except pens, ink, and paper, must be provided by the candidate himself.

* Examinations in Practical Chemistry and Practical Metallurgy are only held in Schools provided with a Laboratory which has been accepted as fulfilling the requirements of the Science and Art Directory. Each candidate must have a separate set of apparatus and re-agents. The examination in the Advanced and Elementary Stages of Practical Inorganic and Organic Chemistry will consist of two parts, viz., a written examination and a practical examination. The written examination will be held from 6 to 7 p.m. The practical examination in the Advanced Stage will be from 7.15 to 10.30 p.m., and in the Elementary Stage from 7.15 to 9.30 p.m. In Laboratories where the Department has specially sanctioned the practical examination of the candidates in two divisions, the first division in the Advanced Stage will be examined from 2.30 to 5.45 p.m., and in the Elementary Stage from 3.30 to 5.45 p.m. The written examination for both divisions will be held from 6 to 7 p.m., as already stated. The examination for Honours will be in practical work only, and will be continuous from 2.30 to 10.30 p.m. In Practical Metallurgy there will be, for all stages, a practical examination only, and will be held as stated in Time Table above. Where the Department has sanctioned the examination of the candidates in the Advanced or the Elementary Stage in two divisions, the examination of the first division will be held from 1 to 5 p.m. for the Advanced Stage, and from 3 to 6 p.m. for the Elementary Stage.

† The City and Guilds of London Institute general Examinations in Technology will probably be held on the evening of Wednesday, 30th April, and the Examinations in the Weaving sections of Textile Fabrics and the Practical Examinations in Typography, Plumbing, and Bread-making on the afternoon following.

‡ The third grade Examinations in Modelling will be held at South Kensington. But they may also be held in any School of Art where Candidates are prepared to cast their own models for transmission to South Kensington. Candidates must provide their own modelling tools. The Department will provide clay for modelling. The examination in Waste Moulding must be taken the day after any other modelling examination for which the candidate may sit.

§ *This Examination may be taken only at Schools of Art having four full length figures of the Antique.*

a. Application for the examination of a School or Class under an approved Local Committee must be made not later than the 25th March, on Form No. 119. For an examination in Practical Chemistry or Practical Metallurgy application must be made not later than the 20th March.

b. Candidates who do not belong to any regularly constituted Science or Art Class should apply before 20th March to the Secretary of the nearest Class which is to be examined in the subject they require. A fee not exceeding 2*s.* 6*d.* per evening may be charged by the Local Committee. Individual candidates who do not reside near any place where a Local Examination Committee has been formed, may be examined at the South Kensington Museum, as far as room will allow. A registration fee of 2*s.* 6*d.* per evening or a composition fee of 10*s.* for any number of evenings (except for the examinations in Practical Chemistry and Practical Metallurgy) will be charged if application (on Form No. 325) is made before 20th March, and of 5*s.* per evening afterwards or a composition fee of 20*s.* for any number of evenings if before 15th April. For Practical Chemistry and Practical Metallurgy the fee will be 5*s.* per examination, if application be made before 20th March, or 10*s.* per examination if made afterwards before 15th April, and these subjects are not included in the composition fees previously specified. If there are more candidates than can be examined, the preference will be given to registered candidates for Exhibitions and Scholarships. Applications for examination at South Kensington cannot be received after 15th April.

c. Schools and Classes cannot be examined at South Kensington.

By order of the
Committee of Council on Education.

*** For pending changes in the Government Grants to Local Schools and Classes, through the Science and Art Department (after May, 1892), see the Minute of the Council of Education at p. 157.

University, Local, &c.	*Examinations.*	*Dates.*	*Latest date for returning forms.*	*Fees.*	*Age Limit.*
London—*continued.*					
Scotch Eductn. Dept., Dover House, Whitehall, S.W. Address Sec., Scotch Education Dept.	Leaving Certifs. for Higher Class Schools Admission into Training Colleges. For Certificate of Merit for Teachers.	About middle of June ... July 6. Early in Dec.	None fixed.	2*s.* 6*d.* for each subject, or otherwise, as may be specially arranged by the authorities of the school.	None fixed.
Royal Agricultural Soc. of England, 12, Hanover Sq., W. Sec.: Ernest Clarke, Esq.	Senior Prizes and Certificates.	May 10 and 14	March 31 ...	Deposit of £1 (returnable).	None.
	Junior Scholarships.	Nov. 8 and 9	Oct. 15... ...	None. ...	Between 14 and 18.
National Art Training School (of the Science and Art Department), Exhibition Rd., South Kensington, S.W. Principal: J. C. L. Sparkes, Esq. Registrar: Maj. Gen. Sussex W. Lennox.	Entrance Examination, on dates named, for those who have not already passed 2nd Grade freehand.	Tuesdays, Jan. 5, and 21; Feb. 9; Mar. 1, 8, 15, 22, 29; April 5 and 26; May 10 and 31; June 21; July 26; Sept. 27; Oct. 11, 18 and 25; Nov. 1, 15 and 29; Dec. 20.	... ...	Entrance Fee, 10*s.*	None.

Surveyors' Institution: J. W. Penfold, Esq., Hon. Sec., 12, Great George St., S.W.	Preliminary for Adm. of Students.	Jan. 26 and 27	November ...	£1 1s.	18 (over).
	Professional Associate and Fellowship.	March 14 to 18	November.	£3 3s. each Exam. respectively.	21 and 25 (over).
	Special (Members) Exam. in Forestry, Sanitary Science, Surveying and Levelling.	June 14, 15 & 16	April 20.	£3 3s.	21 (over).
The Inst. of Chartered Accountants.	Preliminary	June 7, 8 & 9 Dec. 6, 7 & 8	30 days prev.	£2 2s.	None specified.
The Secretary, 3, Copthall Buildings,	Intermediate	June 14 and 15; Dec. 6, 7 and 8.	"	£2 2s.	
London, E.C.	Final	June 21, 22 & 23; Dec. 20, 21. & 22	"	£2. 2s.	
The Soc. of Accountants and Auditors.	Preliminary	June 13; Dec. 5.	28 days prev.	10s. 6d.	
Sec.: J. Martin, Esq., 4, King St., Cheapside, E.C.	Intermediate	June 14 and 15; Dec. 6 and 7.	"	£1 1s.	
	Final	June 13, 14, and 15; Dec. 5, 6, and 7.	"	£1 11s. 6d.	
The Law Society of the United Kingd. Sec.: E. W. Williamson, Esq., Incorporated Law Society's Hall, Chancery Ln.	Preliminary Articles of Clerkship to Solicitors	Feb. 3, 4; May 4, 5; July 6, 7, and Oct. 19, 21.	30 days prev. at least.	£2	None.
	Intermediate Exam. ...	Jan. 14, Apl. 7, Jun. 16, Nov. 10.	30 days prev.	£3	None.
he Honours Exam. [illegible] Friday Final.	*Final Exam.	Jan. 12, 13, Apl. 5, 6, June 14, 15 Nov. 8, 9.	42 days prev.	£5	None.

University, Local, &c.	*Examinations.*	*Dates.*	*Latest date for returning forms.*	*Fees.*	*Age Limit.*
London—*continued.*					
Pharmaceutical Soc. Sec. and Regist.: R. Bremridge, Esq., 17, Bloomsbury Sq., London, W.C.	Preliminary	Jan. 12 April 12 July 12 Oct. 11	14 days prev.	£2 2*s.*	None.
Society of Apothecaries, Blackfriars, E.C. Sec., to the Board of Examiners: C. E. Armand Temple, B.A.,M.B.Cantab. Apothecaries' Hll., Blackfriars, E.C.	Arts	Mch. 4 and 5 June 3 and 4 Sept. 2 and 3 Dec. 2 and 3	14 days	£1 1*s.* for whole exam. or £1 1*s.* each special subject. Candidates will be examined in—I. Eng. II. Lat. III. Arith. IV. Alg. V. Geom. VI. One of the Subjects annexed, at option of Candidate: Gk., Fr., Ger., Log. Italian and other Mod. Langs. are special subjects.	None.
Royal Academy of Music. Sec.: James G. Syme, Esq., W.S., Tenterden Street, W.	Metropolitan Exam. for Licentiate Diploma (L.R.A.M.). Subjects: I. Counterp., Harmony, Plan or Design and Instrmtn. II. Singing. III. Piano. IV. Organ. V. Orchestral Instruments. VI. BandMastership	December ...	October 19 ...	£5 5*s.* each subject.	

Royal College of Music, Kensington Gore, S.W. Hon. Sec.: Charles Morley, Esq.	Certific. of Proficiency, A.R.C.M.	April ...	Feb. 26 ...	£5 5*s.*	
	Free Open Scholarships. Composition, 1; Singing 2; Piano, 2; Organ, 1; Violin, 4; Flute or Oboe, 1.	February ...	Jan. 12. Applications must be on college forms to be obtained from the Regr.		
Associated Board of Royal Academy of Music, and Royal College of Music. Sec: G. Watson, Esq., 52, New Bond St., W.	Local Centre Exams. Preliminary (Paper Work).	Feb. 24.	Jan. 30 ...	£2 2*s.*	Juniors not exceeding 16 years.
	Final: Local School Exams.	On and after March 28.	"		
Guildhall School of Music: Chas. P. Smith, Esq., Victoria Embkt., E.C.	Certificate ... ... (For Students of 3 yrs. standing.)	June	4 weeks prev. to June 1.	£5 5*s.*	None.
College of Organists. Hon. Sec.: E. H. Turpin, Esq., Mus. D., Bloomsbury Mansion, Hart St., New Oxford St., W.C.	F. C. O.	Jan. 12, 13, 14. July 12, 13, 14.	Dec. 31. July 7.	£2 2*s.* for Examination and member's Subscription.	None.
	A. C. O.	Jan. 19, 20, 21. July 19, 20, 21.	Dec. 31. July 7.		
Trinity College, London (Music). Mandeville Place, Manchester Sq., W. Sec.: Shelley Fisher, Esq.	Higher Exams. for Diplomas & Certifs.	Jan. 4-9 ... July 11-16 ...	Dec. 12, 1891. June 18, 1892.	£1 1*s.* to £3 3*s.*	16 is the limit of age for Honours in the Junior Division.
	Local, Musical Knowledge (Theory). (Senior, Intermediate, and Junior.)	Dec. 11, 1891. June 24, 1892.	Nov. 11, 1891. May 24, 1892.	6*s.* to 15*s.*	

University, Local, &c.	*Examinations.*	*Dates.*	*Latest date for returning forms.*	*Fees.*	*Age Limit.*
London—*continued.* Trinity College, London—*cont.*	Local Examinations in Instrumental and Vocal Music (Senr., Junr., and Primary).	Held throughout each term at various Local Centres	28 days before Exam. week.	£1 1*s.*	None.
Natnl. Froebel Union and the Kindergn. Co. (Bedford) Sec. N.F.U.: Miss Clive Bayley, 12, B'k'ham St., Strand. Sec., N. K. Co., 12, Mill St., Bedford.	Certificates : Elementary. Higher.	July.	A fortnight before.	£1 1*s.* ... £2 2*s.* ...	17 (above). 18 (above).
Whitehall, S.W. Education Depart. Training Colleges.	Certificate. Scholarship.	December. July.	October 1.		
Manchester. Victoria University. Regr.: A.T. Bentley, Esq., M.A.	*Prel. (Arts, Sc. and Law).	June 16 ... Sept. 26 ...	June 1. Sept. 9 } with fees.	Matr. Fee £2, includes Fee (£1) for Prel. or Ent. Ex.	None.
	First M.B. Exam.	June 14. ... Oct 1. ...	June 1. Sept. 9.	Fee £5 (Matricula. Fee additional).	
Colleges :— Owens' Col., Mnchstr.	Entr. in Arts (Medicine)	June 20.	June 1.		
Univ. Col., Liverpool.	,, (Music)	Sept. 26.	Sept. 9.		
Yorkshire Col., Leeds. (See Liverpool.) (See Leeds.)					

NEWCASTLE-ON-TYNE. Durham College of Science. Sec. :—H. F. Stockdale, Esq.	Matriculation. Exhibitions.	Sept. 26, 27. Sept. 26-29.	Sept. 17.		
Durham College of Medicine. Sec.: Lieut. Henry Fox, R.N.	Certific. of Proficiency in Gen. Education. Prely. in Arts (M.B.) (at Durham Univy.).	March 22 and Sept. 27. March 29 and Sept. 27.	1 month prev. „ „	£1. £1.	 15 (above)
OXFORD AND CAMBRIDGE. Schools Exam. Bd. Secs.:—E. J. Gross, Esq., M.A., Caius Coll., Camb.; P. E. Matheson, Esq., M.A. 74, High St., Oxford.	Higher Certificates ...	July 11-13.	2 months prev.	£2. Cands. who have already obtained Certifs. will be admitted to a subsequent Examn. on payment of a fee of £1 10s.	
	Lower „ Commercial „	Mon., Jy. 18-23. „ „	„ „ 8 weeks prev.	£1 1s. £1 5s. ...	Adapted for Cands. of about 16 years of age.

MANCHESTER—VICTORIA UNIVERSITY.

* A GILCHRIST SCHOLARSHIP.—Value £50 a year for three years, is awarded to the candidate who stands highest he Preliminary Examination held in June. This Scholarship is tenable at either of the Colleges of the University. conditions of competition apply to the Principals of the College at which it is proposed to study. For information o University Examinations, &c., apply to the Registrar, Victoria University, Manchester.

University, Local, &c.	*Examinations.*	*Dates.*	*Latest date for returning forms.*	*Fees.*	*Age Limit.*
Oxford. The University ... Sec.:—H. T. Gerrans, Esq., Clarendon Building, Oxford.	Locals	Begins Mond. July 11.	May 14.*	£1 (and Local Fee)...	None.†
	Exam. for Women	See note §.	See Note.‖	See Note.¶	
	Prel. for Holy Orders	Apl. 5 & Oct. 11.	Mch. 1 and Sep. 1	25*s.*	None.

Oxford.—The University, Local Examinations.

* Forms of Entry must be obtained from the Local Secretary of the place at which the candidate wishes to be examined. They are procurable from March 1st to May 12th, and must be returned by May 14th, with fees.

† Juniors.—Persons of either sex are admitted without limit of age. Any one born on or after July 1, 1876, may be received as a Cand. for Hons. Anyone born before that day may be received as a Pass Cand. Seniors.—Successful Candidates born on or after July 1, 1873, will receive Certificates signed by the Vice-Chancellor. conferring the title of Associate of Arts. Successful Candidates born before that date will receive Pass Certificates.

Oxford.—The University, Examination for Women.

Information on all points connected with the education of Women in Oxford can be obtained on application to Mrs. A. H. Johnson, 8, Merton Street, Oxford.

§ Responsions on March 17th, June 16th, September 28th, and December 8th.

The First Examination on (1) June 13th.
(2) December 13th.

The Second Examination (Pass) on June 13th.

The Second Examination (Honours)—(1) In Latin and Greek on March 10th. (2) In Mathematics on June 9th and 23rd and Dec. 15th. (3) In Modern History and Literæ Humaniores on June 6th. (4) In Natural Science (Preliminary) in Physiology, Morphology, Botany on March 14th, and December 6th; in Mechanics, Physics, Chemistry on June 2nd and Nov. 24th. (5) In Natural Science (Final) on some day to be hereafter fixed, not later than seven days after the termination of the Preliminary Examination which begins in June. (6) In Music on some days in Hilary Term and Michaelmas Term to be announced in the University Gazette. (7) In sections 7 and 8 on June 13th.

‖ The Forms with the Fees must *in all cases* be returned direct to the Secretary:—

(1) For Responsions in March, June, and December at least three weeks before the day fixed for the commencement of the Examination. For Responsions in Sept., on or before Aug. 16th. For the First Examination in June and December, on or before May 1st and November 1st respectively.

(2) For the Second (Pass) Examination and for the Examination in the Rudiments of Faith and Religion on or before April 1st.

(3) For the Second Examination (Honours):
In Latin and Greek on or before Feb. 23rd.
In Modern History, Natural Science (Final), and Literæ Humaniores on or before May 16th.
In Mathematics, on or before May 16, and Nov. 18.
In Natural Science (Preliminary) on or before Feb. 24th, May 16th and Nov. 1st.
In all other Sections on or before April 1st.

¶ The Fees payable will be—

	£	s.	d.
For the Preliminary Honour Examination in Natural Science in each of the the subjects whether offered separately, or together	0	10	0
For the Examination in the Rudiments of Faith and Religion	1	0	0
For the Final Honour Examination in Natural Science whether taken separately or together with the subjects in the Preliminary Honour Examination	1	10	0
For the First Examination or Responsions	2	0	0
For any other Examination or part of an Examination	2	10	0

No Fee can be returned under any circumstances, or be carried to the credit of a Candidate at a subsequent Examination.

NIVERSITY, LOCAL, &c.	*Examinations.*	*Dates.*	*Latest date for returning forms.*	*Fees.*	*Age Limit.*
ST. ANDREWS.					
The University ... Local Sup.:—Prof. Birrell. * Applications for Prospectus, or Exam. questions, etc., should be made to the Sec., L. L. A. Scheme.	Locals.	May 31, June 1 and 2.	May 13, to Prof. Birrell, Local Superintendent	Preliminary, 5*s.*; Junior Certificate, 10*s.*; Senior Cert., 20*s.* Cands. from public inspected Primary Schools, Prelim., 4*s.*; Jun., 7*s.* 6*d.*; Sen., 15*s.*	No limit.
	* L.L.A. Cands. must hold certif. approved by the University, e.g., Univ. Local., C. P. certif., P. T. Govt. Certif.	June 21, 22, and 23.	Apply Secretary L.L.A. scheme before Mar. 15; return application form before April 1, to Professor W. Knight, the University.	£2 2*s.* Entrance covers two Exams. For a third and every subsequent Examination £1 1*s.* For the Diploma £4 4*s.* additional after qualification. Fees sent with return forms to Prof. Knight.	No limit.
Affiliated College, Dundee; Univ. Col. *see under Dundee.*					
SHEFFIELD.					
Firth College. ... Sec.: Ensor Drury, Esq.	Scholarship and Entrance (if under 17).	October ...	Sept. 25.		
	Free Even. Studentshs.	"	"		

AN ABSTRACT OF THE CHIEF CIVIL SERVICE EXAMINATIONS, 1892.

Showing Age, Subjects of Examination, Salary, and particulars of recent Examinations.

N.B.—The full Regulations for all Open Competitions can be had post free on application to the "Secretary, Civil Service Commission, London, S.W."

All the appointments mentioned below are open to public Competition, except those marked (N), *for which a nomination by the Head of the Department is required.*

The dates are those of the most recent examinations; the figures following in brackets indicate the numbers of appointments.

Assist. Clerks in Navy. 15-17.—(N). Dict. (Spelling and Writg.): Letter Writg.: Writing subst. of chap. read: French: Comp. Addition: Arith.: Geog. and Hist.: Scr.: Alg. and Euc.: Lat.: Ger. or Span. or Ital.: Elem. Physics: Drwg.: Shorth. £45 to £420, &c. Comps. in June and November. June '91 ( ); Nov. '90 (11); June '90 (10). Nov. '89 (12); June '89 (13); Nov. '88 (10); June '88 (9); Nov. '87 (10); June '87 (9); Nov. '86 (9); June '86 (9); Nov. '85 (10); June '85 (4).

Boy Clerks. 15-17.—Writ.: Orth.: Arith.: Comp. Addition: Cop. MS.: Comp.: Geog. 14*s.* per wk., incr. 1*s.* per wk. per yr. Jan. '92 (100); May '91 (153); Jan. '91 (119); July '90 (119); Jan. '90 (103); July '89 (62); Jan. '89 (33); July '88 (63); March '88 (61); July '87 (63); Oct. '86 (54); July '86 (62); Feb. '86 (63). Not retained after 20. If between 17 and 20 eligible for Open Comp. for Men Clerkships without prelim. Exam., and after a time compete among themselves for a certain number of these Appts.

Boy Copyists (Temporary). 14-18.—Writ.: Orth.: Elem. Arith. 4*d.* per hour. Not retained after 20. May '91; Jan. '91; Nov. '90; July '90; Ap. '90 (115); Jan. '90 (106); Nov. '89; Oct. '89 (91); July '89 (74); May '89 (63); Mar. '89 (48); Nov. '88 (110); Sep. '88 (Dublin); July '88 (124); Feb. '88; Nov. '87; July '87; Exams. at short intervals.

British Museum—Assistants. 18-30.—(N). Dict.: Orth.: Arith.: Eng. Comp.: Précis: Geog.: Eng. Hist. or Euc. or Alg.: Transl. from one Anc. and one Mod. Lan.: any other Subj. the Trustees may prescribe. £120 to £450, &c. Sept. '90 ( ); 1888 (2); 1887 (7); 1886 (6); 1885 (3); 1884 (1); 1883 (4); 1882 (6).

Cadets for Ceylon, Hong Kong, and Straits Settlements. 21-24. —Writ.: Orth.: Arith.: Comp.: and Précis: Lat.: not more than 3 of foll.—Grk.: Fr.: Ger.: Ital.: Pure and Mixed Math.: Geog.: Hist.: Const. and Intern. Law, and Pol. Econ.: Geol.: Civ. Engineering, and Surveying. Ceylon Cadets,

Rupees 3,000; Hong Kong and Straits, 1,200 dolls. Aug. '91 (7); Aug. '90 (6); Aug. '89 (10); Aug. '88 (9); Aug. '87 (5); Aug. '86 (2); Aug. '85 (3); Aug. '84 (2); Aug. '83 (4).

Constab. Cadets (Ireland). 21-26.—(N). Arith.: Sep. Addition: Orth.: Writ.: Intelligence in Dict.: Eng. Comp.: Précis: Geog.: Hist.: Lat. or Fr.: Elem. Law: Law of Evidence. £125 to £450. 1891 (6); 1890 (3); 1889 (3); 1888 (9); 1885 (3); 1884 (2); 1883 (22); 1882 (27).

Class I. Clerks. 18-24.—Writ.: Orth.: Arith.: Eng. Comp. and Précis: Eng. Hist.: Eng. Lang. and Lit.: Lang., Lit., and Hist. of Gr., Rome, Fr., Ger., Italy: Math. (Pure and Mixed): Nat. Sci. (5 branches): Moral Sci.: Jurisp.: Pol. Econ. Lowest, £100 to £400, &c.; highest £250 to £600. Dec. '86 (4); Jan. '86 (13); Mar. '85 (10); June '84 (15); Oct. '83 (18).

Customs—Out-door Officers. 19-25.—Height 5 ft. 4 in., chest 34 in., or if height 5 ft. 10 in., then chest 35 in. Writ.: Orth.: Arith. and Mens.; Comp., Geog., Précis. £55 to £100. Eligible for Exam. Officers: £110 to £340, &c. Selection by exam. in official business. July '91 (60); Oct. 87 (30); May '87 (70); Jan. '87 (50); Oct. '86 (100).

Customs—Outport Clerks. 17-20.—Exam. under Men Clerks' Scheme. £70 to £400, &c. Apr. '86 (10); Aug. '80 (85).

Eng. Students (in Navy). 15-17.—Writ.: Dict.: Arith.: Comp.: Gram.: Geog.: Fr. or Ger. or Ital.: Lat.: Alg.: Euc.: Freeh. Drwg.: Very Element. Phys. and Chemistry. £137 to £700. Comps. once a year in April—in Ap. '91 (36); Ap. '90 (31); Ap. '89 (25); Ap. '87 (47); Ap. '86 (36); Ap. '85 (28); Ap. '84 (25).

Excise Assistants. 19-22.—Writ.: Orth.: Arith. and Mensuration: Comp.: Geog. About £80 to £250, with chance of £800. Comps. usually in May and Nov. July '91 (100); Nov. '88 (20); May '87 (50); Nov. '86 (50); July '86 (80); Nov. '85 (70); 1883 (108); 1882 (220).

Female Clerks in Post Office. 18-20.—Writ.: Orth.: Arith.: Comp.: Geog.: Hist. £65 to £190. Sep. '91 (20); Ap. '91 (110); Sep. '90 (50); May '90 (75); Sep. '89 (50); Mar. '89 (30); Mar. '88 (30); Ap. '87 (35); July '86 (60); Oct. '85 (25); Jan. '85 (50); June '84 (20).

Female Sorters in Post Office. 15-18.—Height 4 ft. 10 in. Reading and Copying MS.: Writ.: Orth.: Arith. (1st 4 rules): Geog. of United Kgdm. 12*s.* per wk. to 20*s.*, &c. May '91 ( ); Dec. '90 (25); May '90 (18); Dec. '89 (20); May '89 (12); Dec. '88 (30); Oct. '87 (30); Feb. '87 (20); May '86 (10); Aug. '85 (40); Feb. '85 (60).

Female Telegr. Learners in Post Office. 15-18.—Dict.: Writ.: Arith. (1st 4 rules). Geog. of United Kgdm. After instruction (3 mos.), 10*s.* per wk., to 30*s.*, &c. May '91 (15); Dec. '90 (29);

Sept. '90 (6); May '90 (39); Dec. '89 (36); May '89 (70); Dec. '88 (22); May '88 (44); Nov. '87 (30); May '87 (30); June '86 (80); Nov. '85 (20); Feb. '85 (100); Sep. '84 (20); 1883 (160).

Foreign Office—Clerks. 18-24.—(N). Arith.: Writ. and Orth.: Comp.: Précis: Fr.: Ger.: Lat.: Gen. Intelligence: Geog.: Hist. Europe: Const. Hist.: Ital.: Span.: Anc. Grk. £100 to £600, &c. About two vacancies every year.

High Courts of Justice (Ireland)—Junior Clerks. 20-30.—Writ.: Orth.: Arith.: Cop. MS.: Comp.: Indexing: Hist.: Geog. £150 to £300, £100 to £300. April '91 (1); Oct. '89 (2); Feb.' 88 (1); June '87 (2); Sep. '85 (3).

India Civil Service. 17-19 (on 1st Jan. of yr. in wh. Comp. is held) till June 1891. 21-23 (on 1st April, &c.) in and after 1892.—£300 for two yrs. spent on probation in England. In India, from 400 rupees per month. Comps. once a year. June '91 (32); June '90 (45); June '89 (49); June '88 (44), June '87 (43); June '86 (38); June '85 (41); June '84 (38); June '83 (40).

Male Telegraph Learners. 14-18.—Dict.: Writ.: Elem. Arith.: Elem. Geog. After instruction (3 mos.) 12*s.* pr. wk. to £140 and £190. Comps. generally twice a year. July '88 (40); Jan. '88 (120); June '86 (120); Jan. '86 (30); Sept. '85 (50); Feb. '85 (100); Feb. '84 (100); 1883 (241).

Second Division Clerks. 17-20.—Writ.: Orth.: Arith.: Cop. MS.: Hist. Comp.: Geog.: Indexing: Digesting: Bk-kpg. £70 to £350, &c. Sept. '91 (130); Ap. '91 (104); Oct '90 (81); May '90 (65); Feb. '89 (Special Limited Competition), (20); Aug. '87 (54); Jan. '87 (46); Sept. '86 (60); May '86 (49); Jan. '86 (93); Oct. '85 (89).

Patent Office—Assist. Examiners. 21-25.—Writ.: Orth.: Arith.: Comp.: Précis: Geom.: Mech. Dwg.: Mechanics and Mechanism: Chem., Elec., and Mag.: Hydraulics, Hydrost., and Pneum. £250 to £400. Nov. '85 (9); Dec. '84 (8); Sep. '84 (12); Dec. '83 (12).

Prison Clerks (England). 20-30.—(N). Writ.: Orth.: Arith.: Cop. MS.: Comp.: Indexing: Bk-kpg.: Digesting. £80 to £190. Nov. '84 (7); 1882 (9).

Student Interpreters in China, Japan, or Siam. 18-24.—Writ. and Orth.: Arith.: Eng. Comp.: Précis: Geog.: Euc.: Lat.: Fr.: Ger.: Merc. and Crim. Law. £200 and promotion in the Consular Service. Ju. '91 (5); July '90 (5); June '88 (4); June '86 (6); Dec. '85 (4); Feb '84 (6); June '82 (3); Mar. '81 (1).

Student Interpreters for Turkey, Persia, and Levant. 18-24.—Reading: Writ. and Orth.: Arith.: Eng. Comp.: Fr.: Lat.: Anc. Grk.: Ital.: Ger.: Span. £200, with promotion in the Consular Service. Jan. '88 (3); Apl. '85 (3); May '83 (4); May '81 (6).

UNIVERSITIES' LOCAL EXAMINATIONS SCHOLARSHIPS AND EXEMPTIONS.

UNIVERSITY OF CAMBRIDGE.

December, 1892.

Scholarships and Prizes.

The Marmaduke Levitt Scholarship.—This Scholarship of about £40 a year, tenable at the University of Cambridge for 3 years, will be awarded at Easter 1893 to one among the boys examined as Senior Students in December 1892. As soon as the Class List is issued, candidates should send their names to Dr. J. N. Keynes, Syndicate Buildings. No one will be elected who is not placed in the First or Second Class. By the scheme authorised by the Court of Chancery each candidate must send "satisfactory certificates of his moral character and of the inability of his parent or guardian to send him to the University of Cambridge without such assistance."

St. John's College.—St. John's College offers an Exhibition of £30 per annum for two years with the addition of a Sizarship in suitable cases to the first (or, in the event of his refusal to the second) in Mathematics of the Senior Boys, provided he shall have obtained the mark of distinction both in Pure and in Applied Mathematics; and the like prize to the first (or, in the event of his refusal to the second) in Classics of the Senior Boys, provided he obtains the mark of distinction both in Latin and in Greek. Any Student who accepts such offer shall be required to obtain Admission to the College without delay and to commence residence before the age of nineteen years. In applying for the Sizarship the applicant shall be required to forward a declaration from his Parent or Guardian that he is in urgent need of assistance to enable him to go through a University Course; the Student appointed to such Exhibition with or without a Sizarship shall not thereby be debarred from competition for the Minor Scholarships and Open Exhibitions, nor if successful shall he thereby forfeit his Sizarship, but he shall only receive the £30 so far as his annual emolument does not thereby exceed £80 a year, exclusive of the Sizarship.

Newnham College.—The Stevenson Scholarship of £35 for one year, to be continued for a second year or for a second and third year if the Student is making satisfactory progress, is offered by Newnham College to the best Candidate among the Senior Girls in the First Class. The recipient must commence her studies at Newnham College, Cambridge, either in October, 1893, or October, 1894, and the Scholarship will not be finally awarded without satisfactory evidence as to health.

Girton College.—Two Scholarships each of the value of £30 a year for three years, with augmentation in the case of Students needing further assistance, will be offered by Girton College to the best Candidates among the Senior Girls. The successful Candidates will be required to commence residence in October, 1893, or later, as the College may determine, and to read for a Girton College Degree Certificate in Honours.

Bedford College, London.—The Trustees of the Reid Fund offer a Scholarship of £46 10*s*. per annum, for two years to a Candidate in the First of Senior Girls. The holder of the Scholarship must enter upon residence at Bedford College, London. Further information to be obtained from the Hon. Sec. of the Reid Trust, Bedford College, York Place, London.

The Syndicate will give prizes to the four Candidates who pass the best Examination among the Senior and Junior Boys and the Senior and Junior Girls, £12 to each of the two Seniors, and £8 to each of the two Juniors.

The Council of the Royal Geographical Society offer two silver medals, one for the best Senior in Physical Geography (Section F, division II., *e*), and one for the best Senior in Physical, Political and Commercial Geography (Section B, division *d*), if of sufficient merit. Students can no longer enter for the Medal without taking the Section.

A private donor gives £5 for the best Candidate in Political Economy among the Senior Girls.

Local Examination Scholarships.

The following and other Scholarships at Public Schools will be open to Junior Students (Boys) who distinguish themselves sufficiently in the Examination held in December 1892.

Wellington College. The Scholar will be boarded and educated at an annual charge of £10. Tenable while the boy remains at the School. Open to any boy who shall be under fifteen years of age on the 13th of July, 1892, and who shall obtain distinction in Greek and Latin, or Mathematics, provided that he be a son of a deceased officer who within five years of his death had been either on full or half pay.

N.B.—Immediately on the publication of the Class List, the Parent or Master of any boy who fulfils the conditions and desires the scholarship, must inform the Secretary of the Syndicate that he is a Candidate.

A Local Examination Scholarship will not be given to a boy whose parents are in easy circumstances. If the authorities of a school notify to the Syndicate that their students are not candidates for scholarships, no scholarship will be offered to them.

The Syndicate will communicate with the Masters of such boys as appear suitable for scholarships, and will request the Masters to forward the communication to the parents, for the purpose of ascertaining in each case, whether the parents of the boy are willing to accept the offer of a scholarship, and whether the circumstances of the parents are such as to satisfy the conditions upon which the Scholarships are offered.

The Syndicate will transmit to the authorities of the schools that offer scholarships such certificates, as to the moral character and fitness as may be supplied by the Masters and the parents of the several candidates.

The authorities of the schools offering scholarships reserve the right of deciding whether they will accept a candidate whose name is submitted to them.

The tenure of a Scholarship depends upon satisfactory conduct and progress.

EXEMPTION FROM VARIOUS EXAMINATIONS.

A. The following are the conditions on which a Senior Certificate excuses the holder from parts or the whole of the Previous Examination.

1. To excuse the holder of a Certificate from Part I. of the Previous Examination the Certificate must state that the Candidate has passed in Religious Knowledge, including the original Greek of the Gospel, and has attained a certain standard intermediate between the ordinary pass standard and that of distinction in the Latin and in the Greek division of Section C.

2. To excuse from Part II. of the Previous Examination the Certificate must state that the Candidate has attained a certain standard intermediate between the ordinary pass standard and that of distinction in Religious Knowledge or Logic in Euclid and in Algebra.

3. To excuse from the Additional Subjects for Candidates for Honours the Certificate must state that the Candidate has attained a certain standard intermediate between the ordinary pass standard and that of distinction either in applied Mathematics, or in French, or in German.

B. A Senior Certificate enables a student to become a

Candidate for the degree of Bachelor of Music if the student passes in (1) Preliminary, (2) the English Section, (3) one of the four languages included in sections C and D, (4) Euclid and Algebra.

C. A Senior or Junior Certificate satisfies the preliminary requirements of the General Medical Council if it includes Latin, Euclid, Books I., II., III., Algebra, and one of the following:—Greek, French, German, Logic.

D. Persons who have passed the Cambridge Local Examinations are excused the Preliminary Examination before entering into Articles of Clerkship with Attorneys and Solicitors. The published regulations of the Law Society state no special subjects.

E. A student who holds the Certificate of the Syndicate, and desires to add some one or more subjects to obtain exemption from a Preliminary Examination, can enter for such subject or subjects alone on payment of the ordinary fee for entrance.

HIGHER LOCAL 1892 SCHOLARSHIPS, PRIZES, ETC., FOR WOMEN ONLY.

With a view to meeting the actual expenses of examination of Women who are engaged in tuition as a profession, or are preparing for that profession, the sum of £5 each will be given by the Syndicate to the five Candidates fulfilling these conditions who are placed highest in order by the Examiners in June, 1892.

The Lowman Memorial Prize (the interest on £172 17*s*. 3*d*., 2¾ p. c. Consols) will be awarded to the candidate who stands highest in English Language and Literature among those who are engaged in or are preparing for the work of tuition.

Newnham College.—The Council of Newnham College offer the following Scholarships:—Two, at least, of £50 a year for two or three years awarded either (1) for success in two of the groups—A. (English), B. (Ancient and Modern

Languages), C. (Mathematics), D. (Logic, Pschyology, and Political Economy), E. (Natural Philosophy), H. (History: English, and English Constitutional, and French), provided one at least of the two be either B. or C.; or (2) for distinguished success in Group C. Also the Cobden Scholarship of £50 a year for two years, given by Mrs. Winkworth, for distinguished success in Political Economy and Logic, or in English History and French History, with distinction in Political Economy. Also one or more Scholarships of £35, for one year, to candidates who have not gained one of the larger Scholarships: one of these Scholarships may be awarded for distinguished success in the December Examination. The above Scholarships will be awarded only to Students who have either (1) passed in two Groups of the Higher Local Examination, one of these being Languages or Mathematics; or (2) gained Honours in the Senior Local Examination, and passed in either Languages or Mathematics in the Higher Local Examination; or (3) passed the Previous Examination; and they will not, generally speaking, be awarded to Candidates who have already resided as students for two or more terms, unless they have fulfilled the conditions as to examinations required by the University before admission to a Tripos Examination. The performance, if any, in preceding years, will be taken into account in awarding the Scholarships. All Scholarships will be continued to students for a second or a second and third year, if their circumstances make it important to them, provided they are doing sufficiently advanced work, and are making satisfactory progress. Scholars are required to reside during the terms for which they hold their Scholarships; they must begin residence in the October following their election, unless they have not then attained the age of 19, or unless they are prevented by grave cause to be approved by the Council. Permission to defer residence will under no circumstances be granted for more than a year; and a Scholarship will only be awarded if the Council is satisfied that the candidate's state of health is not such as to prevent her from profiting by a systematic course of study at Cambridge. No two of the above Scholarships can be held simultaneously by the same person. Nor can any of them be held with the Gilchrist Scholarship. Further information, if required, can be procured on application to Miss Gladstone, Newnham College, Cambridge.

Gilchrist Scholarship: A Scholarship of £50 per Annum, tenable for three years, for women desirous of studying at either Girton or Newnham College in preparation for one of the Tripos Examinations of the University, will be awarded by a Committee appointed by the Authorities of the two Colleges jointly, for proficiency in one or other of the following groups:—

B (two languages, of which either Latin or Greek shall be one); C, Mathematics; E, Elementary Chemistry, Physics, and Biology. The Scholar may enter at either of the Colleges. Candidates must either have obtained an Honour Certificate in the Cambridge Senior Local Examination, or be entitled to a Certificate in the Cambridge Higher Local Examination at the time of the award.

The Scholarship will not be awarded unless, in the judgment of the Committee, a satisfactory degree of proficiency is shewn. Printed copies of the complete regulations can be obtained from the Secretary of the Gilchrist Educational Trust, 17, Victoria Street, Westminster, S.W.

Candidates for Gratuities or Scholarships must give notice *in writing* to the Local Secretary at the centre at which they a e to be examined before the end of the Examination.

Communications respecting Instruction by Correspondence should be addressed to Miss Rhodes, 59, Hills Road, Cambridge. The classes, which are under the direction of the Council of Newnham College, re-open in October.

There is a lending library from which books are sent by post for preparation in all the groups. Application should be made to Miss J. Kennedy, Shenstone, Cambridge.

EXEMPTIONS.

A. The Certificate of the Higher Local Examination excuses from Part I. of the Previous Examination, if it states that the Candidate has passed in Religious Knowledge, in Latin, and in Greek: from Part II., if he has passed in Scripture Subjects or Logic, and in Arithmetic, Euclid, and Elementary Algebra: from the Additional Subjects if he has passed in Statics and Dynamics, or in French, or in German.

An Honour Certificate admits to Tripos Examinations members of Girton and Newnham Colleges who have resided during a sufficient number of terms, provided the Student has passed in Group B (Languages) and Group C (Mathematics).

B. Any Certificate of the Higher Local Examinations enables a student if a man to become a Candidate for the degree of Bachelor of Music; if a woman, to enter the Examination for such candidates.

C. The Certificate of the Higher Local Examination satisfies the preliminary requirements of the General Medical Council if it includes Latin and Mathematics.

D. Persons who have passed the Cambridge Local Examinations are excused the Preliminary Examinations before entering into Articles of Clerkship with Attorneys and Solicitors. The published regulations of the Law Society state no special subjects.

UNIVERSITY OF OXFORD.

Local Examination Scholarships.

SCHOLARSHIPS AND PRIZES.

1. Senior Candidates (Boys). The Dyke Exhibition, of not less than £60 a year, tenable for four years at the University of Oxford, open to any boy, born on or after July 1, 1873, who is a native of any of the counties of

Somerset, Devon, and Cornwall, or has for three years past been resident in any of such counties, or has for two years past been educated at any of the Schools in the same counties, provided that he is, in the opinion of the Governors, in need of pecuniary help to support him at the University, will be awarded to such Senior Candidate as the Governors shall think most deserving, having regard to the results of the Examination to be held in 1892. For further particulars, apply to R. Bere, Esq., Milverton, Somerset, clerk to the Governors, on or before February 25th, 1892.

2. Senior Candidates (Girls). One Scholarship, value £46 10*s*., at Bedford College, London, tenable for two years from Michaelmas, 1891, is offered by the Trustees of Mrs. Reid's Fund for the Higher Education of Women to the Candidate who shall obtain the highest place in the First Division. For particulars, apply to the Reid Trustees, Bedford College, York Place, W.

3. Senior or Junior Candidates (Boys), Wellington College. The Scholar will be boarded and educated at an annual charge of £10. Tenable while the boy remains at the School. Open to any boy who shall be under fifteen years of age on the 13th of July, 1892, and who shall obtain distinction in Greek and Latin, or Mathematics, provided that he be a son of a deceased officer who within five years of his death had been either on full or half-pay.

4. Junior Candidates, Trinity College, Stratford-on-Avon. A Scholarship of £50 a year for three years, in part payment of fees, is open to any boy who obtains distinction in Mathematics and is placed in the First Class in the General List. The successful candidate will become a resident pupil in Sept., 1892.

5. Senior Candidates (Boys). The Delegates of Non-Collegiate Students propose to award an Exhibition of £50 a year on the results of the Local Examinations for Senior Candidates in 1892. The Exhibition will be tenable for two years, and the Exhibitioner will be re-elected for a further period not exceeding two years, provided that the

Delegates are satisfied with his conduct and industry. The Exhibition will be awarded to the candidate who has shewn the greatest proficiency either in Latin or Greek, or in Mathematics, at the option of the Delegates. There is no limit of age for the Exhibition. Senior candidates in the Local Examinations of 1892, who desire to compete for this Exhibition, are required to signify their intention to the Censor of Non-Collegiate Students, Students' Delegacy, High Street, Oxford.

6. The Royal Geographical Society offers two Medals, one of silver and one of bronze, to the two Senior Candidates (boys or girls) being under the age of nineteen on July 1st, 1892, who shall give the best answers in Geography, provided that their papers are of sufficient merit.

The authorities of the schools which offer Scholarships reserve the right of deciding whether they will accept a candidate whose name is submitted to them.

The continued or extended tenure of any Scholarship is in every case conditional on the Scholar's conduct and progress being satisfactory.

EXEMPTIONS FROM VARIOUS EXAMINATIONS.

1. Senior Candidates (Boys) who show sufficient merit in translations from *prepared* Latin and Greek authors, in Greek and Latin Grammar, in Latin Prose Composition, and in Mathematics, to be excused from **Responsions**, and Senior Candidates (Girls) who shew sufficient merit in two languages and in Mathematics to be excused from the **First Examination for Women**, receive Certificates from the Delegates to that effect.

Senior Candidates (Boys) who show sufficient merit in French or in German to be excused from the Examination in an Additional Subject at **Responsions**, receive Certificates from the Delegates to that effect.

2. Persons who obtain Exemption from Responsions or the First Examination for Women, are admitted to the First Examination for the Degree of Mus. Bac.

3. Persons who obtain Exemption from Responsions may be exempted from the Preliminary Examination for the Army in all subjects except Geometrical Drawing.

4. A Senior or Junior Certificate satisfies the preliminary requirements of the General Medical Council if it includes Lat., Math. and Mech.; and one of the following —Grk., Fr., Ger., Italian, Chemy., Botany, or Zoology.

5. Persons who have obtained a Junior or Senior Certificate are excused the Preliminary Exam. before entering into Articles of Clerkship with Solicitors. The published regulations of the Law Society state no special subjects.

6. A *Junior* Certificate (if the Candidate was born on or after July 1, 1876) exempts the holder from the Preliminary Examination of the Institute of Chartered Accountants, if it includes Algebra (to Quadratic Equations), Euclid I-IV, Geography, English History, and three other optional subjects, of which one must be a language. A *Senior* Certificate (if the Candidate was born on or after July 1, 1873) is also accepted, if the holder passes in Dictation and in English Composition, in addition to the above subjects. Candidates who seek exemption from the above Examination, should indicate the fact on their Entry Forms.

7. Any Certificate qualifies the holder to compete for admission to the National Training School for Teachers in Schools of Art, if it includes English and either Latin or a modern foreign language.

Persons who wish to gain exemption from the examinations of any recognized public body may be admitted to the Senior or Junior Exams., although they shall not offer all the subjects necessary for a certificate, *but they must in that case apply for a special Form of Entry to the Local Secretary at the Centre at which they desire to be examined.* Such persons shall not receive a certificate, and their names shall not be published in the lists, but the Secretary shall notify the subjects (if any) in which they have satisfied the Examiners to the proper authority of the public body from whose examination they seek exemption.[1]

[1] Only the usual certificate will be accepted by the Incorporated Law Society.

EXAMINATION FOR WOMEN:

Accepted Equivalents for First Examination.

No Candidate will be admitted to the Second Examination unless she has passed the First, or some other Examination accepted by the Delegates as equivalent.

At present the Delegates accept as equivalent (1) Responsions. This Examination is conducted by the University Masters of the Schools, and Candidates must comply with all the requirements of "The Examination Statutes and Regulations" (Clarendon Press) so far as they are applicable to them; (2) the Matriculation Examination of the University of London: the Preliminary Examination in Arts of the Victoria University if the Candidate has passed in the same Examination in two of the languages Latin, Greek, French, or German, and in Mathematics: Cambridge Higher Local Examinations, if the Candidate has passed in Group C and in two languages of Group B: the Oxford Senior Local Examinations, if the Candidate has passed in the same Examination in *either* Algebra *or* Euclid, and (with the special recommendation of the Examiners) in two languages of Section C: the Examination for Higher Certificates of the Oxford and Cambridge Schools Examination Board, if the Candidate has passed in the same Examination *either* in two subjects of Group I and in Elementary Mathematics, *or* in one Greek and one Latin book, in Greek and Latin Grammar, in translation from English into Latin, in Arithmetic, and in either Algebra or Euclid.

OXFORD AND CAMBRIDGE SCHOOL EXAMINATIONS.

Two Scholarships, tenable at Girton College, Cambridge, each of the value of £30 a year for three years, with possibility of augmentation in the case of a Student requiring further assistance, will be offered on the Examination for Higher Certificates, preference being given to Candidates showing proficiency in Classics or Mathematics, or Natural Science. The successful Candidates will be required to commence residence in October, 1892, or later, as the College may determine. The Scholarships will not be awarded unless a sufficient degree of proficiency is shown. A Scholarship, tenable at Newnham College, Cambridge, of the value of £50 for one year, will be offered on the Examination for Higher Certificates in Natural Science. No Candidate will be allowed to take more than three of the six subjects of Group IV. Each Candidate must send in her name, with the fee of £1, before June 1, to E. J. Gross, Esq., Caius College, Cambridge, or P. E. Matheson, Esq., High Street, Oxford. If she offers herself also as a Candidate for a Certificate, the fee will be £2. The successful Candidate will be required to commence residence in October, 1892, or later, as the College may determine. The Scholarship may be withheld or diminished in value if no Candidates of sufficient merit present themselves.

One Scholarship, tenable at Somerville Hall, Oxford, of the value of £30 a year for three years, will be offered on the results of the Oxford and Cambridge Higher Certificates Examination, to be held in July, 1892. The successful Candidate will be required to come into residence in October, 1892, or later, if the Principal of the Hall so advises.

One Free Studentship, at Bedford College, London, of the value of 30 guineas per annum, tenable for two years, will be given in accordance with the results of the July Examination for Higher Certificates by the Oxford and Cambridge Board, regard being had to the age of the Candidates, and to the subjects in which they obtain distinction.

Names of Candidates wishing to compete should be sent in by the Head-Mistresses of their respective Schools to P. E. Matheson, Esq., High Street, Oxford, on or before July 1.

NON-COLLEGIATE STUDENTS.

The Worshipful Company of Clothworkers having announced that they will henceforward give three Exhibitions of £52 10*s*. per annum each, to be awarded for proficiency in Physical Science, and to be tenable by Non-Collegiate Students of the Universities of Oxford or Cambridge, each for three years from the date of election, arrangements have been made by which one of these Exhibitions shall be offered yearly for competition among those who may offer themselves in Science at the Examination held under the authority of the Oxford and Cambridge Schools Examination Board.

Candidates for the Exhibition may be, but are not required to be, at the same time Candidates for the Certificates granted by the Oxford and Cambridge Schools Examination Board; and may either be Non-Collegiate Students of one term's standing, or persons who have not yet commenced residence in either University. All who desire to be Candidates for the Exhibition must send either to E. J. Gross, Esq., Caius College, Cambridge, or to P. E. Matheson, Esq., High Street, Oxford, notice of their names and ages, with certificates of character, on or before the first day of June, for Examination in July. Arrangements will be subsequently made as to the place of Examination for each Candidate. Each Candidate for the Exhibition only will have to pay a fee of £1 to the Oxford and Cambridge Schools Examination Board on entering his name; if, however, the Student offers himself also as a Candidate for a Certificate, the fee will be £2.

The successful Candidate for the Exhibition must on election be admitted, if not already a member of either University, as a Non-Collegiate Student, and begin his residence in the following Michaelmas Term.

HIGHER CERTIFICATES.

EXEMPTIONS.

The Higher Certificates give exemption, under certain conditions, from the following Examinations:—

I. The first Examinations in the University course at Oxford and Cambridge—Responsions and the Previous Examination.

A. A Candidate is exempted from Responsions when he has one or more Higher certificates shewing that he has satisfied the Examiners in Greek, Latin, and Elementary Mathematics. Candidates who pass with distinction in Latin or Greek, or who pass (with or without distinction) in French or German, are exempted from the Examination in an Additional Subject at Responsions, which must be taken by Candidates intending to enter for the Final Honour Schools in Mathematics, Physical Science, or Law, if they wish to be excused from the Classical Subjects hitherto required in the First Public Examination (Pass).

A Candidate may obtain exemption from Responsions, if, although he has not obtained a Higher Certificate, he has satisfied the Examiners appointed by the Board in one Greek and one Latin book, in Greek and Latin Grammar, in translation from English into Latin, in Arithmetic, and in the elements of Algebra *or* Geometry, having satisfied the Examiners in all these subjects at the same Examination for Higher Certificates.

B. (1) The Certificate exempts from the first part of the Previous Examination when it states that the Candidate has satisfied the Examiners in Scripture Knowledge (showing a satisfactory acquaintance with the Greek Text), Greek, and Latin; (2) from the second part when the Candidate has passed in Scripture Knowledge, Elementary and Additional Mathematics; (3) and from the Examination in the Additional Subjects when the Candidate has passed in Trigonometry, Statics, Dynamics, or French or German.

II. At Oxford—the Matriculation Examinations of the following Colleges and Halls: University, Balliol, Merton, Exeter, Oriel, Queen's, New College, Lincoln, Brasenose, Corpus, Christ Church, Trinity, St. John's, Jesus, Wadham, Pembroke, Worcester, Keble, and Hertford Colleges; St. Mary, and St. Edmund Halls: and of the Delegates of Non-Collegiate Students.

Candidates who have passed in one Examination in two of the languages Latin, Greek, French or German, and in Mathematics, are exempted from the First Examination for Women.

The Certificates also under certain conditions qualify for entrance at Lady Margaret Hall and Somerville Hall.

At Cambridge—the Entrance Examinations of all Colleges (including Girton) where such Examinations are held.

The Certificates also admit to the Examination of the Training Syndicate; and, under certain conditions, qualify for entrance at Newnham College.

Candidates wishing to be exempted from the Matriculation or Entrance Examination of any College or Hall, or of the Oxford Delegates of Non-Collegiate Students should apply to the authorities of the College or Hall, or to the Delegates for information respecting the conditions under which such exemption is granted.

III. Holders of Certificates are exempted from the Preliminary Examinations of the Incorporated Law Society.

IV. Such portions of the Examination of the Royal Institute of British Architects as appear from the Certificate to have been included in the Examination passed by the Candidate.

V. Such portions of the Examination of the Surveyors' Institution as appear from the Certificate to have been included in the Examination passed by the Candidate.

VI. The Certificates are also accepted by the General Council of Medical Education as evidence that the Candidate has passed a Preliminary Examination.

The subjects in which the Candidate satisfies the Examiners must include Latin, Elementary Mathematics, and one of the following:—Greek, French, German.

VII. The Higher Certificate of the Board is recognised as exempting *pro tanto* from the Preliminary Examination in General Education required by the Faculty of Medicine in the University of Edinburgh.

VIII. Candidates for first appointments in the Army, and for admission to the Royal Military Academy at Woolwich, who have obtained Certificates, are exempted at the discretion of the Civil Service Commissioners from the non-competitive portions of the Examinations prescribed in the Regulations of April 1873, so far as the Certificate shews that the Candidate has satisfied the Examiners in the subjects included in these portions of the Examinations.

LOWER CERTIFICATES.

EXEMPTIONS.

The Lower Certificates give exemption, under certain conditions, from the following Examinations:—

1. The Preliminary Examination of the Pharmaceutical Society of Great Britain, provided that the Candidate obtains a First Class in Latin, Arithmetic, and English.

2. The Preliminary Examination for admission to the Royal Military College provided that the Certificate show that its Holder obtained a First Class in each of the following subjects, viz., Arithmetic, Additional Mathematics, English and Geography, and in either French or German; and passed in Geometrical drawing.

3. The Certificate is also accepted by the General Council of Medical Education as evidence that the Candidate has passed a Preliminary Examination. The Certificate must show that the Candidate has satisfied the Examiners in English, Latin, Arithmetic, Additional Mathematics and in Mechanics; and also in one of the following optional subjects: Greek, French, German, Chemistry.

4. The Lower Certificate is recognised as exempting

pro tanto from the Preliminary Examination in General Education required by the Faculty of Medicine in the University of Edinburgh.

DURHAM UNIVERSITY.

An Exhibition of £30 will be awarded at the Examination for Certificate of Proficiency in General Education, to be held on Tuesday, September 27th, 1892.

LONDON UNIVERSITY.

There shall be two Examinations for Matriculation in each year; one commencing on the Second Monday in January, and the other on the Second Monday in June.

MATRICULATION EXAMINATION.

Candidates for any Degree in this University must have passed the Matriculation Examination. No exemption from this rule is allowed on account of Degrees obtained or Examinations passed at any other University.

EXHIBITIONS, ETC.

The First Six Candidates in the Honours Division of not more than twenty years of age at the commencement of the Examination shall respectively receive an Exhibition or a Prize as follows:—The First of such Candidates shall receive an Exhibition of £30 per annum for the next Two Years; the Second shall receive an Exhibition of £20 per annum for the next Two Years; and the Third shall receive an Exhibition of £15 per annum for the next Two Years; such Exhibitions to be payable in quarterly instalments, provided that on receiving each instalment the Exhibitioner shall declare his intention of presenting himself either at the two Examinations for B.A., or at the two Examinations for B.Sc., or at the Intermediate Examination in Laws, or at the Preliminary Scientific and Intermediate Examinations in Medicine, within three Academical years[1] from the time of his passing the Matriculation Examination; the Fourth Candidate shall receive a Prize to the value of Ten Pounds in Books, Philosophical Instruments, or Money; and the Fifth and Sixth shall each receive a Prize to the value of Five Pounds in Books, Philosophical Instruments, or Money.

Any Candidate who may obtain a place in the Honours Division at the Matriculation Examination in January shall be admissible to the Intermediate Examination either in Arts or in Science in the following July.

EXEMPTIONS.

This Examination is accepted (*a*) by the College of Surgeons, (*b*) by the Incorporated Law Society, (*c*) by the Pharmaceutical Society, and (*d*) by the Royal Institute of British Architects, in lieu of their Preliminary Examinations. It also exempts Candidates for admission to the Royal Military College from the Preliminary Test, except in Geometrical Drawing. And it is among those Examinations of which some one must be passed (1) by every Medical Student on commencing his professional studies; and (2) by every person entering upon Articles of Clerkship to a Solicitor,—any such person who may have Matriculated in the Honours or in the First Division being entitled to exemption from one year's service.

This and all other Examinations of the University,

[1] By the term "Academical Year" is ordinarily meant the period intervening between any Examination and an Examination of a higher grade in the following year; which period may be either *more* or *less* than a Calendar year. Thus the interval between the *Intermediate* Examinations in Arts, Science, and in Science, and the *Degree* Examinations of the next year in those faculties respectively, is about fifteen months; whilst the interval between the B.A. Examination and the M.A. Examination of the next year, or between the B.Sc. Examination and the D.Sc. Examination of the next year, is less than eight months. Nevertheless, each of these intervals is counted as an "Academical Year."

together with the Prizes, Exhibitions, Scholarships, and Medals depending upon them, are open to Women upon exactly the same conditions as to Men.

THE UNIVERSITY OF EDINBURGH.

LOCAL EXAMINATIONS—June, 1892.

BURSARIES.

A. In connection with the Association for the University Education of Women—June 1892.

To be competed for at the Edinburgh University Local Examinations, and held on condition of studying for the University Certificate in Arts for Women (payable when tickets are taken for the Association Classes in November 1892).

N.B.—These Bursaries cannot be held along with any other Bursary or Scholarship whatsoever. Holders of two years' Bursaries must study in the Association Classes for at least two years.

For Candidates taking Honours in Senior Subjects.

1. The Houldsworth Bursary, about £30 for two years, to be won by the Candidate who takes the highest number of marks in three or more subjects, provided that she has taken Latin as a preliminary subject, one of which must be Latin or Mathematics, and who undertakes to qualify at St. George's Training College, Edinburgh, for the profession of a teacher.

2. The Earl of Zetland's Bursary, about £20 for one year, to be won by the Candidate who takes the highest number of marks in three or more subjects, one of which must be Latin or Mathematics.

3. The Student's Bursary, £5 for one year, the gift of the Association Students, to be won by the Candidate who takes the highest number of marks in three or more subjects.

B. Bursaries Offered through the Committee of the St. George's Oral and Correspondence Classes (late St. George's Hall Classes).

For Oral and Corresponding Students of the St. George's Classes.

1. £10 offered by Miss Urquhart, to the Girl (holder of no other Bursary) who takes the highest marks, not under an average of 70 per cent., in three Senior Subjects, one being Latin or Mathematics, and agrees to study for the Edinburgh University Certificate in Arts for Women..

Competitors must have studied two of the Subjects in the St. George's Classes, during the session 1891-92, for the entire course of the time during which instruction is given in those selected, and must intend to become teachers.

2. £10 offered by the Students of the St. George's Classes, to the Girl (holder of no other Bursary) who takes the highest marks, not under an average of 70 per cent., in *three* Junior Subjects, including Latin or Mathematics, and agrees to study for the Senior Certificate.

Competitors must have studied two of the Subjects in the St. George's Classes, during the session 1891-92, for the entire course of the time in which instruction is given in those selected.

3. £5 offered by Miss Houldsworth to the Girl who having, previous to June 1892, passed in the Preliminary Subjects, takes the highest marks, not under an average of 70 per cent., in *Senior* French, and *Senior* History and Geography, and in one of the three following subjects:—*Senior* Latin, *Senior* Mathematics, Logic.

Competitors must have studied two of the above Subjects in the St. George's Classes, during the session 1891-92, for the entire course of the time in which instruction is given, and the winner must agree to continue her studies in a way approved by the Committee.

4. The Committee's Bursary of £5, tenable for two years, to the Girl (holder of no other Bursary), who takes

the highest marks, not under an average of 70 per cent., in the Preliminary Subjects, including Latin and Scripture.

Competitors do not necessarily require to be members of the Scripture Class, but they must have studied Preliminary Grammar, Arithmetic, History, Geography, and Latin in the St. George's Classes during the entire course of the time in which instruction is given. The winner, if over eighteen years of age, must agree to study for the Senior Certificate; but, if under eighteen, she may agree to study either for the Junior or the Senior Certificate. Candidates taking Special Subjects are not eligible for this Bursary.

All particulars relating to the above Bursaries may be obtained on application to the Secretary, St. George's Classes, 3, Melville Street, Edinburgh.

C. Bursaries offered by the University Local Examination Board.

1. A Bursary of £5 to the Candidate, Boy or Girl (not gaining any other bursary or scholarship, from whatever source derived), who takes the highest aggregate of marks in three Junior subjects, including English and either Latin or Mathematics (the aggregate of marks not being under 70 per cent.).

2. A Bursary of £5 to the Boy (not gaining any other bursary or scholarship, from whatever source derived) who takes the highest aggregate of marks in three Junior subjects (the aggregate of marks not being under 70 per cent.).

3. A Bursary of £10 for one year to the Boy standing highest in the Senior Examination (the aggregate of marks not being under 70 per cent.), and who desires to enter the University of Edinburgh. If he does not purpose entering the University, a prize of £5 will be given.

EXEMPTIONS FROM PRIVILEGES ATTACHING TO THE EDINBURGH UNIVERSITY LOCAL CERTIFICATES.

The Preliminary Certificates of Glasgow, St. Andrew's, Aberdeen, Oxford, and Cambridge, the Government Admission Examination in Training Colleges, and the Matriculation Examination of the Royal University, Ireland, are accepted instead of the Preliminary Examination.

The Junior and Senior Certificates are recommended by the *Medical Council to the Licensing Boards* as a sufficient test of Preliminary Education, so far as they include the subjects demanded by the Council, viz.:—(1) English Language, including Grammar and Composition; (2) English History; (3) Modern Geography; (4) Latin, including Translation from the Original and Grammar; (5) Elements of Mathematics, comprising (*a*) Arithmetic, including Vulgar and Decimal Fractions; (*b*) Algebra, including Simple Equations; (*c*) Geometry, including the first book of Euclid, or the subjects thereof; (6) Elementary Mechanics of Solids and Fluids, comprising the Elements of Statics, Dynamics, and Hydrostatics; Blaikie's "Mechanics" (this paper will be drawn to suit the requirements of the Medical Council); (7) One of the following optional subjects:—Greek, French, German, Italian, any other Modern Language, Logic.

1. *The Junior Certificate is* pro tanto *equivalent to the Medical Preliminary in the University of Edinburgh.*

2. The Senior Certificate, when it bears that the holder has passed in Latin, Greek, and Mathematics, may be presented by a Student at the time of his entrance to the University, and will be accepted by the Professors in the Faculty of Arts as evidence of qualification to attend the higher classes in these subjects. The holder will thus have the advantage of entering for the *Curriculum of Three Sessions in Arts without further examination.*

N.B.—The Senior Certificate is thus equivalent to a

recognised *Schools leaving Certificate* for the Universities of Scotland. It is on the same level as the Government "Higher Grade."

3. Ladies who hold the Senior certificate are exempted from the Entrance Examination for Girton College, Cambridge.

4. Holders of the Senior Certificate above eighteen years of age are recognised as Assistants in State-aided schools.

THE UNIVERSITY OF GLASGOW.

LOCAL EXAMINATION.

Certificates.—The Certificates granted by the Board are as follows, viz.:—

I. Junior, }
II. Senior, } for both boys and girls.
III. Higher, }
IV. Certificate in Degree Subjects, } for women.

They are signed by the Vice-Chancellor of the University, and specify in each case the subjects in which the Candidate has passed.

EXEMPTIONS.—The following privileges are attached to the Certificates granted by the Board:—1. Students under 17 years of age proposing to enter the Faculty of Arts in the University are required to pass an Entrance Examination, but the holders of Junior or Senior Certificates are exempted from examination in the subjects comprised in their Certificates. 2. Students proposing to enter on the study of medicine in this University, or other Medical School, are required to pass a Preliminary Examination in General Education, but the holders of Junior or Senior Certificates are exempted from examination in the subjects comprised in their Certificates.[1]

[1] The General Medical Council have resolved that after 1st Jan., 1892, all the requisite subjects must be passed at the same time.

3. Students holding a Senior Certificate bearing that the holder has passed with not less than 60 per cent. of the marks attainable in Latin, Greek, or Mathematics are qualified to attend, in any of the Scottish Universities, the Higher Classes in the subject or subjects passed, without having previously attended the Junior Classes in the same department, and provided such students have passed with the required percentage in Latin and Greek, they may complete the curriculum for a Degree in Arts in three Sessions. 4. The Senior Certificate—provided that it comprises one or more of the following subjects, viz., Latin, Greek, French, German—is accepted as qualifying for admission to Girton College, Cambridge. 5. Females holding the Senior Certificate, or the Higher Certificate, or the Certificate in Degree Subjects, may act as Assistant Teachers, under Art. 79 of the Scotch Code of the Education Department, and under Art. 47, *b.* 2, may obtain Government Certificates after twelve months' service in a day school receiving Government Grants. It may also be mentioned that Candidates who have passed in the common subjects are exempted by the Glasgow School Board from the examinations prescribed for intended Pupil Teachers in their schools.

ST. ANDREWS LOCAL EXAMINATIONS.

PRIVILEGES ATTACHING TO THE CERTIFICATES.

1. Certificates, signed by the Vice-Chancellor, will be issued to the successful Candidates for the Senior Certificate, conferring the title of Associate in Arts of this University, provided at least one subject be passed with *honours*, and the total number of marks amount to 130. The Senatus has sanctioned the use of an academic badge, which all who gain the title of A.A. will be entitled to wear. Application for the above to be made to Mr. Brown, robemaker to the University, St. Andrews. Price 10*s*. 6*d*.

2. The Senior Certificate, when indicating that the holder has passed *with honours* in Latin, Greek, and Mathematics, may be presented by a student at the time of his entrance to this or any other Scottish University, and will be accepted by the Professors in the Faculty of Arts as evidence of qualification to attend the higher classes in these subjects. The holder will thus have the advantage of entering for the Curriculum of Three Sessions in Arts.[1]

3. By a Regulation of the General Medical Council, Senior Certificates granted at the St. Andrew's University Local Examinations secure exemption, for such subjects as are mentioned in the Certificate, from the Medical Preliminary Examinations in any University or Medical School in the United Kingdom. The Senior Certificate also secures exemption from the Preliminary Examination for entrance to Girton College. The Pharmaceutical Society of Great Britain accepts Junior or Senior Certificates as exempting *pro tanto* from their preliminary examination. They also admit to the L.L.A. Examinations.

4. Under the new Education Code, women over eighteen years of age who have passed the St. Andrews Local Examination for the Senior Certificate may act as assistant teachers.

5. The Committee have to announce the following prizes: (1) A sum of £10 from the University funds, to be divided among the most deserving Candidates, on such conditions, and in such proportions, as the Committee may determine. (2) Five free passes to the first year of the L.L.A. Examinations immediately succeeding the winning of the pass. The passes will be awarded to the girls who shall secure the largest aggregate number of marks on three senior subjects. (3) The Adkins' Prize of a silver lever watch, value *£5 5s.*, for the candidate who gains the highest marks in Latin and Greek for the Senior Certificate.

[1] Special attention is directed to this Section.

ABERDEEN LOCAL EXAMINATIONS

Scholarships.

Junior Certificate.—Five pounds (one half paid directly, the other half on obtaining a Senior Certificate), tenable for one year, to the best Lady Candidate at the Examination in June, 1892—such Candidate not holding any other Scholarship or Bursary for these Examinations, and on condition that she proceed and qualify herself for, and in due time obtain, a Senior Certificate.

Senior Certificate.—Miss Warrack's Scholarship of £5 (one half paid directly, the other half on obtaining the Higher Certificate), to the best Lady Candidate for the Senior Certificate—such Candidate not holding or taking any other Scholarship or Bursary for these Examinations, and on condition that she proceed and qualify herself for, and in due time obtain, the Higher Certificate of this University.

Higher Certificate.—Five Pounds (the gift of an anonymous donor) to the lady ranking first among those (being two or more in number) who may gain the Higher Certificate for Women at the Examination in June, 1892.

The Rank in every case to be determined by the Examination Board of the University, according to the absolute numbers of Marks gained by the Candidates subject to the Rules of the Examiners, and the names of the Prizetakers to be announced in the Examiners' Report.

EXEMPTIONS.

The Holder of a Senior Certificate in Latin, Greek, and Mathematics will be held by the University as qualified, without further examination, to enter the Senior Classes in these subjects without attending the Junior, provided he make 60 per cent. in the Examination.

The General Medical Council have agreed to accept a Junior or a Senior Certificate obtained in these Examinations in any subject as a pass in that subject for the Medical Preliminary Examination in any University or Medical School in the United Kingdom. This privilege is granted by the Pharmaceutical Society of Great Britain, provided that Latin, English, and Arithmetic are among the subjects for which the Certificate has been obtained.

INTERMEDIATE EDUCATION BOARD FOR IRELAND.

EXAMINATION EXHIBITIONS.

(*a*) Exhibitions of such value as the Board may determine, but not exceeding £15 a year each, tenable for three years, and payable as the Board may direct, shall be awarded to such students as the Board shall adjudge to have obtained the highest places at the examination in the Junior Grade.

(*b*) Prizes not exceeding £10 each shall be awarded to such students in the Junior Grade, as the Board shall adjudge to be next in order of merit to the students to whom Exhibitions have been awarded; the number of such £10 Prizes shall not exceed the number of Junior Grade Exhibitions.

No student shall be awarded such £10 Prize a second time.

(*c*) The number of Exhibitions in the Junior Grade shall be such as the Board may determine, but shall not exceed one for every twenty students in the aggregate who shall have passed in that grade in accordance with Rule 15.[1] If, on dividing the aggregate above referred to by twenty, there shall remain a number not less than ten, an additional Exhibition may be awarded.

[1] Rule 15. In the case of boys no student shall obtain credit for the examination generally, in Grades other than the Preparatory, nor shall his name be published in the Schedule of Results, unless he pass in at least four subjects, to each of which

Exhibitions of such value as the Board may determine, but not exceeding £25 a year each, tenable for Two Years, and payable as the Board may direct, shall be awarded to such students as the Board shall adjudge to have obtained the highest places at the examination in the Middle Grade.

No student shall hold two exhibitions at the same time.

Prizes of such value as the Board may determine, but not exceeding £40 each, shall be awarded to such students as the Board shall adjudge to have obtained the highest places at the examination in the Senior Grade. No student obtaining such prize shall retain any exhibition previously obtained.

No exhibition under the Act shall be tenable by, and no £40 prize shall be payable to, any student holding a scholarship, exhibition, or free scholarship from any other endowment.

No student shall receive payment of a £40 Prize, or on account of any Exhibition, until he and a parent or guardian shall have made a declaration, in such form as the Board may direct, that the conditions of this Rule have been satisfied in his case.

No exhibition shall continue to be held by any student unless in each year for which it is tenable he shall obtain credit for the examination generally in a grade superior to that in which he obtained or retained it in the previous

not less than 500 marks are assigned, in which must be included one subject from each of the following groups, viz.:—

(A.)—(1) Greek; (2) Latin; (3) French; (4) German; (5) Italian; (6) Celtic.

(B.)—(1) Euclid; (2) Arithmetic; (3) Algebra; (4) Plane Trigonometry; (5) Elem. Mechanics; (6) Algebra and Arithmetic (Senior Grade).

In the case of Girls, in all Grades other than the Preparatory, it will be necessary and sufficient to pass in one subject from group (A), in English, and in any two or more other subjects of the Programme, to which in the aggregate not less than 1,000 marks are assigned.

year, and pass with honours in subjects to which at least 4,000 marks in the aggregate are assigned.

No student shall be allowed to present himself in a grade in which he has already obtained or retained an exhibition, or in a grade lower than that in which he has formerly presented himself.

Should a student, through illness or other sufficient cause, fail to comply with the conditions of continuing to hold an exhibition, the Board may, at their discretion, permit such student to resume the exhibition on such terms as they may prescribe.

The number of exhibitions in the Middle Grade, and of £40 prizes in the Senior Grade, shall be such as the Board may determine, but shall not exceed one for every ten students in the aggregate who shall have passed in those grades, respectively, in accordance with Rule 15.[1] If, on dividing the aggregate above referred to by ten, there shall remain a number not less than five, an additional £40 prize or exhibition may be awarded.

The Board may award prizes in books to students who may have failed to obtain prizes or retain exhibitions, or to obtain Senior Grade £40 prizes, or Junior Grade £10 prizes. These prizes shall be of the following values in each grade: first class prize, £3; second class prize, £2; third class prize, £1.

The Board may award Medals as follows: to each of the students whom the Board shall adjudge to have obtained first places in each grade, a large Gold Medal; to each of the students whom the Board shall adjudge to be the best answerers in the several grades, in Classics (Greek and Latin taken together), in Mathematics (viz., in the Junior and Middle Grades, Arithmetic, Euclid, and Algebra taken together; in the Senior Grade, Algebra and Arithmetic, Euclid, Plane Trigonometry, and Elementary Mechanics taken together) in English, and in Modern languages respectively, a small Gold Medal, always provided that no student shall receive more than one Medal.

[1] See footnote on pp. 69-70.

No student shall be awarded a medal a second time for the same subject in the same grade.

The Board may award in each year to students who shall have obtained credit for the examination generally, Money Prizes, viz.:

Prizes not exceeding £4 in the Senior Grade, £3 in the Middle Grade, and £2 in the Junior and Preparatory Grades, to a number of students not exceeding three in each grade of boys and of girls, who shall have obtained the highest marks in Composition, in Greek, Latin, English, French, German, Italian, Celtic, respectively.

No such prize shall be awardable to an exhibitioner or winner of a Senior Grade £40 prize.

In case an Exhibitioner or winner of a Senior Grade £40 Prize obtains the highest marks in Composition as above, the Prize will lapse.

In the case of equality of students a larger number of Exhibitions, Prizes, and Medals may be awarded so as to include the students on equal marks.

In case a student, through any mistake, should not be awarded marks to which he is entitled on his answering, and should thereby fail to obtain an exhibition, prize, medal, or pass to which his marks when amended shall entitle him, the Board shall have power to award such student an exhibition, prize, medal, or pass, notwithstanding that the number of exhibitions, prizes, or medals shall thereby exceed the limit hereinbefore prescribed, and to alter the Schedule of Results accordingly.

In awarding all exhibitions, prizes, and medals, honour marks only will be taken into account.

Results fees shall be paid to the managers of schools for students who, having attended their schools from the 1st of November of the year previous to that of examination, and having made at least one hundred attendances from that date to the last day of the month preceding the examination, shall have obtained credit for such examination generally. Such results fees shall be calculated at such rates as the Board may determine, but shall not exceed—Preparatory Grade, 1*s.* per 100 marks assigned to each subject in which the student has been awarded a pass; Junior Grade, 2*s.* per 100 marks assigned to each subject in which the student has been awarded a pass; Middle Grade, 2*s.* 6*d.* per 100 marks assigned to each subject in which the student has been awarded a pass; Senior Grade, 3*s.* per 100 marks assigned to each subject in which the student has been awarded a pass; provided (1) that results fees shall not be paid to the managers of more schools than one on the same student in respect of the same subject in the same year; (2) that the aggregate sum to be paid on any one student shall not exceed, in the Preparatory Grade, £3; in the Junior Grade, £5 10*s.*; in the Middle Grade, £6 10*s.*; and in the Senior Grade, £8 10*s.* In 1892 additional results fees will be payable for students in the Junior, Middle, and Senior Grades.

For the purposes of these rules, a school shall mean any educational institution (not being a school under the National Education Board) which affords classical or scientific education to pupils not exceeding eighteen years of age, of whom not less than ten shall have attended the school from the 1st of November, and each of whom shall have made one hundred attendances at the least in the period between that date and the last day of the month preceding the examination in respect to which the results fees are claimed.

Results fees shall not be paid on the same student in respect of the same subject a second time in the same grade.

Each Manager of a school who expects to be entitled to claim Results Fees in any year shall transmit to the Board, not later than the 15th November of the previous year, a list, in such form as the Board shall direct, certified by him to be correct, of students who were on the Roll of the school on the first day of that month.

No student whose name is not on such list will be taken into account in the claim for results fees.

Managers of schools claiming results fees shall send to the Board, when making their claim, a declaration in the form stated in Schedule B of the Programme, and shall state in their claim the exact number of attendances made by each student. All claims for results fees must be sent in on or before 15th October in the year in respect of which such claims are made.

The decision of the Board on the title of any persons to medals, or upon the title to or the amount of, exhibitions, prizes, or results fees, shall be final and conclusive.

Girls.

These rules, except where modifications are specially indicated, shall apply and relate to the education of girls; the examination of girls shall be held apart from that of boys. There shall not be any competition between girls and boys for exhibitions, prizes, medals, or prizes in books. The number of exhibitions to be awarded in each year to girls shall be determined in the same way as for boys.

General.

Non-compliance by the Board with any of these rules, shall not render void any act of the Board; and the Board may by order enlarge the time appointed by these rules for doing any act, and may make such order although the time appointed shall have expired.

These rules shall take effect and come into operation on 1st January, 1892, from and after which date all prior rules inconsistent with these rules are revoked.

PUBLIC SCHOOLS.

SCHOLARSHIPS AND EXHIBITIONS.

1892.

PUBLIC SCHOOLS.

SCHOLARSHIPS AND EXHIBITIONS, 1892

The Scholarships are held provided that the conduct and diligence of the holder continue satisfactory. In the case of Entrance Scholarships due allowance is made for age.

It is essential in applying for admission to these Examinations to send the register of birth, testimonials of good character, &c., and to make application at least about one fortnight previous to the date of Examination. In the case of the larger public schools much longer notice is necessary.

Usually application should be made to the Headmaster for information respecting Scholarships. An asterisk is prefixed if otherwise.

Public Schools, &c.	*Number of Scholarships, 1892.*	*Annual value of each.*	*No. of years tenable.*	*Subjects.*	*Date of Examination, 1892.*	*Limit of age.*	*Tuition and Boarding, one year.*
Aberdeen—Grammar School. H.M.—Jas. Moir, Esq., LL.D.	12 12 2 3 3	£8 & hf. fees £12 £20 £15 £15	4 years. 3 years. 2 years. 5 years. 3 years.	Lat., Eng., Hist., Geo., Arith. Also Gk., Mths., for last two sets of Bursaries.	3rd Sat. in October 1st Sat. in October Date not yet fixed.	Under 15 None ,, under 13	Tuition, £2 to £7. Board, £40 to £70.
Aldenham—Grammar School. H.M.—Rev. J. Kennedy, M.A. Speech Day, July 28. * Open to all boys under 15 (in the school or out of it).	*4 Junior Platt. 2 House. 3 or 4 Senior Platt. 3 Leaving Exhibitns.	£30 £20 £60 £60, £50, £40.	3 years. Until leavg. school. 3 years.	Clcs. Math., Mod. Lngs.	May.	Under 15 Over 15 & under 17.	£68. Entr. Fee £2 2s. Regs. Fee, 5s.

BARNARD CASTLE.—North Eastern County School. H.M.—E. H. Prest, Esq., M.A. *Bursar—Edwin Wells, Esq.	Entrance. *3 †2	£20 £10	4 years. 2 years.	Ely. Scl. subjects.	Octr.	11 to 14 11 to 14.	£31 and 38.
* For boys who are and have been 3 years at any of the Public Elementary Schools of (1) Northumberland (including Berwick-on-Tweed), (2) Durham, and (3) the North Riding of Yorkshire.	In Schl., 1 each term.	£10	3 years.		Begin. of each term.		
† For boys who are and have been at least 3 years at any Public Elementary School at Barnard Castle and Startforth.	Leaving Exhibitns. 1 for advanced education at places to be approved by the Governors.	£40	3 years.		June.	14 and over.	
BATH COLLEGE. H.M.—T. W. Dunn, Esq., M.A. Speech Day about Aug. 1. Latin Play, Dec. 21.	10	£25 to £85	2 yrs., capable of extension.	Classics Mathmtcs., Science, Modern Languages.	Wednesday July 20.	15 and 17.	Tuition, £25. Boarding, £60.

Public Schools, &c.	*Scholarships, &c., 1892.*	*Annual value.*	*No. of years tenable.*	*Subjects.*	*Date of Examination.*	*Limit of age.*	*Tuition and Boarding, one year.*
Bath—Kingswood School (for the sons of Wesleyan Ministers). H.M.—W. P. Workman, Esq., M. A., B.Sc. Speech Day, Dec. 18.	7 In School. 1 ,, 1 ,, 1 Leaving.	£30 £18 £15 £50	1 year. 1 year. 1 year.	No Exam., determined by position in school.		• 19	
Beaumaris—The School. H. M.—Stephen D. Orme, M. A. Speech Day, July 30.	Exhibitns. 15	£10 to £17		Element'ry	Varies.	14	£55 to £45
	3 Leaving Scholsps.	£40	3 years.	Classics and Maths.	July.	None.	Tuitn. only, £8 to £6.
Bedford—Grammar School. For entrance on Classical side or on Civil and Military Department apply to— H. M.—J. Surtees Phillpotts, Esq., M. A., B. C. L. For Exhibitions apply to— *A. Talbot, Esq., 27 De Parys Avenue, Bedford. Speech Day, June.	8 †Entrance Exhibitns.	To Boarders, £60, £50, £40. To Day Boys, £12.	While at School.	Classics, Mathcs., Science, &c.	March.	4 un. 14. 4 ov. 14.	Under 13, £72. Day boys, £9. Over 13, 75 gs. Day boys, £12.
†Open to all boys in the school or out of it.	2 Leaving Exhibitns.	£70 and £60.	4	Classics, Mathcs., Science, &c.	July.		Entr. Fee £2

Modern School. H.M.—Rev. R. B. Poole, D.D. Speech Day, July 28 (last Tuesday in July).	2 Leaving Exhibitns	£55 and £45.	3 years.	Lat., Fr., German, Mathcs., Sci., & Gen. Eng. Subjt.	July.	Not over 17 on Jan. 1 precedg.	£50 to £70.
Belfast—Royal Academical Institution. Robert M. Jones, Esq., M.A., Chairman of Council of Studies. Registrar.—Edward J. Dowdall, Esq.	In School Exhibitns.			Classics, Mthecs., Eng. and Md. Lgs.	June.	None	£60.
	1 Tennent. 1 Drennan.	£5 each.					
	Leaving Exhibitns.						
	1 Sullivan.	£40	3 years.	"			
	2 Porter.	£25	1 year.	"			
	1 Blain.	£10	1 year.	English			
Berkhamsted—The School. H.M.—Rev. T. C. Fry, D.D. Speech Day, July.	3 Free Scholrshps.			Classics, Mathecs., Science, Mod. Lngs.	July.		£52 10s.
	2 Junior.	£8	3 years.			12 to 14.	
	3 Senior.	£12	3 years.			14 to 16.	
	1 Leaving Exhibition.	£60	3 years.			18	

Public Schools, &c.	*Scholarships, &c.,* 1892.	*Annual value.*	*No. of years tenable.*	*Subjects.*	*Date of Examination.*	*Limit of age.*	*Tuition and Boarding, one year.*
Birmingham—King Edward's School. H.M.—Rev. A. R. Vardy, M.A. Speech Day, July 29.	20 Entrce.	£12	2 (capable of extension).	Eng.Gm., Hist. & Geogy., Ar., Ely. Mathcs., Lat., Fr., Ely. Sci.	June 28 and Nov. 29.	8 to 19	Entrance Fee 10*s*.
	4 In School.	£10, £25.	2 years.	Classics, Mathcs., Fr., & Gr. Eng. Sci.	July 5.	15 to 17	
	4 Leaving.	£50.	4 years.		"	19	
Bishop's Stortford—Nonconformist Grammar School. H.M.—Rev. R. Alliott, M.A. Speech Day, July 22.	*7 Awarded annually or as often as funds permit.	£5 to £25.	2 years.	Vary.	As vacancies occur.	1 und. 10 1 " 12 1 " 14 1 over 15	42 gs. to 56 gs. and extras.

* Of these five are open to pupils on entrance, two (£25) being confined to the sons of ministers, but no one is eligible for the one at £20 who is of less than two years' standing in the School. Full particulars may be obtained of the Head Master, or the Hn. Sec. Schsp. Fund, Rev. Frd. Edwards, B.A., Harlow.

Exhibitions.—One of £40 and another of £25, each tenable for three years, will be awarded on certain conditions as often as funds will permit, to pupils who have been in the School at least two years, and are proceeding to one of the Universities or elsewhere with the sanction of the Directors.

Bradfield—St. Andrew's Coll. Warden and H.M.—Rev. H. B. Gray, M.A. Athletic Sports, April 8, 9. Speech Day, June 16.	*2 or 3 Foundation Exhibitions 1 Warden. 3 Minor.	90 gs. and 80 gs. 50 gs. 30 gs.	While at college if recomded. While at college.	Divinity, L. & G. Gram. L.&G. Tran Lat. Prose &Gen. Ppr., Arth., Alg., Euclid. Sep. paper for those above & under 13. Examd. by O. and C. Cert. Brd.	July 28, 29, 30.	11 to 15 11 to 15	£100 to £115 inclusive of extras. Ordinary Board and Instn. 70gs. to 90 gs.

* Foundation Scholars must be either fatherless or the sons of poor clergymen or gentlemen.

	Stevens' Schp. for boys leavg.	£30	3 years.				
Bradford—Grammar School. H.M.—Rev. W. H. Keeling, M.A.	6	£16 or £10	While at School.	English, Mathcs., Lat., Fr.	July (middle).	13	Tuition £16 to £10.
Brecon—Christ College. H.M.—Rev. M. A. Bayfield, M.A. Speech Day, June.	8 4 Several Exhibitions	£20 £50 £10 10*s.*	4 years, to age of 19.	Classics, or Mathcs., or Science.	July or December.	13 to 16	£52 10*s.*
Brighton—The College ... H.M.—Rev. T. Hayes Belcher, M.A. Secretary—Rev. E. H. Woodward, M.A.	11	*£20 to £75	3 years.	Classics, Mathcs., Mod. Lngs.	July or December.	14 or 15	Jun. under 13, 85 guis. Above 13, 100 guineas (inc. terms.)

* In the case of Boarders who especially distinguish themselves in the exam. this may be augmented to any sum not exceeding £80 a year.

Public Schools, &c.	*Scholarships, &c., 1892.*	*Annual value.*	*No. of years tenable.*	*Subjects.*	*Date of Examination.*	*Limit of age.*	*Tuition and Boarding, one year.*
Bristol—The Grammar School. H.M.—R. L. Leighton, Esq., M.A. Speech Day, Aug. 1.	15 Close Schlarshps.	£14 to £18 11*s.* 6*d.*	3 or 6 years.	General.	July and Decr.	15 and 13	Board £33 to £60. Tuition £9 under 12. £12 over 12.
	1 In School.	£15.	1 year.	,,		Over 17.	
	5 Leaving.	£50.	4 years.	,,	July.	20.	
Merchant Venturers' Boys' School. H. M.—J. Wertheimer, B.Sc., B.A. Speech Day, July. 40 Assistant Masters.	9 City of Bristol	1st yr. £12. 2nd ,, £15. 3rd ,, £18.	3 years.	English and Arithmetic. (French optional.)	July.	13	£35 to £50 a year.
	142 County of Somerset	£15.	2 years.		July.	13	
	9 Elton	£12.	3 years.		Dec.	13	
	12 Bedminster	£15.	2 years.		July.	14	
Bromsgrove—The School ... H.M.—Herbert Millington, Esq., M.A.	4 to 6	£60 to £20	While at School.	Classics, French Mathematics.	Variable.	15	£72 Cl. side. £75 Mod. sd. Entr. Fee £3 3*s.*
Bury St. Edmunds—King Edward's School. H.M.—J. H. F. Peile, Esq., M.A. Speech Day, last Tues. in July. The no. of £10 Scholarships varies with no. of boys.	1 Entrance.	£10.	Re-election Annually	Subjects included in a First Grade School curriculum.	Dec. and July.	9 to 19	Abv. 14 £69 Tuition Day Boys £12.
	3 ,,	£4.					
	5 In School.	£10.					
	3 ,,	£4.					
	5 Leaving Exhibitions	£60.	4 years.				

CAMBRIDGE—The Leys School. H.M.—Rev. W. F. Moulton, M.A., D.D. Speech Day, June.	6 Entrance.	£40 to £70.	3 years.	Classics, Mathematics, Science.	July.	13 to 16	85 gs. nomtd. by Life donors. 95 gs. unnominated.
Perse Grammar School. H. M.—H. C. Barnes Lawrence, Esq., M.A. Speech Day, Dec. 15-20. The school has been recently moved to new buildings with accommodation for 300 boys. A chemical laboratory will be built during 1892.	3 Entrance.	School Fees. £6 to £16	While at School.	Elementy. English and Arithmetic.	January	8 to 11	£56 to £66
CANTERBURY—King's School. H.M.—Rev. T. Field, M.A. Speech Day, July 30.	5 Junior Foundation	15 gs.	5 years.	Classics, Mathematics.	July 21 to 23.	16	Sen. £75.
	5 Probrship	£10 4*s.* 8*d.*	2 years.			14	
* The Examination for the Entrance Scholarships will	* Entrance Schlarships	£75, £40, £30, £20.	Durin' good behaviour.		Dec. 16 to 18.	14	Entr. Fee, Day Boys, £2. Boarders £3
be the same as that for the Junior Scholarships. A Candidate for the Entrance Scholarship is eligible for election to a Junior Foundation Scholarship, which is tenable for five years, or until election to a Senior Scholarship of the value of £30. With the £75 Scholarship a Foundation Scholarship would be tenable only as an honorary distinction.							
CARLISLE—Grammar School. H. M.—Rev. S. M. Crosthwaite, M.A. Speech Day, end of July. Sports, shortly before Easter.	2 In School.	£15.	2 years.	Classics, English, Mathes., French, German,	July (about the middle).	10 to 18	

PUBLIC SCHOOLS, &c.	*Scholarships, &c., 1892.*	*Annual value.*	*No. of years tenable.*	*Subjects.*	*Date of Examination.*	*Limit of age.*	*Tuition and Boarding, one year.*
CARLISLE—Grammar School. (*cont.*)							
* About every other year, for sons of clergy. Competition with other northern schools	* 2 Leaving Exhibitins.	£55	4 years.			12 to 14	
for the Hastings Exhibition at Queen's College, Oxford.	1 Triennial.	£25.	3 years.	Chemistry, Electricity. Shorthand.			
CHARTERHOUSE—Godalming ... H.M.—Rev. W. Haig Brown, LL.D.	10 (not less) Junior.	£75	2 to 4 years. till 16 or election to Senr. Schp.	Grk., Lat., Fr., Arith., and Writing Eng. from Dictation.	July.	11 to 15	£110
Sports, April. Old Carthusians Meeting, July (early).	10 Senior.	£95			Exact date published in April.		
Founder's Day, Dec. 12. The Senior Scholarships are open to all who have been at the school at least a year before the Exam. and are between the ages of 14 and 16 on July 15, and are tenable during time at school.	5 Leaving Exhibitns.	£80.	4 ys. at univ. or elsewhere in preparat'n for the work of life.	1 Classics. 1 Maths. 1 Nat. Sci. 2 Gen. Subjects.			

Five "Leaving" Exhns. are also awarded in July.

CHELTENHAM—The College ... Principal—Rev. H. A. James, B.D. Speech Day, June 26. N.B.—Every boy not nominated by a shareholder, has to pay £3 per annum in addition to the school fees. Shares may be bought through the secretary.	10 (at least) Equally divided between Classical and Mathcl. Scholars.	£80 to £20	3 years.	*Classical Scholrshps.* Gk. and Lat. with Latin verse and prose comp. —	May.	15	£78 14*s.* to £88.
	1 (for sons of Old Cheltonians) alternately to Modern and Classical.	£25	3 years.	*Mathemtcl. Scholrshps.* Arth., Alg., Eucl., Trig —			
One "Leaving" Scholarship of £25, tenable for two years, will be awarded this year.	4 (for boys procdng. to Wlwich. or Sandhurst).	£30 to £27 10*s.*	2 years.	Subjects of Army exams.	June.	16 and 17 respectively.	
Grammar School. H.M.—J. Style, Esq., M.A. Speech Day,	12 Open	Tuitn. Fees.	1 year (renewable).	English, Classics. Mathcs., Science.	July.		£54 to £60 (inclusive) according to age.
The Governors may award Exhibitions of £30 a year for three years tenable at the Universities.	1 Townsend Leaving Scholarship	£100 (abt.).	4 years at Pembroke Coll., Oxf.				
CHIGWELL—Archbp. Harsnett's School (1629). H.M.—Rev. R. D. Swallow, M.A. *See note * on next page.*	3 House, 6 (For Day Boys).	*20 guineas. £10 to £15.	3 years. "		July 14.		60 Guineas. Tuition only 15 Guineas

Public Schools, &c.	*Scholarships, &c., 1892.*	*Annual value.*	*No. of years tenable.*	*Subject.*	*Date of Examination.*	*Limit of age.*	*Tuition and Boarding, one year.*
Chigwell—Archbp. Harsnett's School (1629)—(*contd.*) Speech Day, July 29. Sports, April 9.	1 (Leaving).	£30.	2 years.				

* May be increased in value to 30 Guineas a year in the case of boys who are proceeding to the University. Boys who have been educated at Chigwell School for three years are eligible, and with boys from other Essex Schools to be preferred, *cæteris paribus*, for the Essex Scholarships at Hertford College, Oxford. These are of the annual value of £100 for five years.

Public Schools, &c.	*Scholarships, &c., 1892.*	*Annual value.*	*No. of years tenable.*	*Subject.*	*Date of Examination.*	*Limit of age.*	*Tuition and Boarding, one year.*
Clifton—The College ... ... H.M.—Rev. M. G. Glazebrook, M.A. Sec.—W. D. L. Macpherson, Esq. Prize Day, last Tues. in July. Commemoration in June.	3 Leaving Exhhibtns. to the English Universities.	£25, may be increased to £50.	3 with possible extension to 4 years.	Classics, or Mathcs., or Science, or Mod. Lngs., or for these combined.	July School Examination.	Must have been pupils at the College not less than 2 years.	£98 5*s*.
I. Junior School Scholarships. Open to boys who entered the Junior School before the age of 11.	1 or more.	£25.	2 or until election to a Council Scholarshp.	*See note* ‡ *below.*		Und. 14.	
II. Entrance Scholarships. Open only to boys who have not previously entered. Free	1 or more. 1 or more.	£50†. £25.	While at college.	*See note* § *below.*	Tuesday, June 28, 1892.	Und. 14 on prev. 31 March	

nominations and Entrance Exhibitions securing admission to the College in September, may be awarded to boys who do well in the Exam., but fail to obtain Scholarships.					Names, &c., sent in bef. June 22, 1892, to the Headmastr.		
III. Council Scholarships. Open to members of the College, as well as those who have not yet entered.	The Wilson.	£50.†	2			Under 17 on 31st March, 1892.	
	1 or more.	£25.					
	1 or more.	£50.†	2 or until election to another Scholarship.			Under 16 on 31st March, 1892.	
	1 or more.	£25.					
	2 or more.	£50† or £25.	"			Under 15 on 31st March, 1892.	
IV. The Cay Scholarship	1	£20.	1	Maths.			
V. A Modern Language Scholarship.	1	£20.	1	Eng., Fr., and Ger.			

† May be increased to £90.

‡ The Scholarships I. are awarded for proficiency in the subjects taught in the Junior School.

§ The Scholarships II. and III. may be gained by proficiency in the subjects of either of the following groups : Group 1.—Latin, Greek, English, French. Group 2.—Latin, Mathematics, English, French, and either (*a*) Greek, or (*b*) German, or (*c*) Natural Science. The Natural Science will include (i.) Chemistry, Theoretical and Practical; (ii.) Heat; (iii.) Electricity and Magnetism; (iv.) Mechanics and Hydrostatics. But of these four subjects not more than two may be taken up by any boy. The Examination for the Modern Language Scholarship V. consists of passages for translation, Grammar, and Composition in French and German. In English, it includes a General Paper and an Essay. If they are not already members of the College, the Candidates for Scholarships IV. and V. must pass a qualifying examination in Latin; and Candidates in II. and III. Group 1 must pass an Elementary Examination in Mathematics (Arithmetic, Algebra, first four rules, and Euclid I. 1—20).

COWLEY (OXON.)—Oxford Military College. H.M.—J. P. Kirkman, Esq., M.A.	10	£30 to £60.	3 years.	Eng. (Dictn and Essay), Lat., Fr., or Germ.,	Easter.	16	£84 to £120.

Public Schools, &c.	Scholarships, &c., 1892.	Annual value.	No. of years tenable.	Subjects.	Date of Examination.	Limit of age.	Tuition and Boarding, one year.
Cowley (Oxon.)—Oxford Military College (*contd.*) Speech Day, June.				Chemistry, Mathcs. Euc. i-vi, Alg. to Pro. Trigy. to Solut. of Triangles.			
Cranleigh—County School. H.M.—Rev. J. Merriman, D.D. Speech Day, last Wednesday in July.	1 Entrance. Variable No. of Sch. Scholarshps	£20. School Fees.	2 years. 1 year.	English Divinity, Arith.	Entrance, June. School, as vacs. occur.		£37 16*s*.
Croydon—Whitgift Grammar School. H.M.—Robert Brodie, Esq., M.A. Speech Day, July 31.	6 open to boys in sch. or not.	School Fees.	1 year.	Latn., Eng., Mathcs., and either Fr., Germ., or Chemy. at option of Candidate.	Jan. 16th.	8 to 15	Tuition. £10 Lower School. £16 Upper School. For Board apply to Headmster.
	2 open to boys not already in school.	School Fees.	1 year.	English, Arith., French, Latin.	Jan. 16th.	8 to 12.	
	3 In School 4 Leaving Exhibitions	£15. £50, £40, £30.	1 year. 3 years.			15 to 19 Und. 19.	

DARLINGTON—Qu. Elizabeth's School. H.M.—Philip Wood, Esq., M.A. Speech Day, (last Thursday in July).	4 Entrance. 4 Element. 4 In School. 1 Leaving.	Tuitn. Fees. „ „ £40	1 3 1 3	...	Entrance, Sept. El., July. In School, July. Leaving, July.	Under 14. „ 14. „ 14. „ 17.	£48 Board. £6 to £12 Tuit. Fees.
DAVENTRY—The School ... Warden—Rev. W. H. Logan, M.A. Speech Day, July. Athletic Sports, April.	12 Entrnce. (6 open. 6 sons of clergy only) 2 Parker foundation. 1 Sawbr. Ex.	£20, £35 Education Free. £15	While at School.	Classics, Mathemcs., Mod. Subjs.	Jan. Apr. Sept.	Senior, und. 16. Junior, und. 14.	£45 under 12. £55 over 12. Entr. Fee, £1 15*s.*
DENSTONE—The College .. H.M.—Rev. D. Edwardes, M.A. Speech Day, July 29th. Annual Play (Shakespeare), Nov. 14.	3 Entrance. 10 In Schl. 2 Leaving.	£14 £21 £20	4 2 3	Classics, Mathemcs., English. Modern Langs. and Science.	Entr'nce, Sept. School, Jan. Leaving, J'ly (end).	14 17 19	34 guineas. Hdmaster's house. 48 guineas.
DERBY—The School ... ... H.M.—J. R. Sterndale Bennett, Esq., M.A.	5 House. 3 School, 2 Rowland.	£40 10 gs. £25	3 years. 2 years.		Aug. 1st wk. Sept. 3rd wk.	15	£60 to £70. Entr. Fee. £1 3*s.* 6*d.*
DOLLAR—The Institution ... H.M.—George Thom, Esq., M.A.	8	£5, with Free Edc., Books, &c.	4 years.	Eng. Lit., Classics, Mod. Lans.,	June.	13, 14, or thereby. (Pupils in	£50 to £65.

Public Schools, &c.	*Scholarships, &c., 1892.*	*Annual value.*	*No. of years tenable.*	*Subjects.*	*Date of Examination.*	*Limit of age.*	*Tuition and Boarding, one year.*
Dollar—The Institution (*cont.*) Sec. — Thos. W. M'Donald, Esq. Speech Day, June 30 (about).	1 Univer. or Tech. Sch. Bursary.	£30.	3 years.	Mathcs. and Science. ”	”	Cl. III. J. D.) Open to all.	
Dover—The College ... ... H.M.—Rev. W. Bell, M.A.	3	£73 7*s.* to £79 13*s.*	3 years.	Lat., Gr., *or* Germ., Fr., Mathcs. and General.	March.	Under 14.	
	1	£40	3 years.	Lat., Gk., Fr., Mathcs. and Genl. Paper.	July (last week).	15	£73 7*s.* to £79 13*s.*
	1	10 gs.	3 years.			15	
	1	About £20	3 years.		”	14	
	1	10 gs.	1 year.		”	No limit.	
	1	10 gs.	1 year.	”	”	Under 14.	
	1	10 gs.	1 year.	”	”	Under 13.	
Dublin—The High School ... H.M.—W. Wilkins, Esq., M.A. *Elected by the Governors.	*20.	Tuitn. Free.	5	Usual subjects in School Curriculum.	Elections in June & Dec.	10 to 12.	Tuition, £8 to £16.
Speech Day, April.	1 Leaving.	£30, with Free Rooms.	5		Oct., at Trin. Coll. Dublin.	20	

Durham—The School ...	4 (or more) Junior.	£25	4 years.	Classics, Science, and Mathcs.	June 20.	14	Tuition 16 to 22 gs. Bd. 54 gs. Entr. Fee. 2 gs.
H.M.—Rev. J. M. Marshall, M.A.	1 Senior.	£55	3 years.				
Speech Day, July 29.	2 Senior.	£40			,,	16	
	2 Exhns.	£60	3 years.				
Eastbourne—The College.	1	£40	3	Classics, Math., French, & English	July.	15	Tuition, £20. Boarding, £60.
H.M—Rev. C. Crowden, D.D.	4	£20	3		,,	15	
Speech Day, last Tuesday in July.	2	£10	3		,,	15	
	1 Leaving.	£50	3	Classics or Math.	,,	19	
Edinburgh—Royal High Sch. Rector—Jno. Marshall, Esq., LL.D. Edin., and M.A. Oxon.	A. 2 Open.	£20	2 years in school.	Lat. (Cæsar, &c.), Gk., Fr., Eng. Mathcs.	End of June.	13 to 15.	Day School Tuition abt. £13 13*s*.
Speech Day, about July 20.	B. Not more than 3 in school.	£20	2 years.	Lat. (Sallst. Virgil, &c.), Gk., Eng., Mathcs.	End of June.	14	Tuition abt. £14 14*s*.
	C. Not more than 5 in school.	£20	2 years.	Lat. (Hor., Virg., Livy, &c.), Gr., Eng., Math.	End of June.	15	Tuition abt. £15 15*s*.
	D. Not more than 3 Lvng.	£30	3 years.	Lat., Gr., Eng., Math.	End of October.	Under 19	
The Fettes College ... ... H.M.—Rev. W. A. Heard, M.A. Boys residing in England	5 or 6	£300 in amounts varying from	While at College.	Eng., Lat., Gk., Fr., Arith., Alg., Geometry.	July 12. Names of Cands. to be forwarded	11 to 15	Tuitn. £30. Brd. & Tuit. 100 gs. £60 for

PUBLIC SCHOOLS, &c.	*Scholarships, &c., 1892.*	*Annual value.*	*No. of years tenable.*	*Subjects.*	*Date of Examination.*	*Limit of age.*	*Tuition and Boarding, one year.*
EDINBURGH—The Fettes College—(*contd.*).							
may, if they wish it, be examined in London. Copies of papers set at last Exam. can be obtained from Mr. Jackson, Fettes College, on receipt of eight stamps.		£60 to £20		Boy under 13 will not be req. to compete in Fr., Alg., and Geomy. Gk. is not compulsory in Mathcl. Schlps.	by June 27th.		Day Brdrs. Entr. Fee 5 gs.
George Watson's College ... H.M.—Geo. Ogilvie, Esq., LL.D. Candidates must in all cases have attended at least one year at the school.	8 Foundns. in School.	£31 to £38	Till 16 yrs. of age.	The branches which Cands. have been studying during the Session in the Schl.	End of June.	2 each for boys under 12, 13 & 14 respec., & 2 under 15.	Tuition £5 to £8 8*s*. Foundationrs. Free.
	40 Burses. in School.	Tui. Fee £5 to 8 gs.	1 year.		„	5 each for boys under 9, 10, 11, 12, 13, 14, 15, 16 respect'y.	
	3 Leaving. College Bursary.	£25 £25	4 years. 4 years.				
Daniel Stewart's College. .. H.M.—W. W. Dunlop, Esq., M.A.	6 Foundns.	Tui. Fee and £21	Till 16.	„	June.	1 each for boys under 11, 12,	Tuition £2 10*s*. to £8 8*s*.

Candidates must in all cases have attended at least one year at the school.	20 Bursaries.	Tait. Fees.	1 year.		June.	13, & 14 respect'y, & 2 for boys under 15. 2 each 9, 11, 13, 15; 3 each 10, 12, 14, 16.	
ELY—The King's School ... H.M.—Rev. R. Winkfield, M.A. Speech Day, July. Sports, shortly before Easter. Regatta, July.	6 Junior.	£10	Up to age of 15.	Classics, Maths., M. Languages, Divinity, History, and Engl.	July.	under 14.	£48 in School House. £57 in H. Master's House.
	6 Senior.	£10	Till the Holder leaves the School.				
	1 Bishop's Scholarship	£25	3.				
	3 Leaving.	£40	3.				
EPSOM—The College. H.M.—Rev. T. N. Hart Smith, M.A., late Assistant Master at Marlborough College. 14 Assistant Masters. The Foundation Scholarships, of which there are 50, are confined to the Sons of Medical Men. Founder's Day, on which the Prizes are distributed, is always the last day of the Summer term, about July 25th.	7 Entrnce. Open. In school.	From £40 downwrds.	2 years, or more if satisfactory.	Classics, Maths., and Science.	July.	14	The charges are, in College, £70; Wilson Hse, 75 guis.; for Sons of Med. Men in College, about £50, varying slightly according to age.
	4 Open. 2 Conditnal.	£15	1	,,	,,	Two 14 Two 17 Two unlmtd.	
	12 on leaving.	9 of £100 or over. 3 of £60 or over. There are also a few Exhibitions of about £30, simil'r-ly limited.	From 4 downwards.	,,	,,	19.	

Public Schools, &c.	*Scholarships, &c., 1892.*	*Annual value.*	*No. of years tenable.*	*Subjects.*	*Date of Examination.*	*Limit of age.*	*Tuition and Boarding, one year.*
Eton—The College ... ... H.M.—Rev. Edmond Warre, D.D. Lower M.—E. C. Austen-Leigh, Esq. Clerk—*R. Cope, Esq., Cloisters, Eton College. Commemoration Day (and Speech Day), June 4.	About 12.	Educated and Lodged Free during School time.	Till age of 19.	Gk., Lat., Mathc., Geography, History.	Election, July.	Over 12 under 14.	Oppidani. £132 (abt.). Private Classical Tuition £21 extra. Entr. Fee. 10 gs.

N.B.—It is advisable that parents should communicate with a House Tutor some time previously, with a view to entering their boy's name on his list. As the numbers in the Houses are limited, it is often necessary to enter a name some years beforehand.

Scholarships, Exhibitions, Prizes.

I. *Tenable at School:* One or more Exhibitions, worth £50 a-year, are offered annually to competition by Oppidans between 14 and 16. Tenable till election to Foundation, or till 19.

II. *Tenable after leaving:*—

1. Newcastle Scholarship. £50 for three years: decided annually by special Examination at Easter.
2. Four or five Scholarships at King's College, Cambridge, open yearly to Collegers and Oppidans,
3. 2 Chamberlayne, at present about £60 for four years.
   1 Reynolds, „ „ £59 „
   2 Davies, „ „ £60 „
   1 Berriman, „ „ £43 „
   1 Bryant, „ „ £47 „

Of these one or more are offered for competition each year by the direction of the Governing Body at the July Examination of the First Hundred.

4. Goodall Exhibitions, to which deserving boys are nominated.
5. Two Postmasterships at Merton College, Oxford, open to Collegers or Oppidans.
6. Rous Scholarship: Pembroke College, Oxford, open to Collegers and Oppidans.

III. *Prizes.* There are numerous Prizes; among others,

α. The Prince Consort's, for the encouragement of Modern Languages.
β. The Tomline for Mathematics.
γ. The Strafford Shakespeare Prize.
δ. The Jelf Verse Prize.
ε. The Wilder Divinity Prizes.
ζ. The Brinckman Divinity Prizes (Lower Boys).
η. The Richards Essay Prizes.
θ. The Hervey English Verse Prize,

besides the College Prizes for the encouragement of Science and History, given annually.

EXETER—Grammar School. ... H.M.—W. A. Cunningham, Esq., M.A. Speech Day, July. There are 8 Leaving Exhibitions of £40 a year for 4 years, tenable at Universities, Woolwich, Sandhurst, &c.; 4 of £60 at Exeter College,	4 House Scholarships.	£20 to £45.	While at School, subject to conditions.	Classics, Mathcs., and Mod. Subjects.	About Easter.	14	£46 to £66.

Oxford; and 2 of £30 at St. John's College, Cambridge.

The above are confined to boys educated at Exeter School. The following Exhibitions, &c., are partially close:—

Four Huish Exhibitions of £50 a year for 4 years, limited to Exeter, Sherborne, Blundell's, and Taunton Schools. Ten Stapleton Scholarships of £60 for 5 years at Exeter College, Oxford, and 4 Dyke Scholarships of £60 for 4 years.

Public Schools, &c.	*Scholarships, &c., 1892.*	*Annual value.*	*No. of years tenable.*	*Subjects.*	*Date of Examination.*	*Limit of age.*	*Tuition and Boarding, one year.*
Felsted—The School ... H.M.—Rev. H. A. Dalton, M.A. N.B.—Examination at either Felsted or London, at option of Candidate. Speech Day, July.	1 at least. 3 at least. 1 Leaving Exhibition. 1 „	£40 £20 £60 £50	While at School. 3 years. „	Lat., Gk., or Germ., English, Div., Mathcs.	June 22-24. July.	12 to 15.	£48 at School House. £58 at Boarding House.
Galway.—Grammar School ... H.M.—R. Biggs, Esq., LL.D. * Competes with two other Schools.	No entrance or in school * 2 Leaving	£40, £25.	5 years.	Lat., Gk., Maths., Eng. Lit. and Hist., M. Langs.	Oct. at Trin. College Dublin.	20	£50 to £54
Giggleswick.—The Grammar School of King Edward the Sixth ... ... H.M.—Rev. George Style, M.A. Prize Day, last Wed. in July. Sports, last Sat. of first Term.	1 or 2 Entrance. 1 or 2 In School. Leaving Exhibitns., none yet created.	Tuition Fees. „	While at School. „		As vacancies occur.	13 None.	£60, under 13. £72, over 13.

GLASGOW—High School ... Rector—D. H. Paton, Esq., LL.D. Vacations, July and Aug.	2	Classical, £20;	2 years.	Latin, Gk., Math., Fr., or Ger., Eng.	School Exam., end of June: for Leaving Certs. same date. Names, etc., sent in to J. B. Douglas, Esq., 157, St. Vincent Street, Glasgow, by Aug. 31.	under 16.	Tuition, £3 to 10 gs.
		Modern, £20.	"	Lat. Math., Sci., Fr., or Ger., Eng.			
GLENALMOND—Trinity Coll. Warden—Rev. J. H. Skrine, M.A. Speech Day, Aug. 2nd.	4 to 6 1 Leav. Ex., to be held at any Univ.	£50 (1 of £70.)	While at School.	Lat., Gk., Mathes., Fr., Eng.	July.	15	£105 Seniors. £94 10s. Juniors.
GRANTHAM—The School ... H.M.—W. J. Hutchings, Esq., M.A.	6 Exhibitions.	Exempt from Tui. Fees.	3 years.		July.	14	£51 to £54. Entr. Fee. £1.
HAILEYBURY COLLEGE—Near Hertford. H.M.—The Hon. and Rev. E. Lyttelton, M.A. Speech Day, about June 24.	Junior, 2 " 2 " 1 Nomatn.	£50 £30 £10	3 years. 3 years.	Class. side.—Classics, with paper to test general intellg.	About the middle of December.	Jun., 2 und. 13. 2 " 14.	56 to 76 gs. Entr. Fee £5 5s.
	Senior, 3 " 2	£40 £30	"During good conduct."	Mod. sid.—Lat. & Fr., or Fr. and German, Arith., Alg., Euc. Bk. i.		Sen., 15 to 16, on preceding 1st of October in each case.	

Public Schools, &c.	*Scholarships, &c., 1892.*	*Annual value.*	*No. of years tenable.*	*Subjects.*	*Date of Examination.*	*Limit of age.*	*Tuition and Boarding, one year.*
HAILEYBURY COLLEGE (*continued*). * In some cases elsewhere.	5 Leaving Exhibitions	1 £60 2 £50 1 £40 1 £20	3 years. * At Oxford or Cambridge.	Classics. (1, or at the most 2, may be given for proficiency in other subjects.)	July.	Under 19 on preceding 1st of January.	
HARROW—The School ... ... H.M.—Rev. J. E. C. Welldon, M.A. N.B.—The Governors can, at their discretion, add £20 a year to any Scholarship, should the circumstances of the Scholar appear to make it desirable.	Entrance Schlrships. 1 2 3 or 4	£80 Not less than £60 Not less than £30	While at School, should conduct and diligence continue satisfactory	Classics or Mathcs.	Tues. bef. Easter, March 22.	Open to all boys (not members of the school) born in or after 1878.	Necessary annual expenses. "Large" House, £138 3*s.* "Small" House, £183 3*s.* Entr. Fees. School, £6. House, £10.

Candidates for Classical Scholarships will be examined in the following subjects:—Lat. Passages for Trans. into Eng.: (Books, Latin-English Dictionary). Gr. Passages for Trans. into Eng.: (Liddell and Scott's Small Greek Lexicon). Eng. Passages for Trans. into Latin Prose: Lat. Verses: (Gradus and Dictionary).

N.B. *No Grammars to be brought.* In *one* of the two Translation Papers no books will be allowed.

One at least of the Scholarships will be awarded for success in Mathematics, the Examination including Arith. and Algebra to the Binomial Theorem and Logarithms inclusive; also the Geom. of the straight Line and Circle so far as is represented by Eucl., Books I.—IV. 5, and VI. 1—17.

A Candidate may also be elected for combined proficiency. With this view a Classical Candidate will be at liberty to substitute for Latin Verses, Arithmetic, Algebra, and Geometry; and a Mathematical Candidate will be at liberty to decline the paper of Easy Problems, and to be examined instead in Latin Prose, and in Latin and Greek Translation.

All Candidates for Classical Scholarships will be examined in Mathematics, and all Candidates for Mathematical Scholarships in Latin. All Candidates will be examined also in *not more than one* of the following subjects, out of which they may choose:—French, German, History, and Geography, one branch of Natural Science. The Examiners reserve to themselves the liberty of setting any questions, either on paper or *vivâ voce*, tending to elicit the general intelligence of the Candidates.

The Names and Exact Ages of the Candidates, certified by their Parents, and accompanied by a statement in which of the Voluntary subjects the boys wish to be examined, should be sent to the Head Master, on a printed Form supplied for that purpose, by the Tuesday preceding the day of Examination; also a certificate of good moral character from the Master or Tutor under whom they have last studied.

The Examination will begin *punctually* at 10.15 on the Tuesday before Easter, in the Old Speech-Room; and will end by the evening of the following day. For such candidates as pass the first day's Examination, accommodation for the night will be found (if desired) in the house of the Head Master.

In awarding Scholarships, some allowance will be made for age. No boy can be elected under 12 years of age.

SCHOOL AND LEAVING SCHOLARSHIPS.

Isabella Gregory's, one of £100 a year for four years to either University.
Earl Spencer's, one of £30 a year for three years to either University.
Mr. Beriah Botfield's, one of £60 a year for three years to either University.
Mr. Leaf's, one of £70 for three years.

H

HARROW—The School, *contd.*—

Mr. Douglas Anderson's, one of £50 for three years.
Mr. Sayer's, two of 50 guineas a year for four years to Gonville and Caius College, Cambridge.
Mr. Neeld's, two of £30 a year for three years to any College in Oxford.
†Mr. T. C. Baring's, three of £100 a year for five years to Hertford College, Oxford.
Mr. William Roundell's, one of £40 for three years, awarded for proficiency in non-Classical subjects.
The Clayton Memorial Scholarship, of £30 a year for three years, awarded for proficiency in non-Classical subjects.
The Earl of Bessborough's, " Ponsonby " Scholarship, of £30 a year for three years, awarded for proficiency in non-Classical subjects.

† These Scholarships are competed for at *Oxford*, and are limited to Candidates who have been educated, or are in course of being educated, at Harrow.

PUBLIC SCHOOLS, &C.	*Scholarships, &c., 1892.*	*Annual value.*	*No. of years tenable.*	*Subjects.*	*Date of Examination.*	*Limit of age.*	*Tuition and Boarding, one year.*
HEREFORD — Cathedral Grammar School. H.M.—Rev. T. Thistle, M.A. Speech Day in July. Sports in March. Concert in Dec.	Leaving Exhibitns. (1) 2 (2) 2	£120 to £40.	4	1. Examd. with open Scholars at Brasenose College, Oxford. 2. Examd. with Sizars at St. John's Coll., Ox.	Feb. Oct.	19	£65 Sons of Laymen. £60 Sons of Clergy.

HURSTPIERPOINT—The College. H.M.—Rev. C. E. Cooper, M.A. Speech Day.—May 5. Play (Shakespeare) Nov. 9.	5 Entrance 2 Leaving	£8. 8*s*. £16 13*s*. 4*d*.	While at School. 3 years.	Classics. Maths. English. — Do. & Div.	Jan.		36 gs. 48 gs.
IPSWICH.—Queen Elizabeth's School. H.M.—Rev. F. H. Browne, M.A. Sub-Master.—C. H. Garland, Esq., M.A. In School Scholarships, 2 Pemberton of £20 for boys between 14 and 16. 5 of	10 Queen's Scholarships 4 Entrance 2 Exhibitns.	£15 £40 and £35 £20	While at School. " "		As vacancies occur. Dec.	9 to 15 11 to 16 "	Day Boys, £15 to £18. Boarders, £65 to £75.

£15 awarded yearly, and tenable for a year. Hunt, of £10, Barnes, of £15.

Leaving—Pemberton, Martin, and Sharp, each of £50 a year for three years, one awarded annually; Albert, of £32, Ford Studentship, at Trinity, Oxford.

Foundation Prizes—Rigaud, £10, Pemberton, £12 10*s*., Steward, £3.

ISLE OF MAN.—King William's College. H.M.—Rev. F. B. Walters, M.A. * Sec. H. S. Christopher, Esq. Speech Day in July.	3 Barrow 2 Univer. Several School. 6 Leaving Exhns.	£30 £30 £20 £10 £30	5 years. 3 years. While at School. 3 yrs. at Ox. or Camb.	Clas. and Mathcs. Clscs. and Mathcs.	About Sept. 20. "	14 to 17 12 to 16 3 Classc. 3 Mathcs.	In Hostel. 48 gs. Junior Ho. 43 gs. Entr. Fee 1 g.

Public Schools, &c.	Scholarships, &c., 1892	Annual value.	No. of years tenable.	Subjects.	Date of Examination.	Limit of age.	Tuition and Boarding, one year.
JERSEY—Victoria College. H.M.—Rev. R. H. Chambers, M.A. Speech Day, July. Sports, April.	1 (at least) In School 2 Leaving and 1 every 3rd year.	£20 £30 to £40 £30.	2 renewable 4 and 3 yrs.	Lat., Gk., Mathcs.	July. Variable.	16 19 usually.	53 Guineas.
LANCASTER—Royal Grammar School. H.M.—Rev. W. E. Pryke, M.A. Speech Day.—Wednesday nearest August 1. Sports, Last Thursday in Lent Term. Concert, Last Thursday in Michaelmas Term.	7 Leaving, viz.— 3 Victoria, 1 Storey, 1 Blades, 1 Booker, 1 Queen's.	£30 £50 £40 £32 £15	3 (Victoria, Storey, Blades) 1 (Booker, Queen's)	Classics, Mathcs., Mod. Lngs., Science, or some of them.	July.	19	£60.
LANCING—The College ... H.M.—Rev. H. W. McKenzie, M.A. * The Secretary. Speech Day, July.	3 or more.	£30 to £45.	Renewable with good condct. aftr. 2 yrs., until age of 19.	Lat., Gk., Mathcs., Fr., Genl. Knowledge.	July (beginning) or end of June.	14½	£65. Entr. Fee £3 3s.

LEATHERHEAD — St. John's Foundation School. H.M.—Rev. A. F. Rutty, M.A. Speech Day, July. * Also from time to time the Committee award exhibitions of from £30 to £60 per ann. to Foundationers who gain Open Scholarships.	* 2 Entr. 2 Leaving.	£21 £40 & £25.	While at School. 3	Latin, Gk., and Elem. Mathcs. O. and C. Board Exam.	September.	14	Foundatns. Free. — Supplemen. Foundatns. £31 10s. — £52 10s. Sons of Clergy. — £63 Sons of Laymen.
LEEDS—Grammar School ... H.M.—Rev. J. H. Dudley Matthews, M.A. Speech Day, end of July.	In School. 2 Senior. 4 Junior. 1 Leaving Exhibitn.	 £20 £10 10s. £50	 4 years. 4 years. 4 years.	Classics, Mathcs., Md. Langs., Science.	December. "	16 2 to boys under 12. 2 to boys under 14.	Tuition only, 10 gs.
LINCOLN—Grammar School. H.M.—Rev. Canon Fowler, M.A. Speech Day, July.	3 or 4 Entr. and in School. 1 Leaving.	£10 £60	2 4	Clcs. Mths. Sci., Eng. Mod. Lang., Hist., Lit., &c.	July.	8-19	£36 to £42.

Public Schools, &c.	*Scholarships, &c., 1892.*	*Annual value.*	*No. of years tenable.*	*Subjects.*	*Date of Examination.*	*Limit of age.*	*Tuition and Boarding, one year.*
Liverpool—The College. Principal—Rev. F. Dyson, M.A. * Sec.—Rev. George H. Dayson. Speech Day, November.	5 Entrance. 10 In Coll. 8 Leaving Exhibitns.	£10 £3 to £22 £40 to £50	1 renewable 1 „ 3½ years.	O. and C. Higher Certificate Exam.	July.	14 20	£75 Upper School. — Tuitn. only. Upper Sch., £24. Mid. Sch., 11 Gs. Comcl.Sch., £5.
Royal Institution School. H.M.— Speech Day, Dec.	6 Leaving Exhibitns.	1 £70 2 £20 1 £20 1 £20 1 £25	3 years. 3 years. 1 year. 3 years. 3 years.	Classics, Mathcs, Science, Modern Languages.	May O. and C. Certif. Exam. in July.	None.	£105
The Institute. H.M.—Alfred Hughes, Esq., M.A.	10 9 Exhbitns.	12 Guineas. 1 £60 5 18 Gs.	1 2 or 3				
(Great Crosby) Merchant Taylors' School.	20 "Harrison."	£10 to 14.	2 years in the School.	Classics, Mathcs.,	July. ("Harrison	8 to 18.	

H. M. — Rev. Canon S. C. Armour, M.A. Athletic Sports Day, about June 21. Speech Day, about Nov. 25. The Master and Wardens of the Merchant Taylors' Co. visit the School on these days.	3 "Great Crosby."	£40 each.	3 yrs. at the Univ., or to prepare for technical or professional education.	Modern Science, Modern Languages, & English.	Schps." are also awrded in April and Dec. at the Term Exams.)		£50 to £54. Tuitn. only £10 to £14. Greek, £4 extra.
Llandovery—The College. Warden—Rev. Owen Evans, M.A. Speech Day, July 31. Theatricals, December.	43 Scholarships.	£613	Varies.	Classics, Mathcs., Histy., and Science.	January 15 and 16.	Varies.	48 Guineas.
London—Blackheath—The School.	In School, 2.	£10	1 year.	Eng., Lat., Gk., Ger., Fr., Math., Hist., Gog., and Divin.	End of Lent Term.	1 under 13. 1 under 16.	£86 5s.
H.M.—Herbert Bendall, Esq., M.A.	1 Entrance.	£10	1 year.		May 1.		
Speech Day, July. Sports, End of Lent Term.	2 Leaving Exhibitns.	£50	2 years.	Divn., Clas., Mths., Hst., & Nat. Sc.	End of Summer Term.	1 under 13. 1 over 18.	
Central Foundation School of London, Boys', Cowper St.,	200 Eutnce.	Half-tuitn. Fees.	During stay at School.				
City-road, E.C.	6 Entrance.	£10	2		July.	Entrnce. 14.	
H.M.—R. Wormell, Esq.,	63 in Schol.	£5 to £30	2 or 3				
D.Sc., M.A. Speech Day, July (last Monday in July).	12 Leaving.	£50	4				

Public Schools, &c.	*Scholarships, &c., 1892.*	*Annual value.*	*No. of years tenable.*	*Subjects.*	*Date of Examination.*	*Limit of age.*	*Tuition and Boarding, one year.*
LONDON, *continued*—							
Christ's Hospital, Newgate Street, E.C. H.M.—Rev. Rd. Lee, M.A. Speech Day, July 27. Athletics, April.	5 Leaving Exhibitns.	£70	4 At O. or C.	Classics and Mathcs.	July.	19 years.	Free, on Nominatn.
City School (Day School), Victoria Embankment, E.C. H.M.—A.T. Pollard, Esq., M.A.	1 Entrance.	£20	4 years.	Eng., Arth., Histy. and Geography.	June.	13	Tuition, £12 12*s.* under 12. £15 15*s.* over 12.
Secretary.—George R. Renwick, Esq.	10 others.	Total value £400.	Various.	Various.	June & July.	Various.	

There are also 15 In School Exhibitions to boys under 16, of from £20 to £30 a year, and 32 Exhibitions of £50 for 4 years to Universities or some place of higher education, awarded as vacancies occur.

Public Schools, &c.	*Scholarships, &c., 1892.*	*Annual value.*	*No. of years tenable.*	*Subjects.*	*Date of Examination.*	*Limit of age.*	*Tuition and Boarding, one year.*
Dulwich College ... ... H.M.—A. H. Gilkes, Esq., M.A. * School Sec.—Rev. G. C. Allen, M.A. The number of leaving Exhibitions vary from year to year. There are usually 3 or 4 of £50 to £60.	10 (6 Junior and 4 Senior).	£20	3 years.	Classics, Mathcs., Mod. Lngs., and Science.	June.	Junior, under 13. Senior, under 16.	£85 10*s* Entr. Fee £1 1*s.* Tuition Fee only, £22 10*s.*

Haberdashers' Co.'s Schools:—							
Aske's Schools—Hatcham. H. M. — Alfred Barker, M.A., B.Sc.	In School to 1 boy in 10.	1, 2, or 3 terms' fees.	1 year.	Ordinary Subjects.	During the year.	8 to 18.	
	Leaving Exhibitions 1 or more.	£25.	3 years.	Leaving Exhbns. are not granted to any boy who has not passed the Camb. Local Exam.	,, The Schps., etc., are granted on the report of the whole year's work ending June		
Aske's School—Hoxton ... (Haberdashers' Company.) H.M.—R. W. Hinton, B.A.	About 20 Entrnce. 20 School Exhns	FreeEducn. in School.	1 or 2 years, and renewable.	Eng. Subjs. mainly, Mathemcs., French, Sci.	October.	Entrance 14. Sch. and lvng., 17.	
Exams., Matriculation, Locals, South Kensington, Civil Ser.	Leaving Exhns.	Variable, up to £50 per ann.	2 or 3 yrs.	,,	,,		

There are also Girls' Schools on these Foundations. Forms of application for admission, and further information, may be had of the Head Masters, or of the Clerk to the Managers, R. J. Ellis, Esq.

Highgate School ... ... H.M.—Rev. C. McDowall, D.D. (Prebendary of St. Paul's Cathedral). * For Boarders only. Foundation Scholarships are not confined to Boarders. Speech Day.—July 13. Athletic Sports.—April 9.	In School. * 4 Entrnc. 3 Foundn.	£70, £60, £40. £24 each.	4 years.	Classics and Mathemtcs.	June 18 and 19.	12 to 15	Day Boys, £24. Boarders, £84. Entr. Fee 1 guinea.
	Leaving Schships. 2.	£60, £40.	3 years.				

Public Schools, &c.	Scholarships, &c., 1892.	Annual value.	No. of years tenable.	Subjects.	Date of Examination.	Limit of age.	Tuition and Boarding, one year.
London—*continued.*							
King's College School, Somerset House, W.C. H.M.—C. W. Bourne, Esq., M.A.	6	£25.	While at School.	Classics or Mathcs.	3 each at the beginning of Lent and Mich. Terms.	15	Tuition only, 24 gs.
Mercers' School, College Hill, Cannon Street, E.C. H.M.—Rev. D. L. Scott, LL.D.	† 25 In School altogether.	Tuition Fees.	While at School.	Awarded on the results of Sch. Exm	July.	none.	...
† These Scholarships are filled up as vacancies occur. Speech Day.—July .	3 Leaving Exhibitins.	£25.	3 years.	"	"	Must have been 5 years in the Schl. & entered under 12 yrs. of age	...
Merchant Taylors' School, Charterhouse Square, E.C. H.M.—Rev. W. Baker, D.D. Sec.—*C. Waters, Esq. M.A. ‡ Nomination from members of the Court of the Merchant Taylors' Company must be obtained for outsiders.	2‡	12 gs.	2 years.	Lat. (easy Trasl. and Gram.), Fr., Arith., and Genl. Hist.	April.	12	Tuition only, Lower School, 12 gs. Upper Sch., 15 gs. Entr. Fee £5 5s.
	In School. 6	15 gs.	2 years.			14	

Speech Day.—June. Athletic Sports.—End of April or beginning of May.	4 Leaving Exhibitions	£30.	While at School.			16	
St. Paul's School, West Kensington, W. H.M.—F. W. Walker, Esq., M.A. Sur-Master.—Rev. J. H. Lupton, M.A. * Bursar.—S. Bewsher, Esq. § These are open to all boys whether now in the School or not. Registration Fee 10*s.* to competitors not in the School.	7 § Foundn. Scholarsps. for Juniors and Senrs. Each year, in Jan. from 8 to 6, at Easter 6 to 4 at Michaelmas 20 to 18.	£40 to £100. £24 9*s.* (Foundn. Scholars pay the Entrance Fee, £1, but are exempt from the Tuition Fee, valued as above.)	Juniors until they have reached 16. Seniors until they have reached 19.	Juniors.— 1. Mathics. 2. History, Geog., & Eng. Grm. 3. Latin. 4. Greek. 5. French. 6. Freehand Drawing. Seniors.— The above. With Chemistry, Physics, Geometrical Drawing added. N.B.—No subject is indispensable, and the election is made on the aggregation of subjects.	Jan. 13-15, and 16. April 27-29 and May 2. Sept. 9 and 12.	Junr., 14 (Some to boys under 12, if of marked ability). Senr., 16	Tuition, £24 9*s.* Entr. Fee £1. Several Masters take Boarders at charges varying from 60 to 80 gs.
About 8 "Leaving" Exhibitions are awarded annually, these vary in value from £40 to £80, and are tenable for 4 years. Speech Day.—July 27th.							
Stationer's School (Stationers' Company.) H.M.—H. Chettle, M.A.	1 each.	£80 & £40	1	School subjects.	Dec.	15	
	Exhibitions confined to pupils from public element. schs. 20 in school.	£4	While at School.	Up to 7th Standard.	Aug. & Jan.		

Public Schools, &c.	Scholarships, &c., 1892.	Annual value.	No. of years tenable.	Subjects.	Date of Examination.	Limit of age.	Tuition and Boarding, one year.
London, *continued*.							
University College School, Gower Street, W.C. H.M.—H. Weston Eve, Esq., M.A. Exhibs. to University College, London, value £20 and £10, are annually awarded. Speech Day.—July 29th.	4 annually in School.	12 gs.	3	Eng., Arth., Mathmtcs., Lat., Fr.	End of June.	14	24 gs. Tuition. £80 Board (average).
Westminster School (St. Peter's College, Westminster) ... H.M.—Rev. W. Gunion Rutherford, M.A., LL.D. * The fixed expenses of a Queen's Scholar are £30 annually, payable each term in advance. This charge includes maintenance as well as tuition. There are also several valuable School prizes, and 11 or more "Leaving" Scholarships and Exhibi-	10 Queen's. Several Exhibitions	* £30 £30 to £20.	Average 4 years 2	English and Scriptural Knowledge, Latin and Greek (translations from and into), Latin and Greek Grammar Mathematics.	In July.	14 on Mch. 25 preceding.	Tuitn. 30 gs. Bdrs. 65 gs. Half Brdrs. 24 gs. Dinner in Hall £12. Entr. Fee £5 5s.

tions awarded each year, the annual value varying from £120 to £40, tenable at the Universities for periods varying from 3 to 5 years. Election.—End of July.							
LONDONDERRY—Foyle College H.M.—M. C. Hime, Esq., M.A., LL.D.	14 Open.				March & October.	15	54 gs.
	2 In School Exhibitions	£10.	1 year.	Gen. Subjs.	October.		
	2 Leaving Exhibitions	£30.	5 years.	„	„		
Academical Institution ... H.M.—John C. Dick, Esq., M.A. Speech Day.—Dec. 23.	3 In School. 2 Leaving.	£30 £50	1 year.	Grk., Lat., Fr., Germ., Ital., Arith. Bookkpng., Alg., Eucl., N. Phily., Chemistry, and Drawg.	June 15.	No limit.	44 gs.
MALVERN—The College ... H.M.—Rev. Arthur St. John	1	£99.	While at School.	Classics, Mathmtcs., and Modern Subjects. (Equally divided betwn each.)	End of July and Decr.	Und. 16.	£84 upon passing good Entr. Exam., otherwise £99.
Gray, M.A.	1	£87.	„			„	
Speech Day.—July.	7 (about).	£50.	„			„	
Sports.—March or April.	8 (about).	£30.	„			„	
Concert.—December.							

Public Schools, &c.	*Scholarships, &c., 1892.*	*Annual value.*	*No. of years tenable.*	*Subjects.*	*Date of Examination.*	*Limit of age.*	*Tuition and Boarding, one year.*
Malvern—The College—*cont.*	1 Leaving Exhibition.	£50.	3 beginning 1892.	Classics, Mathmtcs., Mod. Subjs.			
Manchester—Grammar School H.M.—J. E King, Esq., M.A. Clerk and Receiver.—Mr. O. W. Cox. Speech Day.—July.	160 (about).	Tuition Free.	3 years.	Reading, Writing, Compostn., Geogr'phy, Grammar, Arithmtc., and any one of following: Alg. to Quad. Euc. 1 & 2, Fr., Latin.	June and November.	10-13	Tuition only, 12 gs.
Mansfield—Queen Elizabeth's School. H.M.—Rev. E. Johnson, M.A. Speech Day.—August.	1 5 or 6 1	£20 £3 to £9. The latter doubled for Boarders. £20 and accumulations	} While at School. At Keble or Selwyn.	Either Classics, Mathmtcs., Nat. Science or English.	At Entrance (the last day of each vacation).	Various.	£45—£50 Entr. Fee 5*s*.

MARLBOROUGH—The College. H.M.—Rev. G. C. Bell, M.A.	* 16 Foundation.	£30	While at School.	Classics, Mathematics, Modrn. Languages.	December.	10-15	£80
Bursar.—Rev. J. S. Thomas, M.A.	2 Senior.	£50	”		June.	15.	
Speech Day, July.	6 Junior.	£30	2 years.		”	14.	
* For the sons of Clergymen of the Church of England, nominated by a Life Governor or by the Council.	The above are open to pupils at the school and "outsiders."						
† Confined to Candidates not already in the school. Tenable only in one of the large Boarding Houses.	† 1 House.	£80	...		”	14. on Jan. 1 previous to Exam.	
N.B. A list of the Life Governors, price 1*s*., will be forwarded by the Bursar	1 Berens.	£15	While at School.		When vacant.	15.	
upon receipt of stamps.	1 Authors.	£15	1 year.		June.	17.	
Several "Leaving" Exhibitions varying in value from £20 to £50, and tenable for 3 years are awarded annually.	2 Mod. Sch.	£20	”		”	17 and 15.	
	4 Council's nomination	£5	While at School.		”	12.	
	2 Ireland. awarded as they fall vacant for sons of clergymen.	£15	While at School.		June when vacant.	15. Jan. 1 prevsly.	
‡ For sons of clergymen who have served in India.	1 Indian.‡	£16.	2 years.		December.	14 on. Jan. 1 previous to Exam.	

Public Schools, &c.	*Scholarships, &c., 1892.*	*Annual value.*	*No. of years tenable.*	*Subjects.*	*Date of Examination.*	*Limit of age.*	*Tuition and Boarding, one year.*
Mill Hill School. Hendon. H.M.—J. D. McClure, Esq., M.A., LL.M. Bousfield (Leaving) Scholarship, tenable for 3 years, at University Coll., London, or New College, London. Annual value, £50; vacant every 3 years.	6 (or more). Entrance (Ministerl.) Also sev'ral other Entrance.	20 to 46 gs. £30 to £50. according to age.	While at School.	Usual Subj. in School Course.	Middle of Lent and Mich. Term.		60 gs. to 84 gs. in School Ho. 90 to 100 gs. in Boarding House.
	In School.						
	2 Senior.	£20	1				
	2 Junior.	£10	1				
	Leaving (No. vari.).	£30	3				
Monmouth.—Grammar School. H.M.—E. H. Culley, Esq., M.A. Speech Day, end of July.	In School.			Latin, Fr., Eng. Essay, Math. Optional, Sci. or Greek.			Tuit. Fees, £2 to £6. Boarding 26 to 39 gs.
	20 Monmou.	£10	1		Jan.		
	10 Foundn.	£20			”		
	Leav. Exh.						
	2	£50			July.		
	2	£30	3 or 4		”		
Newcastle-on-Tyne. — Royal Grammar School.	Entrance 15	Maximum, £10	According to merit.				From £39 to £54.

H.M.—S. C. Logan, Esq., M.A. Speech Day, Nov. 5 (about).	In School, 1 in every 20 boys. 1 in every 10 boys. 3 Leaving. 1 1 1	 Tuitn. Fees exempt. Part. exem. Tuitn. Fees. £40 £80 £30 £12.	 „ „ „ „ „ „	Class., Sci., Mathcs., Mod. Subjs.			
Newcastle (**Staffs.**)—High School. H.M.—G. W. Rundall, Esq., M.A. Speech Day, July 31st.	4 In School. 1 Leaving Exhibition.	£13 10*s*. £50.	3 3	Lat., Fr., Mathcs., Sci., Eng. Science and Mathcs.	Nov. July 20.	One 15 Three 16 19	£63 10*s*.
Newport (**Salop**).— H.M.—Tom Collins, Esq., M.A. Speech Day, end of July.	4	£40.	10 years at Christ Church.	Greek and Latin.	Easter.	None Defined.	Board £40. Tuition, £7 10*s*.
Newton Abbot.—The College. H.M.—Rev. G. Townsend Warner, M.A. Speech Day, last Tuesday in July Term. Sports, April.	15 Entrnce. 4 Choir. In School 1 Exhibitn. 2 Exhibitn. for Day Boys.	From £40 £22 10*s*. £10	Varies. „	Classics, Mathcs., Mod. Lang., Engl., &c.	Twice Yearly.	Under 14 Over 14.	From £60.

Public Schools, &c.	*Scholarships, &c., 1892.*	*Annual value.*	*No. of years tenable.*	*Subjects.*	*Date of Examination.*	*Limit of age.*	*Tuition and Boarding, one year.*
Norwich.—King Edward VI.'s School.	Entr. and In School,						
H.M.—Rev. E. F. Gilbard, M.A.	8	£6 to £10.	1	Classics, Mathcs,	January and July.	Under 14, 15, 16, 18.	Board, £54. Tuition,
Speech Day.—Last Wednesday in July.	1 Leaving.	£30	3	Fr., Eng.	July.	None.	£16 10*s*.
	1 (close)	£24	3		"	"	
Sports.—Third Thursday in June.	at Co. Chri. Coll., Camb.						
Nottingham.—Gram. School.	4 Entrance.	£9 to £14	3	Schl. Work	July.	Under 11	£9 9*s*. for
H.M.—J. Gow, Esq., Litt.D.	6 In School.	£9 to £19	3	(mostly).	"	" 16	Books and
Speech Day, Easter.							Tuition.
Sports in June.	2 Leaving.	£60.	4		"	" 19	£40 to £50. for Board.
Oakham School.	12	£4C to £15.	2 or more.	Classics or	March		£57 to £67.
H.M.—Rev. E. V. Hodge, M.A.	4 Leaving.	£50.	2	Mathcs. or	Entrance.		
Speech Day, July.	Exhibitns.			Science.	July Leaving.		
Oundle School.	1 Junior	£45	3 years.	Classics,	July.	Under 14	£65 to £75
H.M.—Rev. M. T. Park, M.A.				Mathcs.,		on Jan. 1.	
*J. G. Hornstein, Esq.	2 Foundation.	£35	While at School.	and Mod.	"	"	Entr. Fee
Speech Day, July.				Languages.			£1 1*s*.
	4 Entrance.	£30	3 years.	English.	"	"	
	1 Leaving.	£50	4 years.		"		

OXFORD.—St. Edward's School. Warden—Rev. A. B. Simeon, M.A. Speech Day, June 5. Sports, Easter Monday. Annual Play, Nov. 25.	6 Schps. and Exhib.	From £60 to £25.	During Residence.	Classics and Mathcs.	July.	Details sent on application.	£65 Sons of Clergy. £75 Sons of Laymen.
High School for Boys. H.M.—A. Wilson Cave, Esq., M.A. Speech Day, December. Sports, April.	2 In School. Leav. Exh.	12 gs.	3	Classics, Mathcs.,	December.	Under 12 ,, 15	Tuitn. only, 8 to 15 gs.
	2 every 3 years.	About £36.	3	Eng. Subjs., French and German.	July.	16 to 18	
POCKLINGTON—The School. H.M.—Rev. Charles F. Hutton, M.A. Speech Day, July 30. Athletics Sports, June.	5 Open Foundation Scholrshps,	£20	While at School.	Classics, Mathcs., Heb. & Sc.		Over 12 and under 15.	Fees £53 per annum. School Ho. £48 per ann. in Hostel.
	5 Close* Leav. Exhs.	£20	...	...	..	Under 16.	
* Sons of Clergy preferred.	4 Dowman Exhibitions to Univer.	£40	3 years.	...	...	No Limit to age.	
	8 Exhibtns.	Half Fees.					
	1 Bp. Crewe Exhbn. to Oxford.	£40	2 years.				
PORTSMOUTH.—Gram. School. H.M.—A. W. Jerrard, Esq., M.A.	4	£5	3 years.	Latin, Fr., Mathcs., Chem., Physiography, and Mech.	January.	14	Tuitn. only 9 to 11 gs. Entr. Fee £1 1s. Extras £3.
	1	£6	While at School.		,,	,,	
Speech Day, July.	2 For fatherless boys.	£9	3 years.		,,	12	

PUBLIC SCHOOLS, &c.	*Scholarships, &c., 1892.*	*Annual value.*	*No. of years tenable.*	*Subjects.*	*Date of Examination.*	*Limit of age.*	*Tuition and Boarding, one year.*
RADLEY.—St. Peter's College.	2 Entrance.	£80	4 years.	Usual Clas.	July.	14	90 to 110
Warden—Rev. H. L. Thompson, M.A.	1 ,,	£50	,,	Subjects.			guineas.
	1 ,,	£40	,,	1 Mathcs.			
Speech Day, St. Peter's Day (June 29).	1 In School.	£30	1 }	Classical.	Christmas.	17, 16	
	2 ,,	£20	1 }	1 Mathcs.			
Sports, March.	1 ,,	£15	1 }				
READING.—The School.	Entrance,						
H.M.—F. P. Barnard, Esq., M.A.	6 for Day Boys.	£10		Lat., Gr., Math., Eng.	As vacancs. occur.	Und. 14.	£72 16*s.* 6*d.* under 14.
Speech Day, Oct. 18.	7 for Brdrs.	£30				Und. 14.	£83 6*s.* 6*d.* over 14.
Sports, end of Summer Term.	*4 In School	£10		,,	,,		
* Extra Scholshps. granted by Trustees if necessary.	2 Leaving.	£100	[Coll. Oxon. 4 St. John's				
	Various.	£30, £40					
REPTON—The School	3 or 4 Entrance Exhibitions.	£60 to £20.	While at School.	Classics (unseen trans. and Latin Prose	July (the end).	15	About £91.
H.M.—Rev. W. M. Furneaux, M.A.							Entr. Fee £5
Two Leaving Exhibitions, 1 of £50 tenable 3 years, and 1 of £25 tenable 2 years.	2 Foundatn Schps. in School.	£40	4 years.	Comp. Gen. Papr. containing passage for trans. from French) or Mathcs.	,,	16	
Speech Day, June 23 (Thursday nearest June 20).							

ROCHESTER — Cathedral or King's School. H.M. — Rev. J. Langhorne, M.A. A "Leaving" Exhibition of the annual value of £40 tenable for 4 years, is awarded each year.	2	£20	4	Classics, Mathcs., M. Langs., Eng. Subs.	July.	15	£50 to £60. A reduction for clergymen's sons. Entr. Fee 5s.
2 "Gunsley" Exhibitions of £60 per annum, tenable at University Coll., Oxford, for 5 years. Speech Day, last Wednesday in July.						Under 14 to 16	
ROSSALL—The School ... ... H. M. — Rev. Charles C. Tancock, M.A. Prize Day, July 26 or Aug. 2.	2 Foundation.	60 gs.	While at School.	For Classical Candidates: Grk. Trans. and Grammar, Latin Trans. and Grammar, Prse, Vrse; a Mathematical Paper; General Papr: Easy	First week in April.	Und. 14	60 gs. for Sons or dependent Wards of Clergymen, 70 gs. for Sons of Laymen (with nom. from Life Governor, 10 gs. less). Entr. Fee £2 2s. Other Fees about £6. per ann.
Examination for Entrance Scholarships at either Rossall or at Exeter College, Oxford, as candidates prefer.	5 or 6 Senior, each year.	1 of £40. 1 of £30. others of £20 or £10	...			Und. 15	
Besides valuable school prizes, there are each year 2 "Leaving" Exhibitions awarded annually, 1 of £50, and 1 of £30 a year, tenable at Oxford or Camb. for 3 yrs.	5 Junior, each year.	1 of £40. 1 of £30. others of £20 or £10	2 years, or until elected to Senior Scholarshp.		..	Und. 14	

Questions in History, Geography, Literature, &c. For Junr. Cands. under 13 ignorance of Greek may be compensated by good work in Latin. For Mthmtcl. Cands.: Arithmtc., Euclid, Algbra., Elemntry Trigonometry, & Problems. Lat. Transls. and Genrl. Ppr. as above. A Ppr. in Fr. and Ger. is set to both sets of Candidates with subjects in combination or as alternatives. Further information can be obtained from the Head Master or Bursar.

PUBLIC SCHOOLS, &c.	*Scholarships, &c.,* 1892.	*Annual value.*	*No. of years tenable.*	*Subjects.*	*Date of Examination.*	*Limit of age.*	*Tuition and Boarding, one year.*
RUGBY—The School ... ... H.M.—Rev. John Percival, LL.D. The Scholarships named above are mostly open to both Boarders and Day Boys. Besides these there are 36 Foundationers' places open to *Day Boys only*. Of these Foundationers 12 get free education and 24 pay half fees. Any *Day Boy* who enters the Fifth Form before he is 14 becomes thereby qualified for a Masters' Scholarship giving free education.	10 or more.	£105 to £20, with augmentation if required.	While at School.	Classics or Mathcs. or Nat. Sci. or French & German, together with Eng. and Elem. Mathcs. in all cases.	June 7.	12 to 15	£112. Entr. Fee £7 7*s*.
ST. BEES—Grammar School ... H.M.—Rev. W. T. Newbold, M.A. Leaving Exhibitions (2) £40 per annum. Speech Day, Aug. 4. Old Boys Cricket Match, Aug. 3.	6	£25	While at School.	English, Arithmtc., Mathcs., Latin, Greek.	April 21 and 22.	15	£33 to £52.

Sedbergh—The School ... H.M.—H. G. Hart, Esq., M.A. Speech Day, July (end).	Schlrships. are awarded to deserving boys under certain conditions, but there is no fixed number or value.			Classics or Mathemcs.				£75, and 3 gs. for Bath, Gymnasium, and Sch. Games.
Sheffield—Royal Grammar School ... ... H.M.—Rev. Edward Senior, M.A. Speech Day, during the Spring Term.	Entrance and In School, 16.	£6 15*s.* to £13 10*s.*	While at School.	Classics, or Mathmats., Modern Langs., Sci.	June.	...		£52 10*s.* to £58 10*s.*
		1	£50.	3 at Oxford, Cambridge, Durham, or Dublin.		,, July.	19	
Wesley College. H.M.—Rev. V. W. Pearson, B.A.	Entrance.			Arith., Eng. Eng. Hist., Geogy. The above must be taken by all cands. 2 or more of the follwing may be takn also:—Fr., Lat., Grk. or Ger., Math., Chemy. or Physics (Elementary).	Dec. 10.	None. In case of equality of candidates the younger will be preferred		£50 8*s.*
		2	£36 Brdrs., or £12 Day Boys.	1 year.				
		2	£12	,,				
		2	£16	,,				
		1	£36	,,				
	In School.							
		4	£36 Brdrs., or £12 Day Boys.	,, but renewable while at school.				

PUBLIC SCHOOLS, &c.	*Scholarships, &c., 1892.*	*Annual value.*	*No. of years tenable.*	*Subjects.*	*Date of Examination.*	*Limit of age.*	*Tuition and Boarding, one year.*
SHERBORNE—The School ... H.M.—Rev. E. M. Young, M.A. 1 Leaving Exhibition £40 for 4 years, awarded annually; 1 Huish Exhibition £50 for 4 years, awarded annually, the latter competed for by 3 other Schools also. Commemoration held in last week of June or first of July.	8 Foundation.	£22 10*s.*	2 years, Renewable.	Classics, Mathcs., Divinity, Geography and History.	July.	Varies according to vacancies 13, 14, 15, 16.	£85. Entr. Fee £4 4*s.*
SHREWSBURY—The School ... H.M.—Rev. H. W. Moss, M.A. * The two of the annual value of £27 may be held with another, and are open only to boys under 14. Leaving Exhibns., 1892, 1 of £63, 2 or 3 of £60, 1 of £45, 1 of £22. Prize of £100. Speech Day in the second half of June.	4 or 5.	£27* to £40	2 years, Renewable without further Examinatn.	Trans. into Lat. Pr. & V., Trans. from Gk. and Lat., Grammar, Elem. Alg. to Q. Eqns. (inc.), Eucl. I. II. III.	Probably at the end of March.	13-15	£90 Entr. Fee "School," £2 2*s.* "House," £4 4*s.*

SOUTHAMPTON — King Edward VI. Grammar School ... H.M.—James Fewings, Esq., B.A., B.Sc. Speech Days, Dec. 21-23. Sports, July 21-31.	In School, 6.	£7 10*s.* 0*d.*	4	School Curriculum Classical Modern Mathcl.	Nov., between 21st & 30th.	13-17.	£45 to £51.
STAMFORD—Grammar School. H.M.—Rev. D. J. J. Barnard, M.A., LL.D. Speech Day, July 28. Sports, April 13. Dinner, April 12.	1 Entrance.	£10 & bks.	3	Eng., Lat., & Mathcs.	Septr.	14.	£51.
	1 do.	£9.	3	"	"	13.	
	3 House.	£40, £30, and £20.	While at School.	Classics or Mathmatcs.	July, 1st Week.	15.	
	1 Foundn.	£10.	3	Genl. Subjs.	Midsmr.	15.	
	1 Leaving.	£50.	3	Classics, Maths. & Sci.	"	19.	
TAUNTON—Independent College. H.M.—Rev. F. Wilkins Aveling, M.A., B.Sc. Speech Day, last week in July.	1 in School.	£10.	1	Classics, Mathmatcs.	Lond. Univ. Matr., Jan.	None.	From £34
	1 Wills.	£20.	1	Fr., Eng.,		None.	
	1.	£5.	1	and Natural Science.	Camb. Loc. Seniors.		
	1 Junior.	£5.	1		Camb. Loc. Juniors.		
	3 Prizes.	£3, £2, and £1.	1		Coll. of Pr., 1,2, & 3 class		
	1 Prize.	£5.	1	Eng. Comp.			
	Leaving 1 of	£40.	2		Lond. Univ. Mat. Hon.		

PUBLIC SCHOOLS, &c.	*Scholarships, &c., 1892.*	*Annual value.*	*No. of years tenable.*	*Subjects.*	*Date of Examination.*	*Limit of age.*	*Tuition and Boarding, one year.*
TIVERTON—Blundell's School *. H.M.—A. L. Francis, Esq., M.A.	2 Foundation.	£12	While at School.	Classics or Mathcs.	July 21, 22.	15	£60 to £71.
	3 Entrance.	£20	"		"	"	

* SCHOLARSHIPS AND EXHIBITIONS.—There are attached to the School the following Scholarships and Exhibitions at the Universities of the annual value of £640 :—Five Scholarships, £60 per ann., at Balliol College, Oxford, tenable for five years. Three Exhibitions, £60 per ann., at Sidney Sussex College, Cambridge, tenable for three years. One Newte Exhibition, £42 per ann., at Balliol College, Oxford, tenable for five years. One Ham Exhibition, £30 per ann., tenable for three years at Oxford or Cambridge. One Gilberd Exhibition, £30 per ann., tenable for three years at Oxford or Cambridge. One Down Exhibition, £21 per annum, tenable for three years at Oxford or Cambridge.

Candidates for the Balliol Scholarships must have been at the School for three years before election; for any other Scholarship or Exhibition, two years.

SPECIAL PRIVILEGES.—Besides the above close Scholarships and Exhibitions, the boys educated at Blundell's School are privileged to compete for the following:—Four Huish Exhibitions, £50 for four years, limited to Taunton, Exeter, Sherborne, and Blundell's School. These were founded in the year 1875. They have been won by Blundell's School in 1877, 1878, 1880, 1883, 1884, 1885, 1887, and 1888. They can be held with any other Scholarships. Ten Stapledon Scholarships of £60 for five years, at Exeter College, Oxford, limited to persons born or educated in the old diocese of Exeter. Four Dyke Scholarships, £60 for four years, at any College or Hall in Oxford, limited to persons born or educated in Somerset, Devon, or Cornwall.

*** To illustrate the advantage which the School offers to boys intended for the Universities, it may be mentioned that several pupils of the School who have lately been at Oxford or Cambridge will have received in Scholarships or Government allowances an average of £200 each per annum during residence.

TONBRIDGE—Sir Andrew Judd's School ... ... H.M.—Rev. Dr. Wood. * Secretary—W. G. Toope, Esq., B.A. "Leaving" Exhibitions (6) 1 each of £90, £80, £70, £60 £30 and £27 per annum for 4 years. Speech Day.—Wednesday before the last Thursday in July. † Junior fees.—Foundationers £14 per ann. Non-Foundationers £21.	10	£66 to £18.	4	Classics, Mathmtcs., French.	June.	15	Tuition Foundatrs., £18 or £14. Non-Foundationers, £27 or £21. † — Boarding, &c., £60 to £66. — Entr. Fee £3 Registration, 5*s.* — Founda-
	tioners are those of whom the Parents or Persons occupying the place of Parents reside within 10 miles by the ordinary roads and ways from Tonbridge Parish Church.						
UPPINGHAM—Archdeacon Johnson's School.	2	£70	4 years or more.	Classics or Mathmtcs.	April.	14	£110.
H.M.—Rev. E. C. Selwyn,	2	£50	"	"	"	"	
M.A.	2	£30	"	"	"	"	
Lower School.—H. M.—Rev. W. Vale Bagshawe, M.A. Speech Day.—July.							Lower School, £110.
	1 Leaving.	£50.	3 years.	"	"		Entr. Fee £5

PUBLIC SCHOOLS, &c.	*Scholarships, &c., 1892.*	*Annual value.*	*No. of years tenable.*	*Subjects.*	*Date of Examination.*	*Limit of age.*	*Tuition and Boarding, one year.*
WAKEFIELD—Queen Elizabeth's Grammar School	* Entrance about 4.	£3 3*s.* to £6 6*s.*	2 renewable	Latin, Gk., Fr., Germ., Eng. and Science, any or all (according to age).	Jan. 13.	none.	Boarders £46 to £52 according to age.
H.M.—Matthew H. Peacock, Esq., M.A., B. Mus.	* In School about 10.	,,	1 renewable				
* Foundation Scholarships total number not to exceed one for every 10 boys.							
Speech Day.—Last Wednesday in July or first in August.	24 Storie.	£11 11*s.* to £17 17*s.*	3 or 4.	Elementary Sch. Subjs.	Sept. 13.	under 13.	Weekly Boarders £40 to £46 according to age.
Sports.—May.	† 6 Choral.	£6 6*s.* to £12 12*s.*	Till voice breaks.	Singing only.	Varies.	under 12.	
† For Cathedral Choir Boys.	6 Holgate.	£16 6*s.* to £22 12*s.*	Not fixed.	Elementary Sch. Subjs.		none.	
	Leaving Exhibitions 9	£50.	3		July 20.	over 17.	
WARRINGTON—Boteler Grammar School.	6	£12, and upwards.	3	Classics, Mathmtcs., Modern Languages.	July.	3 und. 14. 3 ,, 16.	£51t o £60. Entr. Fee £1
H.M.—Rev. E. J. Willcocks, M.A. 3 "Leaving" Exhibitions £50 for 3 years at Oxford or Cambridge.							
Speech Day.—Tues. July 26, 1892.							

WARWICK—King's School ... H.M.—Rev. J. P. Way, M.A. 4 "Leaving" Exhibitions of £50 for 4 years.	2 2 2	A half or third remission of Tuitn. Fees (£12).	While at School.	Div., Lat., Grk., Fr., Germ., Mathcs., Eng. Hist., Liter.& Sci.	July.	2 und. 12. 2 ,, 15. 2 over 15.	£52. Entr. Fee 10s.
WELLINGTON COLLEGE, near Wokingham, Berks ... H.M.—Rev. E. C. Wickham M.A. * Bursar.—M. S. Forster, Esq., M.A. Speech Day.—June . * £30 less for Foundationers, Exhibitioners, and Boys not residing in the College.	7 usually.	£50* to £80	2 years or while at School.	Lat., Gk., Fr., Euc., Algebra, general paper on Scrip. Hist. and Geogy. —	October (generally).	Between 12 & 14 on June 1.	£110. Entr. Fee for Non-Fndts. only, £6. —
† No one shall be eligible to these Exhibitions unless his father is, or was within 5 years of his death, or within 5 years of the boy's offering himself for the Exhibitions, an Officer in H.M. Army on full or retired pay. Two Leaving Exhibitions of £50 to £20 awarded annually.	† 10 Exhibitions.	£50	While at School.	Arithmetic, French and Latin for all Candidates. Papers also set in Greek *or* German, and Euclid, Books 1, 2, with Algebra, to simple equations.	Usually the first week in July.	Between 12 & 14 on June 18.	Foundationers,[1] £10.

[1] None other but the Sons of Officers who, within five years of their death, had been either on full or half-pay, are eligible for admission on the *Foundation.* Age 9 to 12. Candidates must pass the Entrance Exam.

PUBLIC SCHOOLS, &c.	*Scholarships, &c., 1892.*	*Annual value.*	*No. of years tenable.*	*Subjects.*	*Date of Examination.*	*Limit of age.*	*Tuition and Boarding, one year.*
WESTWARD HO—United Services College ... ... H.M.—Cormell Price, Esq., M.A., B.C.L. Speech Day.—July. Assault-of-Arms.—April. Christmas Pastimes.—Dec.	Leaving Exhibitions To Pupils who pass into Woolwich or Sandhurst in the first ten places.	£30.				Boarders, 60 to 75 gs. for Board and Tuition only. Junior School for Boys under 12. Boarders, 55 to 65 gs. Day boys, 14 to 18 gs.	Day boys, 18 to 24 gs.
WINCHESTER—The College ... H.M.—Rev. W. A. Fearon, D.D., Canon of Winchester.	12 (about).	* See last column.	While at School.	Elem. Rel. Knowldge., Hdwtg. and Dic., Arth., Alg., Geom., Lat. Comp. (Pr. & V.), Constrg. & pars. in Gk. and Lat., Fr. Gram., (pars. and trans. of easy pas.),	July	12 to 14.	* Scholars, £21. Commoners £112. Entr. Fee, Commoners only, £12.
Second Master. — Rev. G. Richardson, M.A. Domum Day.—July 28th. N.B. Those who wish to enter the names of Candidates for Scholarships must give notice after the first of May, and on or before June 30. Such notice must be addressed to the Rev. G. RICHARDSON, The College, Winchester.	2 Exhibitions. 6 "Leavg." Scholrshps. at New College, Oxford, may be awarded each year, also not less	£40	..		"	"	

Examination Papers set in past years may be obtained from Mr. WELLS, Bookseller, College Street, Winchester; price One Shilling the set.	than 4 Exhibitions of £50 for 4 years.			outlines of Geogy. and Eng. Hist.			
WOLVERHAMPTON—The School H.M.—Rev. Henry Williams, B.A. Speech Day.—Last Friday in July. Sports.—June (third week).	3 Leaving.	£60.	3 years.	Classics, Mathmtcs., Nat. Scien., Modern Languages. Cmcl. Subjs.	July (last week).	19	£47 10s. to £63 10s.
WORCESTER—Cathedral Grammar School. H.M.—Rev. W. E. Bolland, M.A. Speech Day.—Second week in Otober.	King's† Scholrshps. House† Scholrshps.	£20. £50 to £35.	Generally about 5 yrs. While at School.	Lat., Eng., and Maths., with Greek (not compulsory).	November. "	Under 15.	Tuition, 12 gs. under 12, 15 gs. over 12 (unless entrance before 11). Board, £60 (Sons of Clergy, £50). Entr. Fee £1
	Leaving Exhibition.	£40.	3 years.		July.		
† The number varies according to vacancies.	Dean Peel Scholrship. Meeke Scholarship at Hertford Coll. Oxford	" £40.	" "		Every third July. November.		

Public Schools, &c.	*Scholarships, &c., 1892.*	*Annual value.*	*No. of years tenable.*	*Subjects.*	*Date of Examination.*	*Limit of age.*	*Tuition and Boarding, one year.*
York—St. Peter's School ... H.M.—Rev. G. T. Handford, M.A.	2 Open.*	£15	1 year.	Classics and Mathmtcs.	July.	14½.	Board, £45 and £52 10*s.*
Speech Day, July 30. School Play and Old Peterites' Football Match, week before Christmas. Old Peterites' Boat Race, end of Lent Term. Commemoration and O. P. Cricket Match, St. Peter's Day, June 29. Athletic Sports, July 29-30.	1 ,,	£15.	1 year.	Mathmtcs. Lat., Mod. Languages.		,,	Education, 12 & 14 gs.
	* The winner of one of these three open Scholarships is practically certain of getting one of the five following at the end of his first year. All these Scholarships are given every year.						
† At end of one year's attendance at the School.	1 †	Free Board & Educatn.	4 years.	Classics and Mathmtcs.	,,	15½.	
	1 †	Bd. & Edcn. for £20 per annum.	,,	,,	,,	,,	
	2 † 1 †	Education Free.	2 years.	Mths., Lat., Md. Langs.	,,	,,	
Leaving Exhibition Oxford, Camb., or Durham.	1	£50.	3 years.	Classics or Mathmtcs.	,,	19½.	

LADIES' COLLEGES.

Usually application should be made to the Secretary for information respecting Scholarships. An asterisk is prefixed if otherwise.

LADIES' COLLEGES.

Towns, Colleges, &c.	*No. of open Scholarships, 1892.*	*Annual Value.*	*No of years tenable.*	*Date of Examination.*	*Subjects.*	*Limit of age.*	*Board and Tuition, one year.*
CAMBRIDGE. GIRTON. *Mistress*—Miss Welsh. Sec.—Miss Kensington, 122, Gloucester Terrace, Hyde Park, London, W.	Sir Francis Goldsmid Scholarships.	£45	3 (beg. April, 1892.)	March.	I. *Classics*— Latin, Greek.	No limit of age.	£105. There are no extras and no College Bill. Exam. Fee £1. Must be sent when the form of entry, obtainable from the Secretary, is returned, *i e.* not later than Jan. 31 for March Exam. and by April 30 for June Exam. No Fee is charged in the case of candi-
Candidates for Scholarships must have passed an examination qualifying for admission, such examination including Latin and Elem. Mathcs. Scholarships and Exhibitions will be awarded for proficiency in either Classics, Mathcs., Natural Science, and Modern Languages.	College.	£75	3 (beginning Oct., 1892).	June.	II. *Mathematics*— Euclid, Algebra, Trigonometry El. Mechanics, & Analytical Conics.		
	”	£60	”	”			
	”	£45 (2)	”	”			
	”	£30 (2)	”	”			
	”	20 gs.	”	”			
	Clothworkers' Exhibition.	50 gs.	”		III. *Natural Science*— Chemistry, Physics, viz.: Heat, Mechanics, Light, Electricity, & Magnetism. Botany.		
	Classical Foundation Scholarship.	£80	4				
	Old Students' Scholarship.	£45		”			

					Cands. must take Chemy., Heat, and Mechcs., and may take one other Subjct. Exam. will include practical work in Chemy., Phys., and Botany.		dateswho have passed an Ex. qual. for adm.
Scholars will be required to read for a Degree Certificate in Honours. For other Scholarships see under Local Examinations: Cambridge Higher, June, 1892.—Oxford and Cambridge Schs. Exam. (Higher Certificate) July, 1892. — Camb. Senior, Dec., 1891.	1 or more, the amount to be fixed at the discretion of the Executive Committee.	£30 £50	3 (beg. Oct. 1892).		IV. *Modern Languages*— † { French, German, ‡ Italian. † Compulsory. ‡ Optional.	No limit of age.	Particulars as to Entrance Exams. obtainable from the Secretary.

The following examinations may be substituted for the entrance examination:—

1.—The Matriculation Examination of the University of London.

2.—The Cambridge Higher Local Examination, provided that Group B is included.

3.—The Examination for Higher Certificates of the Oxford and Cambridge Schools Examination Board.

4 & 5.—The Cambridge or the Oxford Local Examination for Senior Students, provided that a language is included.

6.—Three Sections, including A and B, or Section A and two languages in Section B, of the Durham Local Examination for Senior Students.

7.—The Preliminary Examination of the Victoria University.

8.—The Edinburgh Senior Local Examination, provided that the Department of languages is included.

9.—The Glasgow Senior Local Examination, provided that one of the optional subjects selected is taken from Department F.

10.—The Aberdeen Senior Local Examination, provided that Department A is taken.

11.—The St. Andrews Senior Local Examination, provided that two languages other than English, or Mathematics and one language other than English are included.

12.—The Matriculation Examination of the Royal University of Ireland.

13.—The Senior Grade of the Irish Intermediate Examination if the candidate has passed in five of the Subjects 1—10, provided that Mathematics, English and one other language are included. A candidate who has passed in Arithmetic in the Middle Grade may substitute some other subject for Mathematics.

14.—The Sydney Senior Local Examination, provided that Sections I., II., III., VIII., one of the Sections in Group II., and one in Groups II. or III. (in addition to Arithmetic) are taken.

15.—The Entrance Examination of the University of Calcutta.

N.B.—Candidates whose certificates are inadmissible owing to a language not having been included, may qualify for admission by passing in a language only, at the Entrance Examination.

LADIES' COLLEGES.

CAMBRIDGE—*continued.*

NEWNHAM COLLEGE EXAMINATIONS.

Principal.—Miss A. J. Clough.

Vice-Principals.—Miss Helen Gladstone. Miss Jane Lee, Miss Katharine Stephen.

Hon. Secretary.—Miss M. G. Kennedy, Shenstone, Cambridge.

Hon Treasurer.—Mrs. H. Sidgwick, Hillside, Chesterton Road, Cambridge.

Entrance Examination.

An Entrance Examination is held annually at Newnham College in March. The Examination will consist of four parts:

(1) Arithmetic, Euclid and Algebra. (3) Latin.
(2) French and German. (4) Greek.

Candidates will be required to pass in part 1 and in one at least of parts 2, 3, 4.

(1) There will be three papers in this part each of two hours, (*a*) Arithmetic, (*b*) Euclid and (*c*) Algebra. In each division the knowledge demanded will be the same as is required in the Previous Examination.

(2) There will be two papers in this part, each of two hours, (*a*) French, (*b*) German. Unseen passages will be set for translation from books of the periods selected for special study in the Cambridge Higher Local Examination of the following June and some knowledge of composition will be required. There will be short questions on grammar.

(3) There will be one paper of two hours, containing (*a*) passages for translation from the book selected for the Previous Examination of the same year, (*b*) questions on Grammar, (*c*) a short piece of Unseen Translation, for which dictionaries may be used.

(4) There will be one paper of two hours, containing passages for translation from (*a*) the Greek classic and (*b*) the Gospel selected for the Previous Examination of the same year, and (*c*) questions on Grammar.

Candidates intending to take this Entrance Examination must send in their names and pay the fee of two guineas before March 1, to Miss Gladstone, Newnham College.

The following are the set subjects for 1892:—

(1) Euclid, Books I., II., III., Definitions 1—10 of Book V., Propositions 1—19 of Book VI.

Elementary Algebra, viz., definitions; addition, subtraction, multiplication and division of algebraical expressions; method of finding H. C. F. and L. C. M.; simple and quadratic equations involving not more than two unknown quantities; elementary parts of theory of indices, ratio and proportion, arithmetical and geometrical progressions.

(2) French A.D. 1650-1715. German, A.D. 1770—1832.

(3) Virgil, VI.

(4) Plutarch, Themistocles; the Gospel of St. Luke, or Xenophon, Memorabilia, Bks. I. and II., Matthew.

CLASSICAL SCHOLARSHIP EXAMINATION.

An Examination in Classics is held annually at Newnham College, in March. The Examination consists of five papers, as follows :—

(1)	Latin Unseen Translation, Prose and Verse.	3 hours.
(2)	Greek " " " "	3 hours.
(3)	Latin Prose Composition.	2 hours.
(4)	Greek " "	2 hours.
(5)	General Questions on Roman and Greek Grammar, History, Antiquities, etc.	3 hours.

The Examination is open to Students of Newnham College in their first year of residence, and to women desiring to enter the College.

Scholars and other Candidates recommended by the Examiners are admitted to the College without any further qualifying examination.

Candidates for entrance intending to take this Examination must send in their names and pay a fee of two guineas, and Students in residence must send in their names and pay a fee of one guinea, before March 1, to Miss Gladstone, Newnham College.

A Scholarship of £50 a year will be offered for competition in 1892, tenable for three years in the case of a Student who has not yet come into residence, and for two years in the case of a resident Student of Newnham College. Should no Candidate show sufficient merit to obtain the £50 Scholarship, a Scholarship of £35 for one year may be granted on the recommendation of the Examiners, or the Scholarship may be altogether withheld.

Scholarships and Exhibitions.

The Council of Newnham College offer the following Scholarships for competition during the year 1892-93 :

(*a*) One of £50, for three years, founded by the late Mr. Stephen Winkworth, called the Winkworth Scholarship.

(*b*) One of £50 a year, for two years, given by the Goldsmiths' Company.

(*c*) One of £50 a year, for two years, given by the Clothworkers' Company, to be held by a student whose resources are inadequate to defray the expenses of residence at Newnham College.

(*d*) One of £50 a year, for two years, given by the Drapers' Company, to be held by a student who is preparing for the profession of teaching.

(*e*) One of £50 a year, for two years, called the Cobden Scholarship, given by Mrs. Stephen Winkworth.

(*f*) One of £50 a year for one year.

(*g*) The Birmingham Scholarship of £35 for one year.

(*h*) One or more of £35 for one year.

These will be awarded as follows:

At the Classical Scholarship Examination to be held at Newnham College in March, 1892, a Scholarship of £50 a year, for three or two years, will be awarded to the best candidate, provided that such candidate attains a standard satisfactory to the Examiners.

At the Natural Sciences Scholarship Examination to be held at Newnham College in June, 1892, a Scholarship of £50 a year, for two years, will be awarded to the best candidate, provided that such candidate attains a standard satisfactory to the Examiners.

(*f*) At the Natural Sciences Examination for Higher Certificates to be held by the Oxford and Cambridge Joint Board in July, 1892, a scholarship of £50 for one year will be awarded to the best candidate, provided that such candidate attains a standard satisfactory to the Examiners.

In all the above Examinations, if no candidates of sufficient merit present themselves, the Scholarships may be diminished in value, or withheld.

At the Cambridge Higher Local Examination to be held in June, 1892:—

Two Scholarships at least of £50 a year, for two or three years, will be awarded either (1) for distinguished success in group C; or (2) for success in two of the groups A, B, C, D, E, H, provided that one of the two be B or C.

(*e*) The Cobden Scholarship will be awarded either (1) for distinguished success in group D, including distinction in Political Economy, or (2) for distinguished success in group H, together with distinction in Political Economy.

(*h*) One or more smaller Scholarships of £35 may be awarded to candidates who have failed to obtain one of the larger Scholarships. And one may be awarded for distinguished success in the Cambridge Higher Local Examination held in December, 1892.

(*g*) The Birmingham Scholarship will be awarded for distinguished success in the Cambridge Higher Local Examination held in December, 1892.

The Scholarships offered in the Higher Local Examination in any year will be awarded only to students who have either (1) passed in two groups of the Higher Local Examination, one of these being B or C; or (2) gained Honours in the Senior Local Examination and passed in either group B or group C of the Higher Local Examination; and they will not, generally speaking, be awarded to candidates who have already resided as students for two or more terms, unless they have fulfilled the conditions as to examinations required by the University before admission to a Tripos examination.

All Scholarships will be continued to students for a second, or for a second and a third year, if their circumstances make it important to them, provided that they are doing sufficiently advanced work and are making satisfactory progress.

Scholars are required to reside during the term for which they hold their Scholarships; they must begin residence in the October following their election, unless they have not then attained the age of 19, or unless they are prevented by grave cause to be approved by the Council. Permission to defer residence will under no circumstances be granted for more than a year; and a Scholarship will only be awarded if the Council is satisfied that the candidate's state of health is not such as to prevent her from profiting by a systematic course of study at Cambridge.

No two of the above Scholarships can be held simultaneously by the same person. Nor can any of them be held with the Gilchrist Scholarship.

The Council award some Scholarships otherwise than by the above examinations to students who have begun residence and whose circumstances make it important to them. Information about all Scholarships will be given by Miss Gladstone.

A certain number of Exhibitions of five guineas a term are awarded to students resident in the College needing assistance, regard being had to intellectual qualifications, and a written statement of circumstances being required. The Tripos fees of these Exhibitioners may be paid by the College on the recommendation of the Principal or the Vice-Principal.

Exhibitions are tenable with Scholarships.

Loan Fund.

There is a Loan Fund at the disposal of the College, from which students of limited means may obtain help towards the payment of their fees. They will be expected to give adequate testimony respecting their intellectual qualifications, and to make a statement of their circumstances.

Towns, Colleges, &c.	No. of open Scholarships, 1892.	Value.	No. of years tenable.	Date of Examination.	Subjects.	Limit of age.	Board and Tuition, one year.
Royal Holloway College, Egham. Principal.—Miss Bishop. Secretary.—J. L. Clifford Smith, Esq.	6 6	£60 £50	2 2	Jan. 6, 7, 8.	Classics, Mathematics, Natural Science, Modern Languages.	Not under 17.	£90.
OXFORD. [illegible]argaret Hall. [illegible]al.— [illegible] Wordsworth. [illegible]rincipal.— [illegible]	4 or more.	£30 to £45	3	October, First week.	Same as Oxford Univer. Women's Honours Examination.	over 18; under 35.	£75 About £15 extra General Assocn. Fees for Instruction.
[illegible]s. [illegible]pal.— [illegible]s C. A. E. Moberly.	2	£25	2	October.		17	£45. about £15 extra for Tuition Fees.

Towns, Colleges, &c.	*No. of open Scholarships, 1892.*	*Value.*	*No. of years tenable.*	*Date of Examination.*	*Subjects.*	*Limit of age.*	*Board and Tuition, one year.*
OXFORD.—*continued.*							
Somerville Hall. Principal.— Miss A. Maitland. Tutors.— Miss C. Pater. Miss E. Powell. Hon. Sec.— Hon. Mrs. Vernon Harcourt, Cowley Grange, Oxford.	1 Clothworkers' Scholarship. 1 1 Student's Scholarship. 2 or more Exhibitions.	£50. £40. £25 each.	3 3 2	April. Subjects selected must be stated in writing to the Principal on or before March 31.	Greek, Latin, Fr., German, Italian (any two of the above). History, English Literature, Math., Natural Science.	over 17. ...	£63. £15 to £20 extra for Tuition Fees. ...
LONDON.							
Queen's College. 43 & 45 Harley Street, W. Principal.— Rev. Canon Elwyn, M.A. Dean and Sec.— H. G. Seeley, Esq., F.R.S. Lady Resident.— Miss C. Crouduce.	8 By Nomination. 5 By Election. 4 Presented by the Governesses Benevolent Inst.	30 gs.	Presentation 2 to 3 years. Election 2 years. —	End of Sept. One presented in June.	Entrance Subjects: New Testament, Eng. Grammar, ,, History, Phys. Geography, Arithmetic, French. —	14-16. The course extends over 6 years.	Board (if desired) 66 gs. Tuition 24 to 30 gs. for 18 hours class teaching a week. Separate fees for single classes. Extra fees for

Assistant Secy. :— Miss E. M. Po le.			Arnott 1 year.		Arnott Subjects: Elem. Physics, „ Chemistry. Plumptre: at the Associateship Examination.		Instrumental Music, Dancing and Calisthenics.
QUEEN'S COLLEGE SCHOOL. H.M.—Miss Hay.	2 By Nomination.	18 gs.	2	Presentation in June.	... ...	12-14	Board (if desired) 22 gs. a term. Tuition, 12 to 24 gs. a year.
BEDFORD COLLEGE. 8 & 9 York Place, Baker Street, W. Hon. Sec.— Miss Lucy J. Russell.	1 Arnott. (Science.)	£40.	2	Fourth Tues. and Wed. in June.	Algebra, Arithmetic, Geometry, and Nat. Phil.	Not more than 19.	From £60 a year.
*Lady Resident and Assistant Secretary.—	1 Professor's. (Arts.)	£30.	2 }		English Language, Latin, and Mathematics.	„	
Miss Harriet Martin. (*See also p.* 113.)	1 Reid. (Arts.)	£30.	2 }			„	
MARIA GREY TRAINING COLLEGE.— Principal.— Miss Agnes Ward, 5, Fitzroy Street, W.	About 10.	Varies	1	Awards made on previous attainments.	Various.	Above 18	Board (if desired) in various houses, from £1 1*s.* weekly. Tuition Fees, £30, £24.

Towns, Colleges, &c.	*No. of open Scholarships,* 1892.	*Annual Value.*	*No. of years tenable.*	*Date of Examination.*	*Subjects.*	*Limit of Age.*	*Board and Tuition, one year.*
LONDON.—*continued.* Westfield College, Finchley Road, Hampstead. Mistress.— Miss C. L. Maynard. Sec. to Council.— Miss S. M. Smee, Bedford Park, Chiswick, W. Candidates for Scholarships must have passed the Matriculation Examination of the University of London.	Uncertain.	Probably £30 to £50.	2	July.	I. *Classics*— Latin, Greek. II. *Mathematics*— Euclid, Algebra, Trigonometry Conic Sect'ns. III. *Natural Science*— Chemistry, Botany, Zoology, Physics, viz.: Heat, Mechanics, Light, Electricity. IV. *Modern Languages*— French, German, Italian.	18 (over).	£105. There are no extras, and the University Examination Fees are paid by the College. Forms of Application and particulars as to Entrance Examinations can be obtained from the Secretary.

BEDFORD COLLEGE.—*continued from p.* 112.

SCHOLARSHIPS OFFERED BY MRS. REID'S TRUSTEES.

One Free Studentship, value £46 per annum, tenable for two years, is offered to the candidate taking the highest place in the First or Second Division of the Oxford Senior Local Examination, by the Trustees of Mrs. Reid's Fund for the Education of Women, jointly with the Trustees of the Bedford College Residence.

One Free Studentship, value £46 per annum, tenable for two years, is offered to the candidate taking the highest place in the First or Second Division of the Cambridge Senior Local Examination, by the Trustees of Mrs. Reid's Fund for the Education of Women, jointly with the Trustees of the Bedford College Residence.

One Free Studentship, value 30 guineas per annum, tenable for two years, is offered to the woman taking the highest place in the Honours Division of the June and January Matriculation Examinations of the University of London.

One Free Studentship, value 30 guineas per annum, tenable for two years, is offered in accordance with the results of the Midsummer Examination for Certificates by the Joint Board of the Universities of Oxford and Cambridge, regard being had to the age of the candidates and to the subjects in which they have obtained distinction.

Bedford College Residence, 8 and 9 York Place, Baker Street, W.—Lady Superintendent, Miss Mary Ashdown.

Further information about these Scholarships may be obtained from the Reid Trustees, Bedford College.

UNIVERSITIES' SCHOLARSHIPS.

OXFORD AND CAMBRIDGE.

OXFORD ENTRANCE SCHOLARSHIPS.

N.B.—Nearly every Scholarship or Exhibition determines at the end of two years, with possible renewal for two years, and under special circumstances for yet another year.

It is generally necessary for candidates to give about a fortnight's notice of their desire to compete, and of the subjects they intend to take up.

Rooms are usually supplied in the Colleges as far as possible.

The dagger denotes to whom applications respecting Scholarships should be made.

Schoolmasters who are in the habit of sending up candidates to Oxford would do well to take in the "University Magazine" (13*s.* a year post free), which keeps them supplied with all information.

Oxford Colleges.	*No. of open Scholarships, &c., 1892.*	*Annual value of each.*	*Subjects of Examination.*	*Date of Examination.*	*Limit of age.*
ALL SOULS. 1437. Warden.—Sir W. R. Anson, Bart., D.C.L.					
BALLIOL. 1263-8	3	£80	Classics.	The end of Nov.	19
Master.—Rev. Dr. Jowett. †Classical Tutor and Senior Dean.—J. L. Strachan-Davidson, Esq., M.A. Classical Tutor, and Junior Dean.—R. L. Nettleship, Esq., M.A. Classical Tutors.—W. H. Forbes, Esq., M.A.; Evelyn Abbott, Esq., M.A.; F. de Paravicini, Esq., M.A., W. R. Hardie, Esq., M.A. Philos. Lect.—J. A. Smith, B A. †Tutor in Mod. Hist.—A. L. Smith, Esq., M.A.	* 1	£80	Mathematics.	"	None.
	* 1	£80	Mod. History.	"	"
	* 1	£80	Nat. Science.	"	"
	* 3 Exhibitions	£70	Classics.	"	"
	* 1 "	£40	Nat. Science.	"	"
	* 1 "	£40	Mod. History.	"	"

†Natl. Sci. Tutor.—Sir J. Conroy, Bt., M.A. †Math. Tutor.—J. W. Russell, Esq., M.A. Law Tutor.—T. Raleigh, Esq., M.A. Theocal. Tutor.—Hon. and Rev. W. H. Fremantle, M.A.	* These are open also to Members of Univ. under 2 years' standing.				
Tutor to the Ind. Probnrs.—Sir Wm. Markby, D.C.L.	1	£100	Classics.	Easter vacation.	For membs. of the College only.
BRASENOSE. 1509	3	£80	Classics.	Christmas vacation.	19
Principal.—†C. B. Heberden, Esq., M.A. Vice Principal.—†R. Lodge, Esq., M.A.	1	£80	Mathematics.	November (usually).	19
Tutors and Lectrs. — R. Lodge, Esq., M.A.; C. H. Sampson, Esq., M.A.; Rev. A. Chandler, M.A.; Rev. L. J. M. Bebb, M.A.; H. F. Fox, Esq., M.A.; W. H. Pater, Esq., M.A.; A. J. Butler, Esq., M.A.; Rev. F. W. Bussell, M.A.	4 Somerset.	£52 to £60	Classics.	Christmas vacation.	19
* For those who require pecuniary assistance to enable them to enter the University.	* 3 Junior "Hulme" Exhibitions.	£80	2 Classics. 1 History.	Christmas vacation.	20
[CHR]IST CHURCH. 1546. ... . [De]an.—The Very Rev. F. Paget, D.D. [Su]b-Dean and Canon.—Rev. C. A. Heurtley, D.D.	5 or 6.	£80	1 Mathematics. 1 Nat. Science. 1 Mod. Hist. 2 or 3 Classics.	Varies.	Not to exceed 19 on election in Math. and Classics. No limit in Nat. Scien. and Mod. Hist.
[Tu]tors and Lecturers.—A. G. Vernon-Harcourt, Esq., M.A., F.R.S.; J. B. Thompson, Esq., M.A., B.Mus.; † Rev. ...pson, M.A.; R. E. Baynes, ...; Rev. W. Warner, M.A.;	2 Exhibitions.	about £85	Vary from time to time; generally 1 Classics, 1 Nat. Science.		

Oxford Colleges.	*No. of open Scholarships, &c., 1892.*	*Annual value of each.*	*Subjects of Examination.*	*Date of Examination.*	*Limit of age.*
CHRIST CHURCH. 1546. (*Cont.*) J. A. Stewart, Esq., M.A.; F. York Powell, Esq., M.A.; A. Hassall, Esq., M.A.; Rev. W. Hobhouse, M.A.; S. J. Owen, Esq., M.A.; Rev. T. B. Strong, M.A.; H. W. Blunt, Esq., M.A.; R. E. Mitcheson, Esq., M.A., B.C.L.; S. G. Owen, Esq., M.A.		(Exhibs.)			None. Candidates to prove that they cannot come to the Univ. without assistance.
CORPUS CHRISTI. 1516. ... ... President.—†Rev. Thomas Fowler, D.D. Tutors.—A. Sidgwick, Esq., M.A.; H. D. Leigh, Esq., M.A.	8 (about).	£80	Classics, Mathematics, Nat. Science, and Mod. History.	About Nov. 1. Classics and Mod. Hist.	19 for Schps. No limitation for Exhibitns.
Dean.—Rev. C. Plummer, M.A. Assis.-Tutors.—T. Case, Esq., M.A.; L. T. Hobham, Esq., M.A. Div. Lect. and Chap.—Rev. C. Plummer, M.A.	2 (about).	£50		Nat. Scien. about June 20. Maths. abt. Nov. 18.	
EXETER. 1314. ... ... Rector.—†Rev. William Walrond Jackson, M.A. Sub-Rector and Tutor.—†L. R. Farnell, Esq., M.A.	12 (open). 1 Carter. 8 Stapledon. (Devon and Cornwall)	£80 £80 £60	Classics, Maths. Classics. Classics, Maths.	January	19 None. 19

Tutors and Lectrs.—Rev. C. W. Boase, M.A., *Mod. Hist.;* J. C. Wilson, Esq., M.A., *Law;* Rev. H. F. Tozer, M.A.; H. F. Pelham, Esq., M.A.; C. J. C. Price, Esq., M.A., *Mathcs.;* Rev. W. Sanday, M.A. *Theoly.;* I. Bywater, Esq., M.A.; P. F. Willert, Esq., M.A.; C. J. Roberts, Esq., B.A.; R. R. Marett, M.A.	2 Haske.	£80	Theology.		None.
	2 King Charles I. (Chann. Islands).	£80			
	Exhibition (Gifford).	£70	Classics.		
	Symes.	£60	Divinity.		
	Michell.	£60	,,		
	2 How.	£30 £40	Classics.		
Tutor and Dean.—A. B. How, Esq., M.A.	Richards.	£30	,,		
Bursar.—Major C. T. Wilson.	Loscombe Richards.	£30	,,		
HERTFORD. 1282. Hostel.	3 or more.	£100	Classics.	November.	No limit of age.
Principal.—Rev. Canon Boyd, D.D.					
Tutors—	2 or more.	£40 to £60	Classics.	,,	
Classics.—C. N. Jackson, Esq., M.A., Rev. J. H. Maude, M.A., Rev. W. R. Inge, M.A., A. J. Greenidge, Esq., M.A., E. B. Poynton, Esq., B.A.	1 or more.	£100	Mathematics.	,,	
Mathematics.—†Rev. G. S. Ward, M.A.					
Senior Tutors.—W. Esson, Esq., M.A., J. E. Campbell, Esq., M.A. *Science.*—C. E. Haselfoot, Esq., B.A. *History.*—Rev. A. H. Johnson, M.A.	6 Exhibitions. For persons in need of assistance.	£30	Classics, Mathematics, or History.	Sept.	

Besides these, it happens that two or more are thrown open annually from the want of "close" Cands., but the ...r cannot be ascertained long beforehand.

...larger Scholarships are limited to members of the Church of England or of Ireland, or of the Protestant ...al Churches of Scotland, the British Colonies, or the United States of America.

...d annual charges, inc. Rent of Rooms, £49 10*s*.

Oxford Colleges.	*No. of open Scholarships, &c., 1892.*	*Annual value of each.*	*Subjects of Examination.*	*Date of Examination.*	*Limit of age.*
Jesus. 1571.	Scholarships, 2 or 3 open.	£80	Classics.	April 19th.	19
Principal.—Rev. H. D. Harper, D.D.		£80	Mathematics.		
Vice-Principal.—Rev. Ll. Thomas, M.A.	4 Welsh.		Nat. Science and Mod. Hist.	...	No limit.
Tutors and Lectrs.—†Rev. W. Hawker Hughes, M.A., D.G. Ritchie, Esq., M.A., J. Griffiths, Esq., M.A., W. M. Lindsay, Esq., M.A., E. R. Wharton, Esq., M.A.	—— Exhibitions, 1 or 2 open. 2 or 3 Welsh.	Not exceeding £50.	...	...	No limit of age.
Keble. 1870.	2 Classical.	£80	Classics.	April 19	19.
Warden.—Rev. R. J. Wilson, M.A.	1 Nat. Science.	£60	Nat. Science.		20.
Sub-Warden and Tutor.—†Rev. W. Lock, M.A.	1 Historical.	£60	History.	"	20.
Bursar.—Col. J. E. P. Jervise.	1 Classical Exhibition.	£60	Classics.		20.
Dean.—D. J. Medley, Esq.					
Tutors.—Rev. F. W. Spurling, M.A.; H. O. Wakeman, Esq., M.A.; Rev. W. J. H. Campion, M.A.; D. J. Medley, Esq., M.A.; J. Tracey, Esq., M.A.; W. H. Jackson, Esq., M.A.; H. B. Cooper, Esq., M.A.					
All Scholarships and Exhibitions are tenable only by members of the Church of England.					

† For Class. Scholsh. apply to the Rev. W. Lock; Nat. Science Scholsh., W. H. Jackson, Esq.; Historical Scholsh., D. J. Medley, Esq.					
Lincoln. 1427.	2 to 4	£60 or £80	Classics.	End of May	None.
Rector.—Rev. W. W. Merry, D.D.					
Sub-Rector.—†W. W. Fowler, Esq., M.A.					
Lecturer and Dean of Degrees.—Rev. Andrew Clark, M.A.	3 to 5 Classical Exhibitions.	£30 or £40.	Mod. History (1 Scholarsh).		
Tutors and Lecturers.—J. A. R. Munro, Esq., M.A., R. Carter, Esq., B.A., *Classics;* W. H. Fairbrother, Esq., M.A., *Phily.;* O. M. Edwards, Esq., M.A., *Histy.;* J. Williams, Esq., B.C.L., *Law;* Rev. J. O. Johnston, *Theology.*					
Magdalen. 1458.	8 or 9 Demyships.	£80	Mathematics.	January.	19
President.—T. H. Warren, Esq., M.A.			Classics.	March 17.	
Senior Tutor.—† G. E. Underhill, Esq., M.A.	2 or 3 Exhibitions.	£10 to £50.	History.	March 17.	
			Nat. Science.	October 13.	
Tutors and Lecturers.—A. D. Godley, Esq., M.A.; D. G. Hogarth, Esq., M.A.; H. W. Greene, Esq., M.A., B.C.L.; C. C. Webb, Esq., B.A.; Rev. W. Lock, M.A.; E. Chapman, Esq., M.A.; C. R. L. [illegible] Esq., M.A.; H. Duff, Esq., M.A., [illegible] H. E. Clayton, M.A.; J. [illegible], M.A.; A. L. Dixon, Esq.,					

Oxford Colleges.	*No. of open Scholarships, &c., 1892.*	*Annual value of each.*	*Subjects of Examination.*	*Date of Examination.*	*Limit of age.*
MERTON. 1264.	2	£80	Classics.	March.	19
Warden.—The Hon. G. C. Brodrick, D.C.L.	1	£80	Mathematics.	January.	19
Sub-Warden.—G. R. Scott, Esq., M.A.					
†Principal of the Postmasters, Lecturer,	1	£80	Nat. Science.	June.	19
and Dean.—T. Bowman, Esq., M.A.	1 Exhibition.	£60	Classics.	March.	No limit
Tutor and Librarian.—William Wallace, Esq., M.A.					
Mathematical Tutor and Senior Bursar.—W. Esson, Esq., M.A.	1 „	£60	Mod. History.	January.	„
Tutor.—G. R. Scott, Esq., M.A.					
Lecturers.—W. W. How, Esq., M.A.; John Watts, Esq., M.A.; Rev. A. H. Johnson, M.A.; Rev. J. O. Johnston, M.A.; A. A. Prankerd, Esq., D.C.L.					
NEW. 1379.	4	£80	2 Classics.	Scholrshps. Classical,	19
Warden.—Rev. J. E. Sewell, D.D.			1 Mathematics.	November.	
Sub-Warden.—E. H. Hoge, Esq., D.C.L.			1 Nat. Science.	Mathmtcl.,	
Tutors.—†E. H. Hoge, Esq., D.C.L.; Rev.				January.	
W. A. Spooner, M.A.; J. B. Moyle,				Science,	
Esq., D.C.L., M.A.; E. H. Hayes,	Exhibitions,	£50	Classics and	June.	
Esq., M.A.; P. E. Matheson, Esq.,	3 or more.		Mod. History.	—	
M.A.; H. A. L. Turner, Esq., M.A.				Matric.,	

Lecturers.—A. Robinson, Esq., M.A.; A. O. Prickard, Esq., M.A.; D. S. Margoliouth, Esq., M.A.; C. W. C. Oman, Esq., M.A.; H. W. B. Joseph, Esq., B.A.; C. A. St. Hill, Esq., B.A.				April. —	
Oriel. 1326. ... ... Provost.—D. B. Monro, Esq., M.A. Tutors and Lecturers.—Rev. A. G. Butler, M.A.; Rev. F. H. Hall, M.A.; Rev. J. R. King, M.A.; J. C. Wilson, Esq., M.A.; Rev. L. R. Phelps, M.A.	3	£80	Classics, with English Essay and History.	Jan. 13.	19
Pembroke. 1624. .. .. Master.—Rev. Canon Evan Evans, D.D. Tutor, Senior Dean, and Chaplain.—Rev. R. G. Livingstone, M.A. Tutors and Lecturers.—†A. T. Barton, Esq., M.A.; C. Leudesdorf, Esq., M.A., *Mathematics.*; G. Wood, Esq., M.A., *Classics.*	5, possibly 6.	4 at £80. 1 of £65.	4 Classics. 1 Mathematics.	Classics, March 22.	19
Queen's. 1340. ... ... Provost.—†Rev. J. R. Magrath, D.D. Senior Tutor.—Rev. T. H. Grose, M.A. Lecturer in Mod. Hist. and Senior Bursar.—Edward Armstrong, Esq., M.A.	4 To one of these Scholarships, which is called the Eglesfield	£80	Classics.* The Eglesfield Scholsps., either Class. or Maths.	Feb. 23.	19

* For one of the Scholarships extra papers will be set with a view to discovering an aptitude for Historical studi[illegible]iency in Modern Languages.

Oxford Colleges.	*No. of open Scholarships, &c., 1892.*	*Annual value of each.*	*Subjects of Examination.*	*Date of Examination.*	*Limit of age.*
QUEEN'S. 1340—*continued.* Tutors and Lectrs.—Rev. E. M. Walker, M.A.; A. C. Clark, Esq., M.A.; E. B. Elliott, Esq., M.A., *Mathcs.*; T. W. Allen, Esq., M.A.; H. W. G. Markheim, Esq., M.A.; C. B. Grant, Esq., *Mod. Hist.*; J. C. Wilson, Esq., *Law*; Rev. A. C. Headlam, *Theol.*; V. H. Veley, Esq., *Nat. Science.* There are besides a number of valuable Exhibitions confined in the first instance to boys from schools in Cumberland, Westmoreland, and Yorkshire; these are thrown open should no competent candidates offer themselves.	Scholarship, no one is eligible who is not a native of Cumberland or Westmoreland unless no competent candidate so qualified offers himself. (See note p. 118.) 1 Jodrell Scholarship.	£80	Classics and Divinity.	Feb. 23.	20
ST. JOHN'S. 1555.	3	£80	Classics, 1892.	Varies.	19
President.—Rev. J. Bellamy, D.D.					
Vice-President.—Sidney Ball, Esq., M.A. Tutors and Lecturers.—*Senior Tutor*, †Sidney Ball, Esq., M.A.; W. G. Smith, Esq., M.A.; Rev. W. H. Hutton, M.A., *Mod. Hist.*; J. U. Powell, Esq.,; T. C. Snow, Esq., M.A.; L. V.	Casberd Scholarships, 1 or 2. (To Commoners of the College.) Casberd	£80 £90	Varies. "	April 19, 1892.	For boys not going for open Scholarshs.

Lester, Esq., M.A.; L. Pullan, Esq., B.A., *Theoly.;* J. C. Wilson, Esq., M.A., B.C.L., *Law;* W. H. Jackson, Esq., M.A., *N. Sci.;* J. W. Russell, Esq., M.A., *Maths.;* Rev. G. A. Cooke, B.A., *Hebrew.*	Exhibitions, several (for those not obtaining Scholarships).				
TRINITY. 1554. ... ... President.—†Rev. H. G. Woods, M.A. Vice-Pres.—Robinson Ellis, Esq., M.A. Tutor and Dean.—Charles Cannan, Esq., M.A.	4 and Exhibs.	£80 £50-£70	Classics (in the case of one excellence in Mathes. may have weight.)	November, (last fortnight.)	19
Tutors and Lectrs.—R. W. Raper, Esq., B.C.L.; F. T. Richards, Esq. M.A.; M. H. Green, Esq., M.A.; Rev. H. E. D. Blakiston, M.A.; H. S. Jones, B.A.; Rev. A. H. Johnson, M.A., *Mod. Hist.;* Members of the Faculty of Law in All Souls College, *Law;* Rev. W. Sanday, M.A., *Theoly.;* Sir J. Conroy, Bart., M.A., *Phys. and Chemy., Millard Lectr.;* [illegible] H. Nagel, Esq., M.A., *Phys. and* [illegible], *Millard Demons.;* Rev. F. J. [illegible] M.A., *Expl. Mechs. and En*[illegible]*g, Millard Lectr.*	1 Millard.	£80	Nat. Science.	"	No limit.

[illegible]bitions, varying in number and value, according to the merit of the Candidates. The same Classical [illegible] as in the Examination for the Scholarships at Wadham College, and the same Natural [illegible]s in the Examination for the Natural Science Scholarships at Balliol, Exeter, and Christ

Oxford Colleges.	*No. of open Scholarships, &c., 1892.*	*Annual value of each.*	*Subjects of Examination.*	*Date of Examination.*	*Limit of age.*
UNIVERSITY. 872. ... ... Master—†Rev. J. F. Bright, D.D. Tutors.—A. S. Chavasse, Esq., B.C.L., M.A., *Clascs. and Theoly.*; R. W. Macan, Esq., M.A., *Lit. Hum., Librarian.*	4 Scholarships.	£80	Classics (3), Mathematics (1).	January. Varies.	19
	3 Exhibitions.	£40 to £82 10s.	Classics (2) and Mod. Hist. (1).	Varies (*Clasc.* Exhibs. same as *Clasc.* Schps.)	21
Lecturers.—F. H. Peters, Esq. M.A., *Clascs.*; L. A. Selby-Bigge, Esq., M.A., *Phily.*; H. M. Barge, Esq., M.A., *Clascs.*; Rev. A. H. Johnson, *Mod. Hist.*; H. Duff, Esq., *Jurisprudence*; J. Campbell, Esq., *Mathcs.*					
WADHAM. 1612. ... ... Warden.—G. E. Thorley, Esq., M.A. Sub-Warden and Tutor.—†Rev. P. A. Wright-Henderson, M.A.	Exhibitions (usually 3 or 4).	£30 to £40	Hebrew.	June.	20 for Heb. Schps.
Tutors.—H. P. Richards, Esq., M.A.; J. Wells, Esq., M.A.	3 or 4 Scholarships.	£80	Classics. Mathematics.	November.	19
Lecturers.—F. A. Dixey, Esq., M.A., *Nat. Sc. and Med.*; G. C. Wilson, Esq., M.A., *Law*; G. H. Wakeling, Esq., M.A., *Hist.*; A. E. Haigh, Esq., M.A., *Clascs.*; C. E. Haselfoot, Esq., M.A., *Mathcs.*; Rev. G. A. Cooke, M.A., *Hebrew.*					

WORCESTER. 1714. ... ... Provost.—†Rev. W. Inge, M.A. Vice-Provost and Tutor.—T. W. Jackson, Esq., M.A. Dean.—W. H. Hadow, Esq., M.A. Tutor and Mathematical Lecturer.—H. T. Gerrans, Esq., M.A. Law Lect.—H. A. Pottinger, Esq., M.A. Theological Lecturers.—Rev. W. Lock, M.A.; Rev. J. O. Johnston, M.A. Lit. Hum. Lecturers.—Rev. J. H. Mee, M.A., *Mus. Doc.*; W. H. Hadow, Esq., M.A.; F. J. Lys, Esq., M.A. Mod. Hist. Lecturer.—J. A. R. Marriott, Esq., M.A.	4 Scholarships.	£80	Classics. Mathematics.	March November.	19
	3 or 4 Exhibitions.	£35 to £21	...	...	No limit.

CAMBRIDGE UNIVERSITY OPEN ENTRANCE SCHOLARSHIPS

AND EXHIBITIONS TO THE COLLEGES,

ALPHABETICALLY ARRANGED.

The following rules are common to all the Colleges, and apply to all Candidates for Open Scholarships :—

1. Age must not exceed 19 at the time of examination.

2ᵃ. Must give notice to the Tutor of the college he proposes to enter at least one week previous to examination, whether he intends to offer Classics or Mathematics. Two weeks' notice if Natural Science is the subject offered.

2ᵇ. Must also send a copy of register of birth, the residence of Parent or Guardian, a certificate of good conduct and character from the Headmaster of his school or his private Tutor.

3. Must begin residence not later than October following the examination.

4. Shall not, after election, offer himself as a Candidate at any other College without permission.

5. All Scholarships are awarded only when Candidates of sufficient merit are forthcoming, and the tenure of nearly all of them is capable of extension provided the College is satisfied with the progress and diligence of the scholar.

6. At the majority of the Colleges, rooms, etc., are provided by the College Authorities; application should be made beforehand.

7. For further details respecting these Scholarships, application should be made to one of the Tutors or to those with a † affixed.

N.B.—The Exhibitions, as distinguished from the Scholarships, are (1) Exhibitions from certain preferred schools which in default of properly qualified Candidates from those schools are considered open : (2) Exhibitions granted from the Scholarship Fund to Candidates (usually with no restriction as to age) that have acquitted themselves creditably in the Scholarship Examinations, and are unable without such help to commence residence at the University.

Candidates for a Classical Scholarship will be examined in Latin and Greek Translation and Composition, both Prose and

Verse: Candidates for a Mathematical Scholarship in Euclid, Algebra, Plane Trigonometry, Geometrical and Analytical Conic Sections, Statics and Dynamics, the subjects being treated without the aid of the Differential Calculus: and Candidates for a Natural Science Scholarship in Chemistry and Physics (including Light, Heat, and Electricity), Botany and Geology. Biology and Animal Physiology in some cases take the place of Botany and Geology; in any case two subjects must be offered, of which Chemistry is usually compulsory. They will also be required to satisfy the Examiners in Elementary Latin, Greek, and Mathematics. Candidates for admission at the Colleges, who acquit themselves satisfactorily in the Scholarship Examinations, will be excused from the Examination for entrance.

In the case of Colleges conducting examinations in common a Candidate for a Scholarship at any one of these Colleges in either Classics or Mathematics or Natural Science may also be eligible without further examination to a Scholarship at either of the other Colleges, in default of properly qualified Candidates at those Colleges. It is, however, to be understood that each College will give the preference to its own Candidates, if properly qualified.

CAMBRIDGE UNIVERSITY ENTRANCE SCHOLARSHIPS.

Cambridge Colleges.	*No. of open Scholarships, &c., 1892.*	*Annual value of each.*	*Subjects of Examination.*	*Date of Examination.*	*Limit of age.*
CAIUS, *see* Gonville and Caius.					
CHRIST'S. 1505. ... ... Master.—John Peile, Esq., Litt.D. †Tutors.—Rev. J. W. Cartmell, M.A.; E. S. Thompson Esq., M.A. Asst. Tutors.—J. A. Sharkey, Esq., M.A.; E. W. Hobson, Esq., M.A.; J. Greaves, Esq., M.A.; Rev. J. A. Robinson, M.A.; A. E. Shipley, Esq., M.A. Law Lectr.—R. T. Wright, Esq., M.A.	Depends upon the merits of the Candidates.	Maximum value £80. (Depends on the merits of Candidates.)	Classics or Mathematics or Natural Science, or any two of the above.	March.	19
CLARE. 1326. ... ... Master.—Rev. E. Atkinson, D.D. Tutors.—†Rev. W. Raynes, M.A.; W. L. Mollison, Esq., M.A.	6	£80 to £40	Classics or Mathematics or Natural Science.	January 12 (Tuesday).	19
CORPUS CHRISTI. 1352. ... ... Master.—Rev. E. H. Perowne, D.D., Preby. of St. Asaph.	4 or 5.	£80 to £30	Mathematics or Classics.	March 16 and 17.	19 (under.)
Sen. Tutor.—†C. W. Moule, Esq., M.A. Jun. Tutor.—Rev. J. T. Lang, M.A.	3 Sizarships.			October 6 and 7.	No limit for Sizarships.

Cambridge Colleges.	*No. of open Scholarships, &c., 1892.*	*Annual value of each.*	*Subjects of Examination.*	*Date of Examination.*	*Limit of age.*
DOWNING. 1800. ... ... Master.—Alex. Hill, Esq., M.D., M.A. Tutor.—†Rev. J. C. Saunders, M.A.	2 (Minor)	£50	Law and Nat. Sc., with Pass Papers in Clcs. & Mathcs.	April 19 and following days.	19 for Natural Sci., no lim. for Law.
EMMANUEL. 1584. ... ... Master.—Rev. S. G. Phear, D.D. †Tutors.—J. Holmes, Esq., M.A., W. N. Shaw, Esq., M.A. Asst. Tutor.—Rev. A. T. Chapman, M.A.	5 Subsizarships 2	1—£80 2—£60 2—£50 £30	Classics or Mathematics or Natural Science, or any two of these combined.	Probably Dec. 9 to 12, 1890 inclus. Application bef. Dec. 5.	19
GONVILLE AND CAIUS. 1348. ... ... Master.—Rev. N. M. Ferrers, D.D., F.R.S. †Tutors.—Rev. E. S. Roberts, M.A.; J. S. Reid, Esq., Litt. D.	* { 2 6 or more with Exhns. of less value.	£80 £70 to £40	Classics or Mathematics or Natural Science.	Dec. (for Oct. 1892.) September	19
Asst. Tutors.—A. S. Lea, Esq., Sc.D.; E. G. Gallop, Esq., M.A. * Each will be tenable for a year, after which the holder will be eligible to a Foundn. Schp. the ann. val. of which may be from £40 to £100 according to the Student's proficiency as tested by Coll. and Univ. Exams.	Entr. Schps. of £50 each are also offered annually for Mediæval & Mod. Langs. and Oriental Langs., and Mod. Hist.	...	...	Dec., 1892 (for Oct., 1893).	
	Choral Entrance 1 Exhibition.	£40.	...	May (for Oct. 24, 1892).	

Jesus. 1496.... ... ... **Master.**—Rev. H. A. Morgan, D.D. **Senior Tutor.**—†Rev. E. H. Morgan, M.A. **Classical Tutor.**—Arth. Gray, Esq., M.A. **Mathematical Tutor.** — William Welsh, Esq., M.A. **Asst. Tutors.**—J. H. H. Goodwin, Esq., M.A.; J. C. Watt, Esq., M.A. **Lecturer in Theology.**—Rev. F. Foakes Jackson, M.A. **Directors of Study.**—J. P. Bate, Esq., M.A., *Law and History*; J. G. Adami, M.A., *Science and Medicine.* **Asst. Lecturer.**—E. Abbott, Esq., B.A.	Several. The number and value depends upon the merits of Candidates.	£80 Maximum.	Classics or Mathematics or Natural Science, or History.	March 16 and 3 following days	19
M **King's.** 1441. ... ... **Provost.**—Rev. A. Austen Leigh, M.A. **Vice-Provost.**—F. Whitting, Esq., M.A. **Deans.**—Rev. A. H. Cooke, M. R. James, Esq. **Tutor.**—†G. W. Prothero, Esq., M.A. **Asst. Tutors.**—Rev. A. H. Cooke, M.A., *Classics*; W. H. Macaulay, Esq., M.A., *Mathcs.*; S. F. Harmer, Esq., M.A., *Nat. Sc.*	2	£80	Classics or Mathcs. or Hist. or Nat. Sc.	December 7	19
	Laurence Saunders' Scholarships.	£75		Names of Candidates should be sent to the Provost.	
	3 Exhibitions at least.	£70 to £50			
	3 Exhibitions restricted to those in need of pecuniary assistance, &c.	£50 to £40			
	1 Exhibition.	£50	Mod. Languags.		

Cambridge Colleges.	*No. of open Scholarships, &c., 1892.*	*Annual value of each.*	*Subjects of Examination.*	*Date of Examination.*	*Limit of age.*
MAGDALENE. 1519. ... ... Master.—Hon. and Rev. Latimer Neville, M.A. President and Tutor.—Francis Pattrick, Esq., M.A. There are also four Scholarships of £65 a year each, to which certain schools have a preference, but which in the absence of qualified candidates from such schools are treated as open scholarships.	6	£70 to £40	Classics or Mathematics.	March 16, 1892.	19
PEMBROKE. 1347. ... ... Master.—Rev. C. E. Searle, D.D. †Tutor.—Rev. C. H. Prior, M.A. When the number of deserving Candidates is large, other Scholarships or Exhibitions are given besides those offered.	6	£80 to £40	Classics or Mathematics.	March. December.	19
QUEEN'S. 1448. ... ... President.—Rev. G. Phillips, D.D. †Tutors.—Rev. W. M. Campion, D.D.; Rev. A Wright, M.A.	6	£60 to £30	Classics or Mathematics.	January, 1891.	19

St. Catherine's. 1473. ... ... Master.—Rev. C. K. Robinson, D.D. President and Tutor.—†Rev. E. T. S. Carr, M.A. Asst. Tutor.—A. W. Spratt, Esq., M.A.	The number and value are determined by the College authorities in accordance with merit shown	£50 to £20	Classics or Mathematics, or both.	May generally.	19
St. John's. 1511. ... ... Master.—Rev. Charles Taylor, D.D. President.—Rev. P. H. Mason, M.A. †Tutors.—J. E. Sandys, Esq., Litt. D.; W. E. Heitland, Esq., M.A.; Rev. J. T. Ward, M.A.	6 Foundation. 4 Minor. Exhibitions and Sizarships are also awarded.	2 £80 2 £70 2 £50 £50 Various values.	Classics. Mathematics. Natural Science. History. Hebrew. * Sanskrit. * A month's notice required.	December.	19 For Exhibitions and Sizarships no limit.
St. Peter's (Peterhouse) 1257 (charter 1284). Master.—Rev. James Porter, D.D. Tutor.—†J. D. Hamilton Dickson, Esq., M.A. Scholarships at this College are open (1) to non-resident candidates (Entrance Scholarships), who must be under 19 years of age on the first day of examination, and must commence residence in the *following* Michael- [illegible] term at latest; and (2) to resident mem- [illegible] the College—not already Scholars—	4 or 5	£80, £60, £40	1 Mathcs. or 2 Classics or 3 Chemistry and Physics.	About Tuesday, October 11.	19 No restriction on Foundation Scholarships, 2 or 3 of which are offered annually.

[illegible] first term of residence (Foundation Scholarships), *irrespective of age*. There is *no competition* between the [illegible]ts of candidates. The emoluments of Foundation Scholars commence in October, 1892, those of Entrance [illegible]rs in October, 1893. Full particulars of the next Scholarship Examination will be published in June. [illegible] may be obtained from the Tutor, Mr. J. D. H. Dickson.

Cambridge Colleges.	*No. of open Scholarships. &c., 1892.*	*Annual value of each.*	*Subjects of Examination.*	*Date of Examination.*	*Limit of age.*
SIDNEY SUSSEX. 1594. ... ... Master.—C. Smith, Esq., M.A. Tutor.—†G. M. Edwards, Esq., M.A.	3 3 Various Exhibitions and Sizarships.	£70 £40	Maths., 1 £70, 1 £40, Classics, 1 £70, 1 £40, Nat Sci. 1 £70, 1 £40.	Dec. 31, 1891, Jan. 2, 1892 inclusive.	19 for Scholarships.
TRINITY. 1546. ... ... Master.—Rev. H. M. Butler, D.D., Vice-Chancellor of the University. Vice-Master.—W. Aldis Wright, Esq., M.A. Senior Tutor.—J. W. L. Glaisher, Esq., Sc.D., F.R.S. Tutors.—Rev. Rd. Appleton, M.A.; Rev. A. H. F. Boughey, M.A.; A. W. Verrall, Esq. Litt.D.	15 (major) 2 at least (mnr.) for profcy. in Cls., in Math., or in both. 2 at least ,,	£80 £75 £50	Greek Translation, Latin Prose Comp., Latin Translation, Greek Prose Comp., Classical Questions, Latin Verse Comp. Mathematics (3 papers)	Dec. 10-16 inclusive. Date not fixed, but about this time. ,,	19 ,,
An unlimited number of Exhibitions of £40 are given, in all the subjects (*i.e.* to candidates who have not yet come into residence). * Depends on the number of existing Sizars elected to Major Scholarships.	* Sizarships.	£90	Nat. Science, English Essay, General Qustns. Gk. Verse Comp.	,,	No limit.
TRINITY HALL. 1350. ... ... Master.—Rev. Hy. Latham, M.A.	6 minor	1 £80 1 £60 4 £30	Classics, Mathematics, Law, and History.	March 17. Dec. 10.	19

† Vice-Master.—E. A. Beck, Esq., M.A. Tutors.—E. A. Beck, Esq., M.A.; A. W. W. Dale, Esq., M.A. Asst. Tutors.—W. G. Bell, Esq., M.A.; G. B. Shirres, Esq., M.A. Dean.—Rev. H. Henn, M.A.	A variable number of Found. Schps. awarded	£80 to £20 after entrance.			
CAVENDISH COLLEGE (Hostel). 1876. ... Master.—J. H. Flather, M.A.					
SELWYN COLLEGE. 1882 Master.—†Hon. and Rev. A. T. Lyttelton, M.A. Tutors.—Rev. H. J. C. Knight, M.A.; Rev. T. H. Orpen, M.A.; H. C. Knott, Esq., M.A.; A. L. Brown, Esq., B.A.	3 or 4	£30 to £50	Classics, Mathematics, and Biblical Knowledge.	March.	19
AYERST HALL (Hostel). †Principal.—Rev. W. Ayerst, M.A. Asst. Tutors and Lecturers.—H. E. Dixon, Esq., M.A.; Rev. W. E. Waddington, B.A.; A. G. Turner, B.A.; T. E. B. Brown, Esq., M.D., C.I.E. £25 a Term Board and Lodging (furnished) Tuition and University charges.	4	£20	Any Tripos. Proof of ability to take honours.	June.	None.
[illegible]OLLEGIATE STUDENTS—FITZWILLIAM [illegible]L. [illegible].—T. F. C. Huddleston, M.A.	1 Clothworkers. 1 ,,	£52 10s. £30	Phys. Science. General.	July. Nov.	None.

SCHOLARSHIPS AND EXHIBITIONS AT THE UNIVERSITIES.

ABERDEEN UNIVERSITY BURSARIES.

Universities.	*No. of open Bursaries,* 1892.	*Annual value of each.*	*No. of years tenable.*	*Date of Examination.*	*Subjects.*	*Limit of age.*
ABERDEEN.—The University ... Prncp.—W. D. Geddes, LL.D.						
Faculties.						
Arts. Secretary.—Prof. Harrower. Dean.—Prof. Minto. ...	About 45.	£4 10 to £30	4	October.	Arts.	None.
Divinity. Dean.—Prof. Milligan, D.D. Sectry.—Prof. Cowan, D.D.	9	£8 to £30.	3	November.	Divinity.	"
Medicine. Dean and Secretary.—Prof. Dove Wilson, LL.D.	8	£7 to £25	4	October.	Medicine.	"
Law. Dean and Secretary.—Prof. Grub, LL.D.	3	£7 to £10	2 or 1	October.	Law.	"
Secretary of the Senatus.—Prof. Stewart, D.D.						
Registrar and Librarian.—Robert Walker, M.A.						

The Gross Annual Value of open and of presentation Bursaries, Scholarships, and Prizes in the several Faculties is :—

	Bursaries.	*Scholarships.*	*Prizes.*
In Fac. of Arts ...	£4,678	... £725	£334, besides Medals and £210 in Class Prizes.
„ Divinity ...	£893	... £35	
„ Law ...	£138	... £70	
„ Medicine ...	£753	... £241	

N.B.—With few exceptions the Bursaries are quite unrestricted as to age, name, or birthplace. The few Bursaries which may be held in more than one Faculty, are placed under each of such Faculties. A Student may not hold two Bursaries at the same time. Full information will be found in the Aberdeen University Calendar, published by A. King and Co., Aberdeen, price 2*s.* 4*d.* by post.

DUBLIN UNIVERSITY.

Universities.	*No. of open Scholarships, 1892.*	*Annual value of each.*	*No. of years tenable.*	*Date of Examination.*	*Subjects.*	*Limit of age.*
DUBLIN.—The University, ... Trinity College, Dublin. Provost.—Rev. G. Salmon, D.D. Vice-Provost.—Rev. J. Carson, D.D.	Entrance Exhibitions. 12 Junior.	£25	2	October.	Classics, Mathematics, English, French or German.	19
Registrar. — G. F. Shaw, LL.D.	Entrance Prizes 1 First in each of 8 subjects.	£5	...	„	1. Lat. V., 2. Gk. V., 3. Lat. Pr., 4. Gk. Pr., 5. Eng. Lit. and Comp., 6. Eng. Hist. and Mod. Geogy., 7. Fr., 8. Ger., 9. Hebr.	
Catechist and Senior Dean.—Rev. Thos. Stack, M.A. Sen. Lecturer.—J. K. Ingram, Esq., LL.D. Bursar.—Rev. J. W. Stubbs, D.D.	1 Second in each of 8 subjects. Open only to those who have entered within the year.	£2	...	Mich. Term.		
For special information apply to some one of the College Tutors. College Tutors.—Rev. T. K. Abbott, B.D.; Rev. Thos. T. Gray, M.A.; Rev. John P. Mahaffy, D.D.; Anthony Traill, LL.D.; Francis A. Tarleton, LL.D.; George L. Cathcart, M.A.; William S. M'Cay, M.A.; Arthur W. Panton, M.A.; Frederick Purser, M.A.; Louis C. Purser, M.A.; William R. Roberts, M.A.; Edward P. Culverwell, M.A.; John B. Bury, M.A.; Alexander C. O'Sullivan, M.A.; John. I. Beare, M.A.; Robert Russell, M.A.; M. W. J. Fry, M.A.	Besides the above, a variable number of Sizarships is annually given for good answering in Classics or in Mathematics to Students of limited means who are exempted from College fees and have certain other privileges.					

DUBLIN.—ROYAL UNIVERSITY OF IRELAND.

Universities.	*No. of open Scholarships, 1892.*	*Annual value of each.*	*No. of years tenable.*	*Date of Examination.*	*Subjects.*	*Limit of age.*
DUBLIN.—The Royal University of Ireland. Secretaries.—J. C. Meredith, Esq., LL.D.; D. B. Dunne, Esq., LL.D.	Matriculation Exhibitions. 10 (First-class). 20 (Second-class)	£24 £12	... ...	June. Matriculation Exam.	1. Lat., 2. any one of—Gk., Fr., Germ., Ital., Sp., Cel., Sans., Heb., Arabic, 3. Eng. Lang., 4. Elem. Mathcs., 5. Nat. Phil. (*optional*).	Not more than 20 on first day of Exam.
	First University Exhibitions. 10 First-class. 20 Second-class.	£30 £15	... ...	June. Honour marks only.	1. Latin, 2. any one of the Langs. enum. in Matric. List, 3. Eng. Lang. and Lit., 4. Mathcs., 5. Expl. Physics.	Not more than 22 on first day of Exam.
	Second Univer. Exhibitions. 8 First-class. 16 Second-class.	£36 £18	... ...	June (end). Honour marks only.	1. Lat., 2. Gk., 3. Eng. Lang. & Lit., 4. any one of Fr., Germ., Ital., Sp., Celt., Sans.,	Not more than 23 on first day of Exam.

Universities.	*No. of open Scholarships, 1892.*	*Annual value of each.*	*No. of years tenable.*	*Date of Examination.*	*Subjects.*	*Limit of age.*
DUBLIN.—The Royal University of Ireland—*continued.*					Heb., Arab., 5. Logic, 6. Mathe., 7. Math. Phys., 8. Expl. Phys., 9. Chem., 10. Biol., 11. Geol.	
	B.A. Examinations. 7 First-class. 14 Second-class.	£42 £21	... ...	Early in July.	1. Lat., 2. Gk., 3. Eng., and any of—Fr., Ger., It., Sp., Celt., Sans., Heb., or Arab., 4. Logic & either Metaph., Ethics, Hist. of Phil., or Polit. Econ., 5. Mathes., 6. Math. Phys., 7. Expl. Phys., 8. Chem., 9. Physiol., 10. Zool. and Bot., 11 Geology.	Not more than 24 on first day of Exam.
These Scholarships may be held together with the Exhibitions awarded at the various	Scholarships Examinations. 2 First-class.	£40	3	October.	Classics.	Under 21 on

University Examinations, but no person shall hold more than one.	2 Second-class.	£20	3	,,	,,	first day of Scholp. Ex.
	2 First-class.	£40	3	,,	Mathematics.	Candidates must have gained Hon. at preceding Matric. Ex. in the subjs. they intend to offer.
	2 Second-class.	£20	3	,,	,,	
*No person shall be eligible for a Scholarship in Modern Literature who is not a natural-born subject of the Crown.	* 1 First-class.	£40	3	,,	Mod. Literature.	
	1 Second-class.	£20	3	,,	,,	
The Studentships shall be awarded in connection with the M.A. Examination for which Candidates may present themselves after the lapse of one Academical Year from the time of obtaining the Degree of B.A., but no person shall be eligible save a Graduate of the University, under twenty-six years of age on the first day of the Examination. No person shall be allowed to hold more than one Studentship.	Studentships offered for Competition in the M.A. Courses. *5	£100	3	,,	One in each of the following:— 1. Anc. Classics, 2. Math. Scien., 3. M. & M. Sci., 4. Expl. Scien.. 5. Mod. Lit.	Under 26 on first day of Examin.
† Provided that an Exhibi-[illegible] shall not be awarded to [illegible]didate at the first Pro-[illegible] Examination if a [illegible]iod than three Aca-[illegible]rs shall have elapsed	†Civil Engineering Exhibitions. First Professional Exam. 1 First-class. 1 Second-class.	£30 £15	... ..	July (towards the middle).	1 Mathcs., 2. Expl. Phys., 3. Drawing and Descrip. Arch.	

Universities.	No. of open Scholarships, 1892.	Annual value of each.	No. of years tenable.	Date of Examination.	Subjects.	Limit of age.
DUBLIN.—The Royal University of Ireland—*continued.* from the time of Matriculation; or at the Second Professional Examination if a longer interval than two Academical years shall have elapsed from the time of passing the first Professional Examination;	Second Professional Exam. 1 First-class. 1 Second-class.	£36 £18	... ...	... ...	1. Mathem., 2. Math. Phys., 3 Chem., 4. Geol., 5. Prac. Engine.	
or at the B.E. Degree Examination if a longer interval than three Academical years shall have elapsed from the time of passing the First Professional Examination.	B.E. Degree Examination. 1 First-class. 1 Second-class.	£42 £21	... ...	... ...	1. Math. Phys., 2. Civil Engineer., 3. Drawing.	

Should a Candidate who has become entitled to an Exhibition have previously gained an Exhibition in either of the Arts Examinations, such shall be deducted from the amount awarded.

Examinations in Medicine Exhibitions.

The following Exhibitions may be awarded annually by the Senate:

At the First Examination in Medicine, Two First Class of £20 each, and Two Second Class Exhibitions of £10 each.

At the Second Examination in Medicine, Two First Class of £25 each, and Two Second Class Exhibitions of £15 each.

At the Third Examination in Medicine, Two First Class Exhibitions of £30 each, and Two Second Class Exhibitions of £20 each.

At the Examination for the Primary Medical Degrees, Two First Class Exhibitions of £40 each, and Two Second Class Exhibitions of £25 each.

Provided that an Exhibition shall not be awarded to any Candidate at the First Examination in Medicine if a longer interval than three Academical years shall have elapsed from the time of Matriculation; or at the Second Examination in Medicine if a longer interval than two Academical years shall have elapsed from the time of passing the First Examination in Medicine; or at the Third Examination if a longer interval than three Academical years shall have elapsed from the time of passing the First Examination in Medicine; or at the Examination for the Primary Medical Degrees if a longer interval than four Academical years shall have elapsed from the time of passing the First Examination in Medicine.

Not more than one First Class Exhibition, and one Second Class Exhibition, shall be awarded in connection with each Examination, so long as each Examination is held twice annually.

Travelling Medical Scholarship.

A Travelling Scholarship in the Faculty of Medicine, valued £100, will be open to competition at the October Examination in the Faculty of Medicine. The subjects will be in rotation—

(1) Anatomy and Histology, and
(2) Physiology and Pathology.

[illegible]rsons who may have passed the Medical Degrees Examination, either in the year of the Scholarship Exami[illegible] or in the year immediately preceding, will be eligible.

[illegible]he successful Candidate will be required to proceed, within the succeeding six months, to some Foreign [illegible]ol of M[illegible] the name of which must first be submitted to the Senate for approval; and he must there [illegible] six months. If desirable, the Scholar may, with the sanction of the Committee, spend three [illegible]l and three months at another.

DUBLIN.—The Royal University of Ireland—*continued.*

The Scholarship will be paid in four instalments—£20 after the successful Candidate has been declared by the Senate; £20 on his arrival at the Foreign place of study; £30 on the completion of his first three months' work, and £30 at the close of the second three months.

The Scholar must produce Certificates from his Foreign Teachers, testifying to his diligence, before the payment of the third and fourth instalments.

The subjects for the Anatomical Scholarship shall be Human Anatomy, including Anatomical Technique, Embryology, Comparative Anatomy of the Vertebrates, Histology, and Surgical Pathology.

The subjects for the Physiological Scholarship shall be Physiology, Theoretical and Practical; Pathology, including Bacteriology, the recognition of morbid specimens by the naked eye, and the various methods which are employed in the preparation of diseased tissues for microscopical examination.

The Scholar will be required to show such a knowledge of the language of the country which he may select as will enable him to take proper advantage of the instruction given.

PRIZES.

The Senate may, at the First Examination in Law, award the following Prizes:—

One First-class Prize of £20. | One Second-class Prize of £10.

The Senate may, at the Examination for the Degree of LL.B., award the following Exhibitions:—

One First-class Prize of £42. | One Second-class Prize of £21.

DURHAM UNIVERSITY.

Universities.	*No. of open Scholarships, 1892.*	*Annual value of each.*	*No. of years tenable.*	*Date of Examination.*	*Subjects.*	*Limit of age.*
Durham.—The University ... **Warden.**—The Very Rev. W. C. Lake, D.D., Dean of Durham. **Sub-Warden.**—Rev. R. J. Pearce, D.C.L., Professor of Mathematics. **Registrar.**—W. K. Hilton, Esq., M.A. **Tutors.**—Rev. A. Plummer, D.D.; Rev. A. Robertson, M.A.; F. B. Jevons, Esq., M.A.	3 Foundation.	£70	2	(1) Jan. 20. (2) Oct. 12.	Classics or Mathematics.	None.
	1 ,,	£40	2	Oct. 12.	Classics or Mathematics.	None.
	1 ,,	£30	2	Jan. 20.	Classics or Mathematics.	None.
	1 (for those with limited means).	£20	2	Oct. 12.	Classics or Mathematics.	None.
	1 Classical.	£30	1	Easter.	Classics or Mathematics.	None.
	1 Mathematical.	£30	1	Easter.	Classics or Mathematics.	None.
	1 Thorp. (For those of limited means nominated by the Warden.)	£15	3	No Exam.		
	1 Newby.	£25	Until the Scholar is of standing to present himself for Final B.A. Exam.	Oct. 12.	Classics.	None.
N.B.—The Annual necessary Expenses at University College, including Board, Lodging, and Tuition, vary from £82 to £109; at Bp. Hatfield's Hall, from £65 to £79. Th[illegible] other expenses [illegible] as, Entrance, [illegible] &c., amounting [illegible] about £10.	1 Medical.	£25	4	,,	Lat., Eng. Hist., Arith., and Eng. Comp.	,,

Universities.	No. of open Scholarships, 1899.	Annual value of each.	No. of years tenable.	Date of Examination.	Subjects.	Limit of age.
DURHAM The University continued.	1 Theological.	£40	2	Oct. 18.	1st. Gk. Test., Script., &c.	None.
	1 "	£60	2	Jan. 20.		
	2 "	£60	2	Oct. 19.		
	1 "	£30	1	Jan. 20.		
	3 Theological Exhibitions.	£20	2	(1) Jan. 20. (2) Oct. 19.	Awarded at Entr. Exam. to those of limited means.	"

EDINBURGH UNIVERSITY.

Fellowships, Scholarships, Bursaries and Prizes open in Session 1891-92.

Universities.	*Name of Fellowship, &c.*	*Annual value.*	*No. of years tenable.*	*Date of Examination.*	*Subjects of Examination.*
Edinburgh.—The University. Principal.—Sir William Muir, K.C.S.I., D.C.L., LL.D.	*Faculty of Arts.*				
Faculty of Arts. Dean.—George Chrystal, LL.D., Professor of Mathematics.	Scholarships—				
	Vans Dunlop in Polit. Econ.,	£100	3	Nov. 1891.	
	" Nat. Philos.,			Apr. 1892.	
	" Maths., Mor. Philos.,				
	" Sanskrit & Cmp. Philol.,				
	" Agriculture,				
	" History.			Oct. 1892.	
	Gray	£44	2	Apr. 1892.	
	Ferguson (3) (open to Edinburgh graduates).	£80 each.	2	Oct. 1891.	Cls., Maths., and Men. Phil. respectively.
	Steven in Agriculture ...	£75	1	Apr. 1892.	
	J. E. Baxter in Maths. ...	£90	3	Dec. 1891.	

N

Universities.	*Name of Fellowship, &c.*	*Annual value.*	*No. of years tenable.*	*Date of Examination.*	*Subjects of Examination.*
EDINBURGH.—The University—*continued.*	Rhind in Classics. ...	£98	3	Dec. 1891.	
	,, Philosoph. ...	£98	3	Dec. 1891.	
	Bruce of Grangehill and Falkland's in Classics.	£100	3	Apr. 1892.	
	Neil Arnott in Exp. Physcs.	£38	1	,,	
	Mackay Smith in Nat. Phil.	£25	2	,,	
	BURSARIES (First Year)—				
	John Welsh, Classical (2) .	£20 each.	4	Oct. 1891.	Lat., Grk., and Mathics., Eng.,
	,, Mathemat. (2)	£20 each.	4	,,	Gk., Lat., Math., Eng., Fr., Ger.
	Heriot (5)	£30 each.	3	,,	Greek, Latin, Math., English.
There are several other valuable Bursaries restricted in the first place to pupils from Schools in Ayrshire and other localities. These are thrown open when candidates of sufficient merit fail to present themselves. A number of Bursaries are also in the gift of Edinburgh Town Council.	Tyndall Bruce	£20	3	,,	
	Grierson (3)	1 of £24 & 2 of £20 each.	4	,,	,, ,,
	Whitelaw (3)	£22	3	,,	,, ,,
	Edin. Univ. Endowment (2)	£20 each.	3	,,	,, ,,
	Thomson	£25	4	,,	,, ,,
	Sibbald	£30	4	,,	,, ,,
	Mann	£26	3	,,	,, ,,
	Mackinnon	£19	3	,,	,, ,,
	Jardine of Thorlieshope ...	£35	4	,,	,, ,,

Johnstone of Harthope ...	£19	4	„	„ „
Bursaries (Second Year)—				
Spence (2)	£10 each.	3	„	Latin, Greek, Mathematics.
Tyndall Bruce	£35	3	„	„ „
Stewart (open to Edinburgh Students).	£30 for 1st year, £40 for 2nd.	2	„	Latin, Greek, Math., and Brit. History.
Bursaries (Third Year)—				
Macpherson	£43	2	„	Clcs., Mth., Log.
Harrison	£34	2	„	„ „
Horseliehill Scott	£33	2	„	„ „
Renton (any year)... ...	£20	1	Nov. 1891.	Eng. and Math.
Prizes—				
Lord Rector's	£26 5s.	...	„	Essay (for subj. see E. U. calr.).
Gray (3)	£20, £10 & £5 resptvly.	... ...	Sept. 1891.	„ „
Bruce in Logic and Metphcs.	£20		Apr. 1892.	
Muir in Sansk. and Comp. Phil. (several).	Aggregate of £25.	...	„	
Cousin in Fine Art ...	£15	...	„	
Neil Arnott in Nat. Phil. (for Medical Students).	£42	...		
Newton (2)...	£21 each.	2	„	1 Profcy. in Sen. (2nd) Class Maths.; 1 Prof. in Junr. Class of Nat. Phily.

Universities.	*Name of Fellowship, &c.*	*Annual value.*	*No. of years tenable.*	*Date of Examination.*	*Subjects of Examination.*
EDINBURGH.—The University—*continued.*	PRIZES (*cont.*)				
	Univ. Club of London ...	£21	...	Dec. 1891.	Essay (for subj. see E. U. calr.).
Faculty of Divinity.	*Faculty of Divinity.*				
Dean.—Rev. M. C. Taylor, D.D., Professor of Ecclesiastical History.	Scholarships—				
	Jeffrey ... end of first year.	£77	1	Apr. 1892.	Divinity.
	„ „ „	£77	1	„	Heb. & Gr. Lang.
	Glover	£34	3	„	B. D. Subjects.
	BURSARIES—				
	Webster	£36	3	Nov. 1890.	Classics, Math., Philo., Heb. Apol., Gk. Tests.
There are also several Bursaries in the gift of private persons.	Ettles ... first year.	£35	3	„	„ „
	Thomson ... first year.	£25	4	„	„ „
	Buchanan ... first or second year.	£10	3	„	„ „
	Ramsay ...first or second year.	£16	3	„	„ „
	R. Hunter end of first year.	£17	2	Apr. 1892.	Div. Ecc. Hist., Bib. Crit., and Jun. Hebr.
	Mylne	£30	3	...	
	King William III. „	£35	2	„	„ „

	Grierson (3) first, second and third year.	£26 each.	1	Nov. 1891.	See E. U. calr.
	Simeon (2)	£25	3	„	„ „
	Hepburn (2)	£13			„ „
	PRIZES—				
	Hepburn	£25	...	...	Essay (for subject see calndr.).
	Barty (open to entrants) ...	£25	...	...	Hebrew and Hellenistic Greek.
Faculty of Law.	*Faculty of Law.*				
Dean.—J. Kirkpatrick, Esq., M.A., LL.D., Prof. of Hist.	SCHOLARSHIP—				
	Vans Dunlop in Public Law Civil Law & Constit. Hist.	£100	3	Oct. 1892.	
	BURSARIES—				
	Cairns ... second year	£19	1	Oct. 1891.	Lat., Mor. Phil. and standing in law classes.
	Grierson ... first „	£26	1	„	Lat.& Mor. Phil.
	„ ... second „	„	1	„	Lat., Mor. Phil. and standing in lawclasses.
	„ ... third „	„	1	„	
	Thomson ... first „	£25	4	„	Lat.& Mor. Phil.
	PRIZE—				
	Forensic	£10	...	„	Civil Law.
Faculty of Medicine.	*Faculty of Medicine.*				
Dean.—T. R. Fraser, Esq, M.D., Prof of Materia Med.	FELLOWHIPS—				
	Leckie-Mactier	£70	3	Nov. 1892.	Med. Surg. and Gen. cases in Rl. Infirmary.
Secretary of the Senatus Academicus.—Prof. Kirkpatrick.	Freeland Barbour	£100	1	July	Anat. Phy. Path.

Universities.	*Names of Fellowship, &c.*	*Annual value.*	*No. of years tenable.*	*Date of Examination.*	*Subjects of Examination.*
Edinburgh.—The University—*continued.*	Scholarships—				
	Ettles (for Graduates on graduating).	£35	1	May, 1892.	Most distinguished M.B. & C.M. of the year.
	Vans Dunlop in Nat. Hist. (inclu.) Geol. and Botany.	£100	3	Apr. 1892.	
	Vans Dunlop (for Students at end of third year).	£100	3	Mar. 1892.	Anat., Phy., Mat. Med., Path.
	Murchison Memorial (for Students from 4 to 6 years' standing).	Annual proceeds of £1,000.	1	July, 1892.	Clinical Medicn.
	Buchanan (for Graduates on graduating).	Annl. prcds. of £1,000.	1	"	Midwifery and Gynecology.
	James Scott (for Graduates on graduating).	£45	1	"	Midwifery.
	Hope Prize (for Students at end of first winter in Chemical Laboratory).	£25	1	Mar. 1892.	Chem. Laboraty.
	Coldstream (Medical Missionary).	£25	4	Awarded in Oct. 1891.	Medical Prelim. subjects.
	Mackay Smith (Scholarsp).	£25	2	Mar. 1892.	Chemistry.
	Bursaries—				
	Sibbald (two) (for Students entering).	£30	3	Awarded in Oct. 1891.	Latin, Greek, Math. and Eng.

Grierson (1st yr.) do.	£20	1	„	Med. Prel. subjts.
„ (2nd yr.) ...	„	1	„	Chem., Bot., and Nat. History.
Grierson (3rd yr.) ...	„	1	„	Anatomy and Physiology.
„ (4th yr.) ...	„	1	„	Materia Medica and Pathology.
Thomson (two), (for Students entering).	£25	4	Mar. and Oct. 1892.	Medical Preliminary subjcts.
Mackenzie (two), (for Students at the end of first and second winter).	£21 5*s.*	1	Mar. 1892.	Junr. Anatomy and senior Anatomy.
John Aitken Carlyle (two), (for Students at end of first and second winter).	£28	1	„	Anatomy and Chemistry, Anatomy & Physlgy.
Mackie Bursaries (2) ...	£30 each.	2	Oct. 1892.	Students who have completed their first or second *annus medicus* and are in need of pecuniary assistance.
Prizes—				
Neil Arnott (for 2nd or 3rd year Students).	£42	1	Oct. 1892.	Nat. Philosphy.
Robert Wilson (for 2nd year Students).	£8 16*s.* 2*d.*	1	Mar. 1892.	Chemistry Class (Senior).

Universities.	*Names of Fellowship, &c.*	*Annual value.*	*No. of years tenable.*	*Date of Examination.*	*Subjects of Examination.*
EDINBURGH.—The University—*continued.*	Wightman (for Students about to Graduate).	£10 10*s.*	1	May, 1891	Clinical Medcn.
	Beaney (for Students on graduating).	£37 10*s.*	1	"	Anat., Surg., and Clin. Surg.
	Cameron (for Practitioners or Members of the Medical Profession).	£98	1	"	Practical Therapeutics.
	Gunning (for Graduates of not more than six years' standing), (Four Prizes).	£50 each.	1	"	Zoologs, Materia Medica, Obstetrics, Public Health, Jurisprudence.
	Goodsir Memorial	£60	1	July, 1892.	Anatomy and Physiology.

GLASGOW UNIVERSITY.

BURSARIES, ETC., OPEN IN 1892-3.

Universities.	*No. of Bursaries.*	*Foundation.*	*Yearly value.*	*Years of tenure.*	*Examinations.*
GLASGOW.—The University. Principal.—J. Caird, D.D., LL.D. Sec.—James Coutts, Esq., M.A. Professors.—W. P. Dickson, D.D., LL.D.; Sir W. Thomson, LL.D., D.C.L., P.R.S.; R. Grant, LL.D., F.R.S.; W. T. Gairdner, M.D., LL.D.; G. G. Ramsay, LL.D.; J. Veitch, LL.D.; E. Caird, LL.D.; J. Young, M.D.; Alex. Moody Stuart, Advoc.; W. Leishman, M.D.; Sir G. H. B. Macleod, M.D.; P. A. Simpson, M.A., M.D.; W. Stewart D.D.;		I. *In Faculty of Arts.*	N.B.—Changes may be made in dates, &c., owing to new regulations of the Scottish Universities Commission, or otherwise. The General Examination for Bursaries in Arts will take place on Tuesday, 25th Oct., and three following days. Names to be given in to Assistant Clerk (Matriculation Office) on or before the 18th October.		
	1	Breadalbane Scholarship ...	£50	3	For Students at end of Arts or B.Sc. Course in Engineering Exam. Maths., Nat. Philos.
	1	Eben Brown Bursary ...	£37	3	
	1	Buchanan	£13	3	
	2	Clark (Mile-end) Scholarsh.	£50	4	For Students at end of Arts Course. Honours examination in respective departments for M.A.
	1	Crawford or Bishop's Bursary	£13	4	
	1	Exhibition Scholarship ...	£150	2	

Universities.	*No. of Bursaries.*	*Foundation.*	*Yearly value.*	*Years of tenure.*	*Examinations.*
GLASGOW.—The University —*continued*. George Buchanan, M.A., M.D., LL.D.; T. M'Call Anderson, M.D.; J. Ferguson, M.A., LL.D.; R. Herbert Story, D.D.; J. G. M'Kendrick, M.D., LL.D., F.R.S.; J. Robertson, D.D.; J. Cleland, M.D., LL.D., D.Sc., F.R.S.; W. Jack, LL.D.; M. Charteris, M.D.; F. O. Bower, M.A., D.Sc., F.R.S.; A. C. Bradley, M.A.; G. G. A. Murray, B.A.; Archibald Barr, D.Sc.; James Moir.; John Harvard Bills.	1	Wm. Ewing Fellowship ...	£80	3	Honours Exam. in Maths.
	1	Forfar	£30	4	
	1	Foundation...	£10	4	
	1	General Council	£20	3	
	1	General Council (Park) ...	£20	2	
	1	Ferguson (J.) Bursary ...	£80	2	Honours Exam. in Classics.
	1	Lloyds Register Schp. ...	£50	3	For Naval Architecture Special Exam.
	1	Lorimer (Philosophy) ...	£25	3	Special Examination.
	1	Lorimer (Mathematics) ...	£25	3	" "
	1	Luke Fellowship	£110	3	Special Exam. Hist. and Eng. Lit.
	1	McEwen (Arts or Science).	£16	4	
	1	MacGrouther	£20	4	
	2	Metcalfe Bursaries ...	£25	2	Maths., Mechs., & Astron.
	1	Metcalfe Fellowship ...	£100	3	Honours Exam. in Maths. and Nat. Philos., after Arts Course.
	1	Monteith Bursary	£14	3	Special Exam. in German.
	2	Muir (Engineering) Bursary	£12 10*s*.	1	For distinction in work of Engineering Class.
	1	Muir (Mathematics, Senr.).	£18	1	For distinction in work of Senior Math. Class.

1	Muir (Mathematics, Junr.).	£9	2	For distinction in work Junior Math. Class.
1	Scott Bursary	£25	4	
1	Scott Scholarship	£80	2	Mental Philos. and Eng. Lit.
1	Thomson Phil. Bursary ...	£11	2	Exams. in Mental Philos.
1	Williams Bursary	£40	3 or 4	Cands. to be natives of Eng. and to be studying with view to ministry of Protestant Dissenting denomination in England.
	II. *In Faculty of Medicine.*			
1	Davidson Bursary	£40	3	For eminence in 1st Professional Exam.
1	Lorimer	£25	3	Exam. in earlier subjects of Medical curriculum.
1	Mackintosh	£30	1	For Exam. on Insanity.
1	Marshall	£17	4	
1	Monteith	£21	2	Eminence in Anatomy and Physiology.
1	Rainy	£20	2	Exam. in earlier subjects of Medical curriculum.
1	Weir	£18	1	Eminence in 2nd and 3rd Professional Exams.
	III. *In Faculty of Law.*			
1	Cunninghame Scholp. ...	£32	2	For Graduation in Law (LL.B.) of year most distinguished in conveyancing.

Universities.	*No. of Bursaries.*	*Foundation.*	*Yearly value.*	*Years of tenure.*	*Examinations.*
GLASGOW.—The University —*continued.*					
	1	Walkingshay and Young Bursary	£18	2	
	1	Young Fund Bursary ...	£20	2	
		IV. *In Faculty of Theology.*			General Exams. for Theol. Bursaries on 10th and 11th November, 1891.
	1	Black	£42	3	
	1	Brown or Ettles	£21	3	
	1	Findlater Scholarship ...	£38	1	Special Examination.
	1	Hastie Bursary	£25	3	
	1	Lorimer	£25	3	
	1	Muir, William	£25	2	
		V. *In Theology, Law, or Medicine.*			
	1	Armagh	£25	3	Awarded to most disting. Graduate in Arts entering on course in Law, Medicine, or Divinity.

N.B.—As new regulations are in course of being framed by the Scottish Universities Commission, for dates and other particulars Candidates for Bursaries should consult the University Calendar, or apply to Mr. Addison, Matriculation Office. Candidates should be careful to send in their names in time.

LONDON UNIVERSITY.

Universities.	*No. of Scholarships, &c., 1892.*	*Value.*	*No. of years tenable.*	*Date of Examination.*	*Subjects.*	*Limit of age.*
LONDON—The University.	MATRICULATION.					
Registrar and Librarian.—Arthur Milman, Esq., M.A.	* Exhibitions					
* Open to both men and women, who must pass in the Honours Division of the Matriculation Examination.	1 (First).	£30	2	Monday, Jan. 11, and Monday, June 13.	(1) Lat. (2) One of the following, Greek, Fr., Gr., Sanskrit, Arabic. (3) Eng. Lang. and History. Mod. Geog. (4) Mathes. (5) Mechanics.	Not more than 20 at the commencement of Exam.
	1 (Second).	£20	2			
	1 (Third).	£15	2			
	Fourth, a prize value £10.					
	Fifth and Sixth, value £5 each.					
The Exhibitioner shall declare his intention of presenting himself either at the two Examinations for B.A., or at the two Exams. for B.Sc., or at the Intermediate Examination in Laws, or at the Preliminary Scientific and Intermediate Examinations in Medicine, within Three Academical Years from the time of his passing the Matriculation Examination.	† *Gilchrist Exhibitions.*					
	1	£30	2	Awarded annually at June exam. (Honours).	(6) One of the following branches of Expl. Science:—Chem., Heat & Light, Magn. and Electy.	
	1	£20	2			
… le Candidates, to … in pursuing their						

Universities.	*No. of Scholarships, &c., 1892.*	*Value.*	*No. of years tenable.*	*Date of Examination.*	*Subjects.*	*Limit of age.*
LONDON—The University (*cont.*) studies at some Collegiate Institution approved by the Trustees.						
For other Scholarships awarded on the results of the Lond. Univ. Matr. Exam. (Honours Division). See Owen's Coll., Manchester, Univ. Coll., Bristol, Univ. Coll., London, Bedford Coll., London.	*Gilchrist.* *West.* *Reid.*					
* The Exhibitioner must declare his intention of presenting himself at the Degree Exam. within two academical years from the time of passing the Intermediate Examination in Arts or Sciences.	INTERMEDIATE ARTS. * Exhibitions. 1 in Latin.	£40	2	Monday, July 18.	(1) Classics.	22
	1 in English.	£30	2	,,	(2) Fr. or Ger.	22
	† 1 in Mathcs.	£40	2	,,	(3) Eng. Lan., Litre. & Hist.	
	1 "Ger." Prize.	£10	...	,,		
† Candidates for either the Intermediate in Arts or Science may compete for this exhibition.	1 "Fr." Prize.	£10	...	,,	(4) Mathcs.	
‡ For Female Candidates, to	‡ *Gilchrist Exhibitions.* 1	£40	2	Awarded		

assist them in pursuing their studies at some Collegiate Institution approved by the Trustees.	1	£30		July annually.		
	B.A.:— Scholarships.					
These Scholarships are open to both B.A. and B.Sc.	1 "Mathcs."	£50 with style, Univ. Sch.		Monday, Oct. 24.	(1) Lat. with Hist. (2 papers). (2) Greek with Hist. (2 papers).	23
	1 "Mental and Moral Science.	£50 with style, Univ. Schr.	3	"	(3) Eng., Fr. Ger., Italian,	
	1 "Classics."	£50 and Univ. Scholar.	3	"	Arab., Sanskrit, (2 papers in each) one of the above.	
	1 "Fr." Prize.	£15	...	"	(The *above* 3 are	
* An option is given in the case of the Branches 4 and 5.	1 "Ger." Prize.	£15	...	"	compulsory.)	
	1 "Eng." Prize.	£15	...	"	(4)* Mathcs. Pure or Mixed.	
	1 Gilchrist Prize of books (for female cands).	£10	...	Annually awarded	(5)* Mental or Moral Science. Pass and Honrs.	
† Open to Intermediate Arts candidates also.	INTERMEDIATE IN SCIENCE: Exhibitions. † 1 "Mathcs."	£40	2	Monday, July 18.	(1) Inorg. Chem. (2) Experimental Physics. (3) Mathcs. (4) General	22

Universities.	*No. of Scholarships, &c., 1892.*	*Value.*	*No. of years tenable.*	*Date of Examination.*	*Subjects.*	*Limit of age.*
LONDON—The University (*cont.*).						
Open to Preliminary Sc. (M.B.) candidates also.	1 "Neil Arnott" in Expl. Physics.	£40	2	Monday, July 18.	Biology for pass only.	22
	1 Chemistry.	£40	2	"	Optional:—	
	1 Botany.	£40	2	"	Bot. and Zoolgy.	
	1 Zoology.	£40	2	"	for Honours.	
	B.Sc.:— Scholarships. 1 "Mathcs."	£50 and Title Univ. Schr.	3	Pass commences:— Monday, Oct. 17. Honours commences. Mon. in the week next but one after conclusion of Pass. Exam.	Any 3 of the 9 follow. subjs:— Pass. (1) Pure Mathcs. (2) Mix. Mathcs. (3) Experimental Physics. (4) Chemistry. (5) Botany. (6) Zoology. (7) An. Phys. (8) Phys. Geog. and Geol. (9) Mental and Moral Science.	23
See under B.A.	1 "Mental and Moral Science."	£50 and Title of Univ. Schr.	3			

For Particulars see Intermediate in Science Examination on previous page.	1 "Experimental Physics." 1 "Chemistr." 1 "Botany." 1 "Zoology." 1 "Physiology." 1 "Phys., Geog. and Geology."	£50 each, and Title of Univ. Scholar.	2	Exams. for Honours in Zoology on Wed. and Thurs. in week after Exams. for Honours in Chemistry.		
	Preliminary Science (M.B.). 4	£40 each.	2	Twoexams. ineach year. 3rd Mon. in July (Pass & Honours) 3rd Mon. in Jan. (Pass only.)	Pass. (a) Inorg. Chem. (b) Experimental Physics. (c) General Biology. Pass only. Optional:— Botany and Zoology. For Honours.	22
	—					
	Medicine.— Int. (1st M.B.). Exhibitions.			Pass and Honours.		
	1 "Anatomy."	£40	2	Monday,	...	Must be over 19.
	1 "Physiology and Histology."	£40	2	July 11. Pass only		
	1 "Org. Chem."	£30	2	Monday, January 18.		

Universities.	*No. of Scholarships, &c., 1892.*	*Value.*	*No. of years tenable.*	*Date of Examination.*	*Subjects.*	*Limit of age.*
LONDON.—The University (*contd.*)	MEDICINE.—Int. (1st M.B.). Exhibs.(*cont.*)—					
	1 "Mat., Med. and Ph. Chem."	£30	2			
		6 Gold Medals value £5 each.	...			
	M.B.:—Scholarships.					
	1 Medicine.	£50 and Title Univ. Schr. in Med.	2	Pass. Monday, October 31. Honours. week next but one fol. Pass Exam.		
	1 Obs. Med.	£30 Univ. Schr. in Obs. Med.	2			
	1 Forensic Med.	£30 Univ. Schr. in For. Med.	2			
	B.S.:—					
	1 Scholarship.	£50	2	Pass. Tuesday, Dec. 6. Honours.	Surgery.	

	and Title of Univ. Schr. in Surgery.		Tu. in week fol. Pass Exam.	
INTERMEDIATE IN LAWS. 1 Exhibition.	£40	2	Pass. Monday, January 4. Honours. Tu. in the week next but one following Pass Exam. *See* p. 7 *et seq.*	(1) Jurisprudence. (2) Roman Law. (3) Constitutional History of England.
LL.B.:— 1 Scholarship.	£50 and Title of Univ. Law Scholar.	2	Pass. Monday, January 4. Honours. Tues. in wk. next but one follow. Pass Exam.*	(1) Common Law. (2) Equity. (3) Real and Personal Property. (4) Roman Law.

*For exact dates, see Calendar commencement of this

OWENS COLLEGE, MANCHESTER.

Universities.	*No. of Scholarships, &c., 1892.*	*Value.*	*No. of years tenable.*	*Date of Examination.*	*Subjects.*	*Limit of age.*
OWENS COLLEGE, VICTORIA UNIVERSITY, MANCHESTER. Principal —Professor A. W. Ward, Litt. D. Registrar and Secretary.—H. W. Holder, Esq., M.A.	Entrance Schlps. and Exhibitions. 1 Manchester Grammar Sch. Schp.	£18	3	June 13-15	Classics and Mathematics.	15-20.
	1 Crace-Calvert Scholarship.	£25	2	June 13.	Chemistry.	Under 25.
	1 Ramsbotton Scholarship.	£40	2	June 14.	Mths., Mechs., Engineering, etc.	16-23.
	1 Rumney Schp. To artisan memb'rs of Lanc. and Cheshire Institutes.	£45	3			
	3 Hulme Exhibs.	£12	2	Oct. 4 & 6.	Classics, or Fr. & Ger., & Eng.	15-20.
	* 1 Rogers.	£20	1	"	"	
	* 1 Seaton.	£15	2	Oct. 5 & 6.	Classics, English and Mathcs.	
	* 1 Dalton Mathematical. Scholarships open to all per-	£15	2	Oct. 5.	Mathematics.	

* These are for women as well as for men. † June Prel., Ex. of Vict. Univ., 1st Division, or Lond. Univ. Matr. Ex.	sons who satisfy certain conditions prescribed, whether students or non-students at the College :—					
	* 1 Shakspere.	£40	2	Oct. 6 & 7.	Eng. Lang. and Litre.	21 Jan. 1, '92.
	* 2 Bp. Fraser.	£40	2	Oct. 7, 8, 10.	Gk. and Rom., Classics & Hist.	20 Oct. 1, '92.
	* 1 Oliver Heywood.	£50	2		As in Fraser.	20
	* 1 Gilchrist † (Biennially).	£50	3	Oct., 1893.	...	18
	* 1 Gilchrist.	£50	3			
	1 Dauntesey. Medical.	£100	1	Begin Oct. 4, 1892.	Cands. will be examined in (1)	18

Gen. and Comp. Anat. (inc. pracl. work); (2) Outlines of Physcl. Bot.; (3) Chem. (inc. the prin. of Inorg. and Org. Chem. & a prac. exam. in the Qual. Anal. of Inorg. Bodies). Every cand. will also be required to offer himself for exam. in one of the 2 follwg. subs.: (*a*) Maths. (Alg., the El. of Geom. and Pl. Trg.); (*b*) Lat. (trans. from Cla. Auths. into Eng. Lat. Pr. Comp. and Gram).

Universities.	*No. of Scholarships, &c., 1892.*	*Value.*	*No. of years tenable.*	*Date of Examination.*	*Subjects.*	*Limit of age.*
OWENS COLLEGE, VICTORIA UNIVERSITY, MANCHESTER, *contd.*	2 Robt. Platt.	£50	2	Oct. 3, 4, 5.	Comp. Anatomy, and Human Physiology.	18 to 25
* For women also. † Cands. must have passed the Prelim. Exam. of the Victoria Univ. in the June or Sept. immediately preceding the competition.	* 1 Walters.†	£30	2	October (1893).	French & Germ.	

ST. ANDREWS UNIVERSITY.

Universities.	*No. of Scholarships, &c., 1892.*	*Value.*	*No. of years tenable.*	*Date of Examination.*	*Subjects.*	*Limit of age.*
ST. ANDREWS—The University. Principal.—James Donaldson, Esq., LL.D. Librarian, Registrar, &c.—J. M. Anderson, Esq.	About 20.	£10 to £30	1 to 4	End of October.	Latin, Greek, Mathematics, English Literature.	None.

UNIVERSITY COLLEGES.

SCIENCE AND TECHNICAL COLLEGES AND INSTITUTIONS.

UNIVERSITY COLLEGES.—SCIENCE AND TECHNICAL COLLEGES.

It is necessary for Candidates to send in their names to the Registrar of the College at which they are about to compete about a month before the date of Examination. *Vide* Calendar, p. 7 *et seq.*, for particulars as to dates.

University, Science, and Technical Colleges.	*Entrance Scholarships, 1892.*	*Value.*	*No. of years tenable.*	*Date of Examination.*	*Subjects.*	*Limit of age.*
Aberystwith—University College of Wales. Principal.—T. F. Roberts, Esq., M.A. Registrar and Librarian.—E. P. Jones, Esq., M.A., B.D.	1 Scholarship. 1 „ 2 „ 5 „ 2 Exhibitions. 10 „	£40 £30 £25 £20 £15 £10	Renewable at the end of First and Second Session if merit is shewn.	Tuesday, Sept. 15 to 22.	Maths. English. Classics. Mod. Langs. Nat. Science. Oriental Lang. Logic, Psychly., and Ethics.	Must be over 16. Open to men and women.

1. *Candidates are allowed to choose five papers, of which not more than two may be advanced papers. In no case will a high Scholarship be awarded to a candidate who does not take one or more of the advanced papers. Candidates are not allowed to choose Advanced and Elementary papers in the same subject.*

2. *All the candidates will be expected to write an Essay in English or Welsh, in addition to the papers, on one subject selected by the candidate from a given list.*

3. All Scholarships and Exhibitions are tenable from term to term and renewable (subject to the restriction specified in the next paragraph) at the end of the first and second Sessions, provided (*a*) that the holder has made good progress in his studies as shown in the class examinations at the end of each Term; (*b*) that his conduct and diligence have been satisfactory; and (*c*) that he pursues a course of study approved by the Senate.

4. The tenure of all Scholarships and Exhibitions ceases on the attainment of the degree of B.A. or B.Sc. but special assistance may be given, on the recommendation of the Senate, to graduates preparing for other examinations.

5. Scholars and Exhibitioners receiving smaller sums than £40 may, in case of special excellence, receive an increase at the end of the first and second Sessions.

6. Exhibitions of £10 (or, in case of special merit, of £15) will be awarded on the results of the class examinations to students not already holding any scholarship or exhibition.

7. The Scholarships and Exhibitions are open without restriction as to nationality or age, with the exception of a few close Scholarships offered by private benefactors.

Bangor—University College of North Wales. Principal.—H. R. Reichel, Esq., M.A., Fellow of All Souls' College Oxford. Secretary and Registrar.—W. Cadwaladr Davies, Esq.	1 Scholarship. 1 Exhibition. 2 ,, 5 ,,	£30 £20 £15 £10	3 years.	Sept. 15 to 18. The Exam. is held at Bangor only.	(1) Greek. (2) Latin. (3) English. (4) Welsh. (5) French. (6) German. (7) Logic & Phil. (8) Mathcs. (9) Physics. (10) Chemistry. (11) Phys. Geog. and Geoly. (12) Biology. Not less than two or more than five of the above. A Scholarship or Exhn. may be awarded for special excellence in a single subject.	20 Open to men and women.
	In College Scholarships.	£70	1 or 2 years.			
	5 Scholar Assistantships.	£30	1 year. (Annual)			
	H. Tate, Science Scholarships.	Amontg. to £100 in all.	1 year. (Annual)			
	Dean Edwards Memorial Prize.	£25.	1 year.			

REGULATIONS.

1. The Scholarships and Exhibitions are tenable for three years, but their continuance during the second and third years is conditional on good conduct and satisfactory progress, according to which the Senate may also increase or diminish their value at the end of each session.

2. One half of the Scholarships and one half of the Exhibitions will be confined to Welsh candidates, *i.e.*:—

i. Welsh-speaking candidates.

ii. Candidates of whatever nationality who have been domiciled in Wales for three years immediately preceding the date of Examination.

BANGOR—University College of North Wales, *continued.*

3. Candidates other then Welsh candidates must not have exceeded the age of twenty on the first day of Examination.

4. The Senate reserves the right of withholding Scholarships and Exhibitions unless candidates of sufficient merit present themselves. In awarding, especially where there is no limit of age, account will be taken of the promise shown by candidates.

Candidates below the age of sixteen may compete for Scholarships and Exhibitions, but may not enter the College until they attain that age, and the tenure of the Scholarship or Exhibition awarded to any such candidate will date from entrance to the College.

UNIVERSITY, SCIENCE, AND TECHNICAL COLLEGES.	*Scholarships, &c., 1892.*	*Value.*	*No. of years tenable.*	*Date of Examination.*	*Subjects.*	*Limit of age.*
BIRMINGHAM—The Mason Science College. Principal.—R. S. Heath, M.A., D.Sc. Secretary and Registrar.—G. H. Morley.	2	£25	1	September.	One in any *four* of the fol. subjs.: Class., Eng., Fr., Ger., Math.; and one in any *four* of the fol. subjs.: Maths., Phys., Chem., Zoology, Bot., Physiog., Fr., or German.	18
BRADFORD—The Technical Coll. H. M.—Day Sch. Dept. J. Spencer, B.Sc., F.C.S.						
H.M.—Art Dept. Chas. Stephenson.	50	£5	2	July.	General.	None.
H.M.—Textile Dept. T. R. Ashenhurst.	6	£3	1	Sept.	Technical.	

H.M.—Chemistry and Dyeing Dept. C. Rawson, F.I.C., F.C.S.	4	£12 10	1	,,	,,	
H.M.—Mechanical Dept. G. F. Charnock, C.E.	2	£15	1	,,	,,	
Sec.—John Nutter, Esq.						
BRISTOL.—Merchant Venturers' Technical School.	36 City of Bristol.	1st & 2nd yr. £25 3rd yr. £30	3	July	Mathematics, English, Mod. Languages	16
Principal.—J. Wertheimer, B.Sc., B.A.	30 Co. of Glouc.	£20	3	July	Science.	16
Secretary.—G. H. Pope, M.A., B.C.L., J.P.	4 Colston	£25	2	May	Science.	16
	1 Moseley	£20	2	May	Science.	16
Charter Day.—Nov. 11th.	80 Evening Cl.	£2 & £3	1	July	Eng. & Science.	None.
University College. President.—[ ] Principal—Professor C. Lloyd Morgan. Sec.—James Rafter, Esq.	1 Chemical, open to men and women.	£25	1	† June.	Chem., Mathcs., Mechs., and Engnerng., Nat. Sc., Pol. Econ., Logic, Philospy., Eng. Gk., Lat., Fr. and German.	Not under 16
	1 Engineering, open to men.	£25	1	,,		,,
	* 1 Gilchrist, open to men and women.	£50	3	Awarded on the results of Lond. Un. Matr. Mids. Exam. (Honours)	...	16-18
	2 Cath. Winkworth, for women only.	£15	1	† June.	,,	Not under 16
	‡2 John Stewart.	£20	1	† ,,	,,	,,

* Candidates must apply to the Principal before June 4th and submit to him certificate of birth, age, and satisfactory testimonials to character.

† Candidates must send in ...ames and list of subjects by ...day, June 11th, to the ...ary.

...pen to men and women.

University, Science, and Technical Colleges.	*Scholarships, &c.*, 1892.	*Value.*	*No. of years tenable.*	*Date of Examination.*	*Subjects.*	*Limit of age.*
Bristol—University College—*continued.* ‡ Open to men and women. § The next Exam. in June, 1893. ¶ Nomination by Council.	‡1 Hugh Conway.	£40	2	§ June.	Eng. Lit., with that of Greece, Rome, France, and Germany, as subsidiary.	Not under 16 open to Students in Science in Univ. Coll., Bristol.
	1 Science.	£150	2	¶ May		
	2 Evening Class.	£2 10*s.*	1	† „	Chem., Maths., Nat. Sci., Eng., Gk., Lat., Fr., Germ.	Not under 16.
Cardiff—University College of South Wales and Monmouthshire.	1 Entrance.	£35	1	September.	Two Parts. Part I. Gr., Lat., Eng., Math., Physics, Chem., Botany, Welsh, French, and Ger. Part II. (*a*) Clscs. (*b*) Mathcs. (*c*) Sc. (Physics, Chem., Biology). Only one section *a*, *b*, or *c*. of Part 2, in Section C. any two, Logic and Philosophy.	16
Principal.—J. Viriamu Jones, Esq., M.A., B.Sc.	4 „	£25	3			
Registrar.—Ivor James, Esq.	25 Exhibitions.	£10	1			

DUBLIN—Royal Coll. of Science. Dean of Faculty, 1891-92.—T. F. Pigot, Esq. C.E. M.R.I.A. Secretary.—J. P. O'Reilly, Esq., C.E., M.R.I.A. * *See* London, Science and Art Department, S.K., p. 153.	3 Royal Exhibitions. * 22 National Scholarships, tenable either at the College or at the Royal College of Science, London.	£50 And Instruction, Lectures and Laboratories free.		Science and Art Dept. Exams. in Sc., May, Annually. Coll. Sessnl. Exams. 1st week in June.		
DUNDEE—University College. Principal.—W. Peterson, Esq., M.A., LL.D. Secretary.—G. W. Alexander, Esq., M.A.	2 Entrance.	£20 to £25	1	October 9-10.	Mathes., Latin, Greek or Fr., or Ger., English.	
	2 Second year's.	£20 to £25.	1	,,	1 for Art Studts. Math., Classics, and English. 1 for Science Students. Math., and in 2 of Higher Maths., Chem., Physics, Engineering, Biology.	
	2 Engineering	£18 to £20	1	October.	Arith., Algebra, Geom., Trigy., Nat. Phil., Geometrical and Mech. Drawing.	16 to 25.
	1 Smart Bursy 2 Laing	£18 to £20	1	October.		
	1 Chemistry	£30	1	Awarded		

University, Science, and Technical Colleges.	*Scholarships, &c.*, 1892.	*Value.*	*No. of years tenable.*	*Date of Examination.*	*Subjects.*	*Limit of age.*
Dundee—University College, *continued.*	(Forster Research).			to best student in Chemical Dept. in each year.		
Glasgow—The Glasgow and West of Scotland Technical College.	3 Day.	£25	3	April.	Maths., Drawg.,	16 (above).
	4 ,,	£10	1 to 2		Mechs., Physics,	
	65 Evening.	£2	1		and Chemistry.	
Secretary—John Young, Esq., M.A., B.Sc.	1 Day.	15 guineas	3	Oct.	Natural Philos.	
The Bursaries are confined to students of the College.	,,	£15	3	Oct.	Botany.	
Lampeter.—St. David's College.	Scholarships.—					
Empowered to confer the degrees of B.A. and B.D., and	1	£40	During satisfactory behaviour while at College.	Names sent in. Sept. 19,	Either a general examination in several subjects, or a special examination in any one of the following:—	None.
to its biennial Theological Students a Licence in Divty.	1	£30				
(Affiliated to the Universities of Oxford and Cambridge.)	1	£27	,,	Ex. b. about		
Principal.—Ven. C. G. Edmondes.	3	£22		Sept. 28.		
Vice-Principal.—Rev. W. H.			...	...		

Davey, M.A. Professors :— Gk. and Theol—The Principal. Theol. & Heb.—The V. Princ. Mathcs. & Nat. Sci. } A. W. Scott, M.A. Eng.—H. Walker, M.A. Welsh and Hist.—Rev. R. Williams, B.A. Lat.—Rev. G. W. Wade, M.A. Lecturers.—*History*, Rev. E. T. Green, M.A.; *Pure Mathcs.*, S. G. Mostyn, B.A.	2 1 1 Exhibition. 1 ,, 1 ,, 2 ,, Other Scholarships may be vacated by election to higher ones.	£20 £18 £15 £13 £9 £8	During good behaviour. 1 year.	... ...	Theol., Clasc., Mathcs., Phys. & Chem., Hist., Welsh or Heb.	
Leeds—The Yorkshire College, (one of the Colleges of the Victoria University, Manchester). Principal.—N. Bodington, Esq., M.A. Registrar and Secretary.—W. F. Husband, Esq., LL.B. Professors :— Mathcs.—L. J. Rogers, M.A. Physics.—W. Stroud, D.Sc., B.A. [C]hem.—A. Smithells, B.Sc., F.I.C. [G]eology.—Lecturer—	2 Brown. 1 or 2 Akroyd.	£30 £30	2	April 27.	Brown: (1) Eng. Dict., Comp. (2) Eng. Hist. (3) Either Fr., Ger. or Lat. (4) Mathcs. (Arith., Alg., Euc. i. and ii.). (5) Either Higher Mathcs., Physics, Chem. (non-metals), or Botany. Akroyd: Arith., Alg., Euc. i. and ii., short essays. Any two of the	18

Science and Technical Colleges, &c.	*Scholarships, &c.*, 1892.	*Value.*	*No. of years tenable.*	*Date of Examination.*	*Subjects.*	*Limit of age.*
Leeds—Yorkshire College (*continued.*).						
Coal Mining.—A. Lupton, M. Inst. C.E.				Forms of entry must be sent in to Registr. by April 20.	following. (1) Mathcs. (2) Physics. (3) Chem.	
Biology.—L. C. Miall, F.L.S.	1 Baines.	£20				
Civil and Mechcl. Engineering.—J. Goodman, M. Inst. M.E., A.M. Inst. C.E.	Open only to Candi. from Pub. Elem. Schools of Leeds.				Baines and Emsley: (1) Eng. (2) Lat. (3) Either Gk., Fr. or Ger. (4) Mathcs.	
Classics and Literature.—The Principal.	1 Emsley.	£20				
Ancient Hist.—Lectr.—B. M. Connal, M.A.	1 Craven.	£25			Craven: Eng., Mathcs.	16
Mod. Hist. and Eng. Litr. and Lang.—C. Ransome, M.A.	Open only to Cands. who have resided 5 years in Leeds.					For Day-Scholsps. 16 to 24.
French.—Lecturer — P.H.M. du Gillon.						
German.—Lecturer—A. W. Schuddekopf, Ph.D., M.A.						
Heb.—Lecturer—J. Strauss, Ph.D., M.A.					For textile Industries Department only.—Day Schps. are awarded upon examination in Eng. Comp., Elem. Maths., and Freehand Drawing, and a further com-	
Spanish.—Lecturer—A. R. Alvarez, B.A.	Cloth-workers'. Textile.					
Text. Indus.—Roberts Beaumont.	4 Day.	£15 15*s.*	1			
	6 Evening.	£2 2*s.*	1			

Art.—Lecturer and Master—F. Suddards.					petitive exam. in Textile Manfacturing Processes. Even. Schps. Cands. are examined in Textile Man. Proc. and in Elemy. Designing.	
Dyeing.—J. J. Hummel, F.I.C. Physiology.—De Burgh Birch, M.D., F.R.S.E. Italian.—Lectr.—R. I. Isnard. Leather Industries. — Lecturer—Henry R. Proctor, F.I.C. Agriculture by Prof. Muir.	Dyeing.	£20	2		1. Eng. Comp., 2. Arith. & Alg., 3. Chem., 4. Either Physics, French, Germ., Lat., or Gk.	19
Education. — Lecturer and Master of Method—James Welton, M.A.	1 Medical. 1 Infirmary.	£63 £42		Sept.	Chem., Physics, Biol.	23
Extension Lectures. — Lecturer in Science—V. Perronet Sells, M.A. Sanitary Engineering.—W. Spinks, A.M.Inst.C.E. …and. — Teacher — J. …ton. …ping.— Teacher —G. …, A.C.A.	There are several valuable Scholarships open, only to students of the College, offered for comp. annually.			June. Last day for entering about May 15.	(1) Latin. (2) Maths. (3) Eng. (4) Eng. Hist. (5) either Fr., Ger., or Greek.	
—The Univ. Coll. …the Colleges of the …University, Man-…)	1 Bibby. 1 Ranger.	£20 £20	3 2	May 9-14. (Names sent in with Cert. of Birth by	Latin, Gk., Fr., Ger., Eng. Hist. and Comp., Math.,	18 (not more than), on Oct. 1, 1892.

Science and Technical Colleges. &c.	*Scholarships, &c.*, 1892.	*Value.*	*No. of years tenable.*	*Date of Examination.*	*Subjects.*	*Limit of age.*
Liverpool.—The Univ. Coll. (*contd.*) Principal.—Professor Rendall, M.A. Registrar.—Chevalier E. Londini, D.C.L.	1 Commercial.	£25	2	April 23.)	Mechs., Physics, Chem.	18.
	1 Elizabeth James	£40	3	„	„	None
	1 Tate Tech. Sci.	£35	3	„	„	None
	1 Ladies Educnl. Assn. Sch.	...	3	„	„	18
	A limited number of College Studentships.	Fee £6.	Renewable for 3 years.	„	...	18 (over).
	1 T. Hornby.	£20	...	„	Greek only.	None
London—City and Guilds of London Institute for the Advancement of Technical Education. Head Office, Gresham College, E.C. Hon. Sec.—John Watney, Esq. Asst. Sec.—Mr. A. L. Soper. Central Institution, Exhibition Road, S.W. Dean U. C. Unwin, F.R.S.	1 Clothworkers'.	£60	3	September.	(1) Mathcs. and Mechs. (2) Mechl. Drawing.	Not under 16
	3 Institute.	Sufficient	3	„	(3) Physics. (4)	„

		value to cover student's fees.			Chem. (5) Fr. or German.	
	Siemens.	£50	3	„		„
South Lond. Technical and Art School, 122 Kennington Park Road, S. Superintendent.—J. C. L. Sparkes, Esq.	Classes in Modelling, Design, Wood-engraving, Drawing from the Life, Art and Metal Work, Decoration, Plaster Work, &c,					None
Technical College, Finsbury, Leonard Street, E.C. Day and Evening Classes. Principal.—S. P. Thompson, D.Sc.	2 Saddlers'. For pupils from public Elementary Schools.	£30	2	October.	Mathemats. and English.	Not under 14
	1 Institute.	Sufficient value to cover student's fees.	2	„	... ..	Between 15 and 18.
	2 Institute. For pupils from public Elementary Schools.	„	2	„	... ...	Not under 14
	Technological Examinations are conducted once a year at various of the Institute's centres.					
King's College. Principal.—Rev. Henry Wace, D.D. Secretary.—J. W. Cunningham, Esq.	Theo. Dept.—Sambrooke Exhibition.	£20	1 or 2 yrs.			
	Gen. Liter. and Sc. Dept.—1 Sambrooke	£25	2 years.	October.	Classics.	17

SCIENCE AND TECHNICAL COLLEGES, &c.	*Scholarships, &c.*, 1892.	*Value.*	*No. of year tenable.*	*Date of Examination.*	*Subjects.*	*Limit of age.*
LONDON.—King's Coll.—(*cont.*).	Exhibition. ENGINEERING AND APPLIED SCIENCE DEPT.					
	2	£15	...	October.	(*a*) Arith.. Alg., Plane Trigy.	None.
	2	£10	...	"	(*b*) Euclid.	
* For members or non-members of College.	*Science Exhns. open to all Depts.					
	1 Cloth-workers'.	£50	2	October.	(*a*) Mathcs. (*b*) Elemy. Mechs.	19
	1 "	£25	2	"	(*c*) Physics. (*d*) Inorg. Chem. (*e*) Botany. (*f*) Zoology. (*g*) Geology. (*h*) Mineralogy. (Any four of above subjects.)	
	EVEN. CLASSES. Clothworkers' Company. 2 Prizes.	£5 each	1	At close of Winter Session.		None.

	Med. Dept.—Warneford, and other Schps, see Med. Schps, p. 166.				Chem., Mechs., Exp. Phys., Pr. Phys., Geol., Mineral. Phys.Geog., Physl., Compr., Anat., Metallurg., Pr. Metallurg., Agric.	None.
College of Preceptors, Bloomsbury Square. Dean.—H. W. Eve, Esq., M.A. [illegible]—C. R. Hodgson, Esq., [illegible]A.	4 (2 for Male and 2 for Female Candidates.)	£30 for 2 years. £45 for 1 year.	2 years or 1 year.	June	Those of the Certificate Examinations.	Between 17 and 21.
[illegible]ce and Art Department, [illegible] Donnelly, [illegible] Roy.Col. [illegible] of Mines. [illegible] C. A. Mac-	Science Exhibitions.—4 Royal. Tenable at the Roy. Coll. of Science.	£50 per ann.and Instructn., Lectures, andLaboratories Free.	3	Apr. 30 to May 28th.	1. Practical Pl. and Sol. Geom. 2. Math. Constr. and Drawing, 3. Build. Constr., 4. Naval Architec.,	

SCIENCE AND TECHNICAL COLLEGES, &c.	*Scholarships, &c., 1892.*	*Value.*	*No. of years tenable.*	*Date of Examination.*	*Subjects.*	*Limit of age.*
LONDON—Science and Art Dept. South Kensington (*contd.*)	3 Royal, tenable at the Roy. Coll. of Sci., Dublin.	”	”	”	5. Mathcs., 6. Theoret. Mechs., 7. Applied ditto, 8. Sound, Light, Heat, 9. Magnet. & Electricy., 10. Inorg. Chem. (Theo.), 10P. Do. (Prac.), 11. Org. Chem. (Theo.), 11P. Do. (Prac.), 12. Geol., 13. Mineralog., 14. Animal Phys., 15. Bot., 16, 17. Biol., incl. A. & V. Morph. & Phys., 18. Prin. of Min., 19. Metallurgy (Theo.), 19P. Do. (Pr.), 20. Navig., 21. Nautcl. Astr., 22. Steam, 23.	
* These Scholarships are only open to students of the Industrial Classes as defined below:— (*a*) Persons in the receipt of weekly wages, and their children not gaining their own livelihood; (*b*) Teachers and pupil-teachers of elementary schools in connection with the English or the Scotch Education Departments, or the National Board of Education, Ireland, and their children if not gaining their own livelihood; (*c*) Persons in the receipt of not not more than £400 per annum from all sources, and their children if not gaining their own livelihood;	* National Scholarships.—22 Tenable either at Royal College of Sc. and Royal Sch. of Mines, or at R. Coll. of Sc., Dublin.	Instrctn. at Lectures & Laboratrs. Free, with maintenance allowance of 30*s.* per wk. for Sess. (about 40 wks.) 3rd Class Rail. Fare each day during session between home and London or Dublin.	3	April and May. *See also pp.* 14 & 31.		

(*d*) Scholars in Public Elementary Schools within the meaning of the Elementary Education Acts; and Scholars who on leaving the Elementary School are proceeding with their education in Science and Art Schools or Classes. (*e*) Students in an organized Science School under public management, or in a night class for industrial students which meets after 6 p.m., or, on Saturdays, after 2 p.m.					Physiogrph., 24. Prin. of Agric., 25. Hygiene.	
	Free Studentships. 6 Tenable at the Royal College of Sc. or Roy. Sc. of Mines.	Instruction, Lectures and Laboratories Free, but not to any maintenance, &c.	About 3.	May.		
† The Candidate must be of sound bodily constitution. He must have been engaged in handicraft in the workshop of a mechanical engineer for at least three years on the 1st of May of the year in which he competes, and have been at work at the vice and lathe, or the forge, or the bench, during ordinary working hours for at least six consecutive months in each of those years. He must have worked for at least twelve months at the vice and lathe, not less than three months having been spent at the vice and three months at the lathe. The whole of the qualifying work must have been completed before the 1st of May of the year in which he competes.	† Whitworth Scholarships and Exhibitions.	30 Exhibns. of £50. 4 Schlrps. of £125.	1 year. 3 years.	May. Apply before Apr. 15.	The following are the subjects of competitn:—Practic. plane & solid Geomet., i.; Machine Construction and Drawing, ii.; Bldng. Constn., iii.; Naval Arctr., iv.; Maths., v.; Theotl. Mechs., vi.; Applied Mechanics, vii.; Sound, Light & Heat, viii.: Magnetism & Electy.,	Must not have comleted the 26th year of his age on the 1st May of the year in which he competes.

Science and Technical Colleges, &c.	*Scholarships, &c.*, 1892.	*Value.*	*No. of years tenable.*	*Date of Examination.*	*Subjects.*	*Limit of age.*
London—Science and Art Dept. South Kensington (*contd.*)					ix.; Inorganic Chemsty. x. and x*p*.; Inorganic Metallurgy, xix. and xix*p*.; Steam, xxii.; Freehand Drawing (2nd Grade Exam. in Art). *See* S. and A. Exams. (p. 31). for explan. of numerals.	

* After the May Examinations of 1892 the payments of £1 for the Second Class elementary stage in each Science subject will be discontinued, the Council of Education having decided that it will be best in future to rely upon the local efforts in this direction which are expected to be put forth through the powers and means given to County Councils, etc., under the Local Taxation Act of 1890. It is stated, however, that the payments on the results of the examinations in 1892 will not be affected. (See the full text of the Minute on our p. 157.)

Summary of Principal Grants made by the Department of Science and Art.

Science.	*Art.*
I. Payments to the Local Committees of Schools and Classes on the results of instruction, as tested by Examination, of Students of the Industrial Classes.	
(*a*) £2 and £1 for a 1st and 2nd Class respectively in the Elementary and Advanced Stage of each subject.* (*See above*, note *.) (*b*) £4 and £2 for a 1st and 2nd Class respectively in Honours.* (*See above*, note *.) (*c*) In Practical Chemistry and Practical Metallurgy £2 and £1 for a 1st and 2nd Class respectively, in the Elementary Stage, £3 and £2 in the Advanced Stage, and £4 and £3 in Honours.† (*d*) 10*s*. for passing in Section I. (Geometrical Drawing) of the Elementary Stage of Practical, Plain, and Solid Geometry.†	(*a*) £1 and 10*s*. for a 1st and 2nd Class respectively in each subject of the 2nd Grade Examination, including Modelling. (*b*) £3, £2, and £1 10*s*. for excellent 1st and 2nd Class respectively in 3rd Grade Examination. (*c*) £3 or less per student for works executed in local classes. (*d*) £3 for a Student (an artisan) obtaining a Local Scholarship or Free Studentship. (*e*) £15 each for not more than two Art Pupil Teachers. (*f*) £5 for each student who obtains a Royal Exhibition or National Scholarship, or who obtains admission to Training Class.
[illegible]I. Prizes and medals are awarded to candidates.	
[illegible] Prizes to students obtaining a 1st Class in the [illegible]ced Stage of each subject, and bronze medals to [illegible] [illegible]st Class in Honours. Certificates or [illegible]ul candidates.	(*a*) Prizes of books or instruments, to the value of 8*s*. and 12*s*., to students obtaining the mark "excellent" in the 2nd and 3rd Grade Examinations, respectively; and Gold, Silver, and Bronze Medals, and other prizes

[illegible]creased grants after May 1892, see Minute of the Council of Education at p. 157.

SUMMARY OF GRANTS MADE BY THE DEPARTMENT OF SCIENCE AND ART—(*continued*).

Science.	*Art.*
	of Books, for the best works submitted in the National Competition of works of all the Schools of Art and Art Classes.

III. Science and Art Scholarships for Students of the Industrial Class, held locally, £4, £7, and £10, for the 1st, 2nd, and 3rd year respectively, on condition that a local contribution of £5 a year is made.

IV. Local Exhibitions, to be held by Students of the Industrial Classes at the Royal College of Science or Royal School of Mines, the National Art Training School, South Kensington, the Royal College of Science, or School of Art, Dublin, or at an approved Provincial Science College or School of Art, £25 to meet an equal sum locally raised.

V. Grants for Buildings, Fittings, and Apparatus. (Grants for fittings, &c., are now suspended, except in Ireland, while the Local Taxation (Customs and Excise) Act, 1890, continues in force).

(*a*) Not exceeding 2*s*. 6*d*. per square foot of internal area up to a maximum of £500 for buildings.

(*b*) Grants towards the purchase of apparatus, examples, &c., not exceeding 50 per cent. of their cost within certain limits, and towards the purchase of fittings, not exceeding 33⅓ per cent. of their cost.

VI. Special Grants to Organized Science Schools in addition to the foregoing, 10*s*. and 5*s*. respectively for each student who attends a day or an evening school not less than 250 or 60 times in the year.*

* For increased grants after May 1892, see Government Minute at p. 157.

VII. Aid to Students in attending the Royal College of Science or Royal School of Mines, London, the National Art Training School, London, and the Royal College of Science, Dublin.

(*a*) 21 Royal Exhibitions (seven awarded each year) with maintenance allowance of £50 a year tenable for three years.

(*b*) 66 National Scholarships (twenty-two awarded each year), with maintenance allowance of 30*s*. a week for 40 weeks in the year tenable for three years.

(*c*) 18 Free Studentships (six awarded each year) tenable for three years, at Royal College of Science or Royal School of Mines, London.

(*a*) National Scholarships tenable for not more than three years at National Art Training School with maintenance allowance of 25*s*. a week.

(*b*) Free Studentships in National Art Training School.

VIII. Aid to teachers and persons preparing to become teachers in attending the Royal College of Science or Royal School of Mines, London, the National Art Training School, London, the Royal College of Science and School of Art, Dublin, and Provincial Colleges at which advanced instruction in Science is given

(*a*) Grants of £3 each, with travelling expenses, to local teachers selected to attend short courses of instruction at Royal College of Science or Royal School of Mines.

(*b*) Grants of 21*s*. a week each, with travelling expenses, to teachers in training selected to attend the sessional courses of the Royal College of Science or Royal School of Mines.

(*c*) Grants in aid of fees to local teachers selected to attend Provincial Science Colleges.

(*d*) Free admission (subject to payment of examina- fee) to courses of lectures at Royal College of nce or Royal School of Mines to Science teachers.

(*a*) Grants to enable masters and students to visit various metropolitan Art Institutions, and, in special cases, foreign towns, schools, and galleries.

(*b*) Grants of £3 each with travelling expenses to local teachers and students selected to attend short courses of instruction at National Art Training School and South Kensington Museum.

(*c*) Grants of from 10*s*. to 35*s*. a week, with travelling expenses to teachers in training selected to attend the National Art Training School.

Summary of Grants made by the Department of Science and Art.

Science.	*Art.*
IX. Grants to Local Museums and Loans of Works of Science and Art, Books, and specimen sets of teaching Apparatus to Local Museums, Temporary Exhibitions, and Science and Art Schools.	
X. Aid to Training Colleges for instruction in Science and Art.	
(*a*) Grants on results of the Examination in November or December on the same scale as the May Examinations of Science Schools and Classes generally. (*b*) Grants not exceeding 50 per cent. of the Cost for apparatus and fittings.	(*a*) Grants of 10*s.* in respect of each subject of examination in which a resident student passes. (*b*) Grants of 50 per cent. towards the cost of examples.
XI. Aid to Elementary Schools for Instruction in Drawing.	
	(*a*) Grants of 1*s.*, 1*s.* 6*d.*, or 2*s.* on average attendance of Schools examined in Drawing. (*b*) Grants of £1 and 10*s.* for a 1st and 2nd class respectively in each subject of the 2nd Grade Examinations, and 10*s.* for each pass in Geometrical Drawing. (*c*) Grants of 6*s.* or 7*s.* for each scholar receiving Manual Instruction.

The Department's grant for Technical Instruction supplemental to the amount contributed from the local rates, is suspended, except in Ireland, while the Local Taxation (Customs and Excise) Act, 1890, continues in force.*

* See Minute at p. 157.

SCIENCE AND ART DEPARTMENT.

Minute of the Privy Council of Education on Examinations after May, 1892.

(*Issued November*, 1891.)

1. My Lords consider the subject of the examinations of the Science and Art Department in science in relation to the funds applicable to science and art and technical instruction placed at the disposal of county councils and county boroughs under the Local Taxation (Customs and Excise) Act, 1890, and in relation to the operation of the Technical Instruction Act, 1889.

2. It appears that the number of candidates presenting themselves for examination in science is already so large—about 190,000 papers in various branches of science were worked at the examination in May last, besides above 14,000 practical examinations, that the machinery of examination and registration is already severely strained. These numbers will in all probability soon be so increased as to render it impossible to make satisfactory arrangements for the examination of the candidates at the local centres or for the examination of the worked papers under any system of central examination.

3. At the same time the means recently placed at the disposal of local authorities for providing or aiding instruction seem to render it unnecessary for the Science and Art Department to continue to give direct aid for very elementary instruction in science. Such instruction can now be more effectually organized and maintained locally. It is very desirable that the payments for imparting it should, to some extent at least, not be made on the results of individual examination. Local authorities, with their local knowledge and knowledge of local needs and requirements, are in a position to make capitation grants or payments for general efficiency in a manner which a central authority whose rules must be the same for all parts of the country, cannot adopt; and my Lords feel assured that they may count on having the support and assistance of these bodies in forwarding the arrangements for placing instruction in science—the necessary foundation for any sound technical education—on a satisfactory footing.

4. Under these circumstances my Lords have decided that after the May examinations of 1892 the payments of £1 now made for the second class in the elementary stage of each science

subject shall cease.* An elementary paper will continue to be set in each subject, but the results will be recorded simply as pass or fail, the standard for passing being about the same as that now required for a first class—i.e., about 60 per cent. of the marks obtainable.

5. At the same time with a view to encourage more advanced instruction, which does not seem to be adequately provided for at present, the payments of the advanced stage and for honours will be considerably increased. The payments on results will then be £2 for a pass in the elementary stage; £5 and £2 10*s.* for a first or second class respectively in the advanced stage; and £8 and £4 for a first or second class respectively in honours, in each subject of science, and in each sub-division of subject 6, theoretical mechanics, or of subject 8, sound, heat, and light, with the following exceptions:—The payments for practical chemistry will be £3 for a pass in the elementary stage, and £6 and £3 10*s.* respectively for a first or second class in the advanced stage; the payments for mathematics will be £2 for a pass in stage 1, £3 and £2 respectively for a first or second class in stages 2 and 4, £4 and £3 for a first or second class respectively in stage 3, £5 and £4 for a first or second class respectively in stages 5, 6, and 7, and £8 and £4 respectively for a first or second class in honours. The payment for section 1 (geometrical drawing) of subject 1 will remain as at present, 10*s.*

6. The payment for attendance in an organized science school will be increased to £1 in the day school and 10*s.* in the night school.

7. As it is of great importance to prevent large numbers of wholly unqualified candidates being presented at the examinations, the examiners will be instructed to note the papers of all such as would not obtain above 25 per cent of the marks, and a deduction will be made from the grant to each school for each such paper sufficient to cover the cost incidental to its examination.

8. The committee of a science school in a place in Great Britain with less than 5,000 inhabitants which does not receive aid from the local authority, or of any science school in Ireland, will be allowed to continue until further notice on the present system, if they so desire it.

By order,

J. F. D. DONNELLY.

* The payments on the results of the examinations in 1892 will not be affected by this minute.

Science and Technical Colleges, &c.	Scholarships, &c., 1892.	Value.	No. of years tenable.	Date of Examination.	Subjects.	Limit of age.
London—Royal Agricultural Society of England. Sec.—Ernest Clarke, Esq., 12, Hanover Square, W.	Senior Prizes— 1 First. 1 Second 1 Third. 1 Fourth.	 £25 £15 £10 £5		May 10-14. Forms must be returned by Mar. 31.	I. Pract. Agric. II. Chemistry. III. Bookkeepng. IV. Land Srvy. V. A. Engnrg. VI. Botany. VII. Geology. VIII. Anatomy. IX. Agricultrl. Entom.	None
	Junior Scholarships—10.	£20	...	Nov. 8 & 9 Forms must be returned by Oct. 15.	Agriculture. Chemistry. Mechanics. Land Surveying.	Between 14 and 18.
London—University College. President.—J. E. Erichsen, Esq., LL.D., F.R.S. Vice-President.—The Rt. Hon. Sir Ughtred J. Kay Shuttleworth, Bart., M.P. Treasurer.—Hon. L. W. Rothschild. Lady Superintendent.—Miss Rosa Morison.	3 Andrew Scholarships.	£30	1	May. Notice sent in on or before April 30.	1 Classics. 1 for any two of 3 subjects:—Mathcs., Physc., and Chemistry. 1 for 2 langs., and a science to be chosen from:— (a) English, Fr.,	

SCIENCE AND TECHNICAL COLLEGES, &c.	Scholarships, &c., 1892.	Value.	No. of years tenable.	Date of Examination.	Subjects.	Limit of age.
LONDON—University College (contd.) Secretary.—J. Macdonald Horsburgh, Esq., M.A.					Germ., Italian (b) Physics, Chemy., Elem Phys.	
Faculty of Arts and Laws. Dean.—W. P. Ker, M.A., Prof. of English. Vice-Dean.—M. J. M. Hill, M.A., Prof. of English.	1 Gilchrist.	£35	2	May. Notice sent in on or before Sept. 23.	1 Maths. 2 Any two of the following: (a) Mechanics. (b) Mechanical Drawing. (c) Physics, Chemistry. Optional Subj., Trigonmy.	19
Faculty of Science. Dean.—W. Ramsay, F.R.S., Prof. of Chemistry.	1 Hollier.	£60	1	June.	Greek.	21
Vice-Dean.—T. H. Beare, B.Sc., Prof. of Engineering. *Faculty of Medicine.* Dean.—E. A. Schäfer, Esq., F.R.S., Prof. of Physiology.	1 ,,	£60	1	July. Notice in each case sent by June 16 preceding Examinatn.	Hebrew.	21

Vice-Dean.—V. A. H. Horsley, M.D., B.S., F.R.S., Prof. of Pathology. * For the sons of deceased indigent professional men. Candidates whose means are limited and whose high moral character is proved, will be preferred to all others.	* 1 Morris Bursary.	£16	2	Notice of application must be sent in on June 1.	No Exam.	20
N.B.—There are many valuable Scholarships and Exhibitions including the Slade Fine Art and Travelling Scholarships and the Tufnell Scholarships in Chemistry annually awarded to Students at the College.						
Manchester—Technical Sch., Princess Street. Secretary.—J. H. Reynolds, Esq. The school is registered under the Examination Scheme of the Victoria University.	City Council Scholarships, 27 Day, 18 Evening, and other similar Scholarships from Local Authorities surrounding the City.	(Day) £30 per annum. (Evening) £5 per annum.	2 2	Beginning of September. „	Mechanics and Mechanical Engineering, Physics & Elec. Engineering, Sanitary Engineering and Builder's Work; Pure & Applied Chem. Spinning and Weaving, Industrial Draw. and Design, Foreign Languages and Commercial Knowledge.	None.

Science and Technical Colleges, &c.	No. Scholarships, &c., 1890	Value	How long tenable	Date of Exam.	Subjects	Fee
NEWCASTLE. Durham Coll. of Science. Principal, W. Garnett, Esq., M.A., D.C.L. Secretary, H. F. Stockdale, Esq.	1 1 1	£[illegible] £[illegible] £[illegible]	[illegible] (or alternately)	Sept. [illegible]	Cands. must pass the Entrance Matr. Exam. Subjects, [illegible] I, II and III, one of the following: Geol., Phys., Chem., Nat. Hist.	
NOTTINGHAM. University College. P. H. Stevenson, Esq., F.S.A. Prepares for Lond. Univ. Exams., Cambridge Higher, Pharmaceutical Society, &c.	3 open Scholarships General Scholarships to students 1 yr's standing	£15 to £30 £10 to £100	1 year, but renewable for [illegible]	June	No list of subjects [illegible]	None
SHEFFIELD. The Firth College. (Affiliated to Oxford and Cambridge Universities.) Principal, Dr. Hicks, F.R.S., &c.	1 1 8 Sheffield Corporation Scholarships	£[illegible] £[illegible] £[illegible] each	1 year Not more than 3 years	October (1st week) "	Classics, Maths., Eng., Phys., and Chem. Eng., Classics, Maths., Phys., and Chem. Must be 3 subjs.	£1

Registrar and Secretary.—Ensor Drury, Esq.	4 Mechanics Inst. Exhns. There are also a number of *free* evening studentships, varying up to £3.	£2	3	October (1st week).	Eng., Arith., & another subject. Candidates must take three.	over 17
	The Earnshaw Scholarship. (Candidates must be inhabitants of, or educated at, Sheffield.)	£50 (at least).	3 years (conditionally.)	June. Names sent in 7 days previously. If subjects other than Mathcs. or Classics are offered, 14 days.	Mathcs. or Classics.	
Research Scholarships given by H. M. Commissioners for the Exhibition of 1851, £150 tenable for two years on nomination of Firth College.						

SCHOLARSHIPS GIVEN IN AID OF MEDICAL STUDY.

The following list is as nearly complete as the Editor has been able to make it, and gives such prizes as would enter into a Student's calculation of the cost of Medical education. It does not contain prizes of less value than £10, or prizes of greater than this value which are given in any form except money or necessaries of medical study and research:—

Institution.	*Medical Scholarships, &c.*	*Annual or total value.*	*How long tenable.*	*How obtainable.*	*Conditions attached to tenure.*
Oxford University.	Radcliffe Trav. Fellowship.	£200 per annum.	3 years.	Competitive Examination.	Foreign Travel for purpose of Medical Study.
London University. See page 138.					
Edinburgh University ... See page 132.					
St. Bartholomew's Medical School	Entrance Scholarships No. 1.	£65.	...	Open Competitive Examination in Physics and Chemistry.	Full course at St. Bartholomew's Hospital.

St. Bartholomew's Medical Sc., *contd.*	Entrance Scholarships. No. 2.	£65.	...	Open Competitive Examination in Biology and Physiology.	Ditto.
	" No. 3.	£130	...	Open Competitive Exam. in Physics, Chemistry, and Biology.	Ditto.
	Preliminary Scientific Exhibition.	£50.	...	Open Competitive Exam. in Physics, Chemistry, and Biology.	Ditto.
	Jeaffreson Exhibition.	£20.	..	Open Competitive Examination in Latin, Mathematics, and Greek, French, or German.	None.
	Shuter Scholarship.	£50.	...	Competitive Exam. among Camb. Graduates in Anatomy, Phys., and Materia Medica.	None.
	Junior Scholarship. " No. 1.	£40.	...	Competitive Examination among Students in Anatomy and Physiology.	None.
	" No. 2.	£20.	...	Ditto.	None.
	Senior Scholarship.	£50.	..	Competitive Examination among Students in Anatomy, Physiology, and Chemistry.	Study at St. Bartholomew's Hosp.
	Kirkes' Scholarship.	£30 and Medal.	...	Competitive Exam. among Students in Clinical Medicine.	
	Brackenbury Scholarship. No. 1.	£30.	...	Competitive Examination among Students in Medicine.	
	" No. 2.	£30.	...	Competitive Examination among Students in Surgery.	
	Lawrence Scholarship.	£42 and Medal.	...	Competitive Examination among Students in Surgery, Medicine, and Midwifery.	None.

[illegible]	[illegible]	[illegible]	[illegible]	How obtainable	Conditions attached to tenure
[illegible]	[illegible]	[illegible]		[illegible] Competitive Examination [illegible]	
[illegible]	[illegible]	[illegible]		Open Competitive Examination in the following groups of subjects: [illegible] Statics and [illegible] Animal and [illegible]	Full Course [illegible] Hospital
	[illegible]	[illegible]		Competitive Examination among [illegible]	Completion of [illegible] Charing Cross Hosp.

	Llewellyn Scholarship.	£25.	...	Competitive Examination among Third-year Students in Anatomy, Physiology, Materia Medica, Medicine, Surgery, Therapeutics, and Midwifery.	None.
	Golding Scholarship.	£15.	...	Competitive Examination among Second-year Students (both General and Dental) in Descriptive Anatomy, Physiology, and Chemistry.	
St. George's Hospital.— Sec.—C. L. Todd, Esq., Hyde Park Corner, S.W.	Entrance Scholarships. No. 1.	£125.	...	Competitive Examination among First-year Students, being the sons of medical men, in Latin, French, or German, and Elementary Physics.	Course at St. George's School.
	" No. 2.	£65.	...	Competitive Examination among students being First M.B.'s of Oxford and Second M.B.'s of Cambridge, in Anatomy and Physiology.	Ditto.
	" No. 3.	£65.	...	Ditto.	Ditto.
	" No. 4.	£50.	...	Competitive Examination open to all Students who have commenced medical study not earlier than the previous May, in the same subjects as Entrance Scholarship No. 1.	Complete Course at St. George's School.
	" No. 5.	£50.	...	Ditto.	Ditto.

INSTITUTION.	*Medical Scholarships, &c.*	*Annual or total value.*	*How long tenable.*	*How obtainable.*	*Conditions attached to tenure.*
ST. GEORGE'S HOSPITAL, *continued.*	Wm. Brown Exhibition.	£100 per annum.	2 years.	Competitive Examination among Perpetual Students having registrable qualification in the Practice of Medicine, Midwifery, and Surgery.	None.
	"	£40 per annum.	3 years.	Competition among Third year students in respect of fitness for Medical Profession.	None.
	Brackenbury Prize in Medicine.	Interest on £1077.	...	Competitive Examination among Students of not more than four years' standing.	None.
	Brackenbury Prize in Surgery.	Interest on £1077.	...	Competitive Examination among Students of not more than four years' standing.	None.
	Treasurer's Prize.	£10 10*s*.	...	Proficiency in Clinical Examination of three Medical and three Surgical Cases.	None.
	H. C. Johnson Memorial Prize.	£10 10*s*.	...	Competitive Examination among Second year Students in Practical Anatomy.	None.

Pollock Prize.	Interest on £372.	...	Competitive Examination among Second-year Students in Physiology, Physiological Chemistry, and Histology.	None.
General Proficiency Prizes. No. 1.	£10 10s.	...	Competitive Examination among First-year Students in Elementary Anatomy and Materia Medica, Elementary Physiology, and Chemistry.	None.
,, No. 2.	£10 10s.	...	Competitive Examination among Second-year Students in Anatomy, including Histology, Physiology, and Physiological Chemistry.	
,, No. 3.	£10 10s.	...	Competitive Examination among Third-year Students in the Principles and Practice of Medicine and Surgery, Pathology, and Midwifery.	None.
Thompson Medal.	Interest on £185	...	Proficiency in Clinical Examination of three Medical and three Surgical cases.	None.
Brodie Prize.	Interest on £220	...	Surgical pupil, who shall deliver best report of 12 Surgical cases.	None.
Acland Prize.	£5.	...	Medical pupil, who shall deliver best report of 12 Medical cases.	None.
Sir Charles Clarke's Prize.	Interest on £209	...	For General Good Conduct.	None.

INSTITUTION.	Medical Scholarships, &c.	Annual or total value.	How long tenable.	How obtainable.	Conditions attached to tenure.
GUY'S HOSPITAL, St. Thomas' Street, Borough, S.E.	Entrance Scholarships. No. 1.	£105.	...	Open Competitive Exam. among Candidates under 20 years of age in Lat., Grk., Fr., Ger., Arith., Euclid, and Algebra.	Course at Guy's Hospital.
	" No. 2.	£52 10s.	...	Under 25 years of age, ditto.	Ditto.
	" No. 3.	£131 5s.	...	Open Competitive Examination among Candidates under 25 years of age in Inorganic Chemistry, General Biology, and Experimental Physics	Perpetual Course at Guy's Hospital.
	" No. 4.	£52 10s.	...		
	Arthur Durham Prizes.	£15.	...	Dissection done by Students of more than one year's standing	
	"	£5.		Dissection done by First year Students.	Ditto.
	First Years Students.	£50.		Competitive Exam. among First year Students in Anatomy of Bones, Ligaments, and Muscles, Physiology, and Chemistry.	None.
	"	£25.		Ditto.	Ditto.
	Second Yrs. Students.	£25.		Competitive Examination among Second year Students in Anatomy, Physiology, and Materia Medica.	Ditto.

		£10.		Ditto.	Ditto.
	Michael Harris Prize.	£10.		Competitive Examination among Second-year Students in Human Anatomy.	Ditto.
	Sands Cox Scholarship.	£15 per annum.	3 years.	Competitive Examination among Second-year Students in Physiology, Histology, and Physiological Chemistry.	Course at Guy's Hospital.
	Third Yrs. Students.	£25.		Competitive Examination among Third-year Students in Anatomy (Med. and Surg.), Diagnosis, Operative & Minor Surg., Midwifery, and Therapeutics.	None.
		£10.		Ditto.	Ditto.
	Fourth Yrs. Students.	£25.		Competitive Examination among Fourth-year Students in Medicine, Surgery, Diseases of Women, and Medical Jurisprudence.	None.
		£10.		Ditto.	Ditto.
	Golding Bird Prize.	£20 and Medal.		Competitive Examination among Fourth-year Students in Diagnosis.	Ditto.
Treasurer's Gold Medals in Medicine and Surgery for Students in Fourth and Fifth Year.	Gurney Hoare Prize.	£25.		Original Reports on Three Medical and Three Surgical Cases.	None.
	Beaney Prize.	£31 10s.		Competitive Examination among Students in Pathology.	Ditto.
	Gull Studentship.	£150 per annum	3 years.	Particulars on application.	

INSTITUTION.	*Medical Scholarships, &c.*	*Annual or total value.*	*How long tenable.*	*How obtainable.*	*Conditions attached to tenure.*
KING'S COLLEGE. Strand, W.C. Dean of the Medical Department.—Prof. Curnow, M.D. See also at p. 151.	Warneford Scholarships. No. 1.	£25 per annum.	3 years.	Competitive Examination among Matriculated Medical Students in Divinity, English, History, Latin, Greek, French, German, and Mathematics.	Perpetual Course at King's College.
	" No. 2.	£25 per annum.	3 years.	Ditto.	Ditto.
	" No. 3.	£25 per annum.	2 years.	Ditto.	Ditto.
	" No. 4.	£25 per annum.	2 years.	Ditto.	Ditto.
	" No. 6.	£25 per annum.	2 years.	Competitive Examination among Matriculated Medical Students in the Third year.	
	Sambrooke Exhibitions. No. 1.	£60.	...	Competitive Examination among resident Matriculated Students in Mathematics, Elementary Physics, Inorganic Chemistry, Botany, and Zoology.	Course either as Science or Medical Student at King's Col
	" No. 2.	£40.	...	Ditto.	Ditto.
	Rabbeth Scholarship.	20.	...	Competitive Exam. among Matriculated Students in Science.	Ditto.
	Science Exhibitions. No. 1.	£30 per annum.	2 years.	Competitive Examination among Candidates under 19 years of age in Mathematics, Me-	None.

				chanics, Physics, &c., or alternative subjects.	
	" No. 2.	£20 per annum.	2 years.	Ditto.	None.
	Medical Scholarships. No. 1.	£40 per annum.	2 years.	Competitive Exam. among Third and Fourth-year Students.	
	" No. 2.	£30 per annum.	1 year.	Competitive Exam. among Second and Third-year Students.	
	" No. 3.	£20 per annum.	1 year.	Competitive Examination among First-year Medical Students.	
	" No. 4.	£20 per annum.	1 year.	Ditto.	
	" No. 5.	£20 per annum.	1 year.	Ditto.	
	Sambrooke Registrarship. No. 1.	£50.	year.	Matriculated Medical Students who have filled certain appointments at King's Coll. Hosp.	Election by Council of King's Coll.
	" No. 2.	£50.	...	Ditto.	
	Daniel Scholarship.	£20 per annum.	2 years.	Open Competitive Examination among six months' Chemical Laboratory Students.	
	Tanner Prize.	£10.	...	Competitive Examination in Obstetrics and Diseases of Women and Children.	None.
	Carter Prize.	£15	...	Competitive Examination among Matriculated Students.	None.
LONDON HOSPITAL MEDICAL COLLEGE, Turner Street, Mile End, E. Warden:—Munro Scott, Esq.	Entrance Scholarships. No. 1.	£75.	...	Competitive Examination among Students in Subjects of Preliminary Scientific M.B. Examination at Univ. of London.	
	" No. 2.	£50.	...	Ditto.	
	Buxton Scholarships. No. 1.	£30.	...	Compet. Exam. among Students in Subjects of Prelim. Exam.	

INSTITUTION.	*Medical Scholarships, &c.*	*Annual or total value.*	*How long tenable.*	*How obtainable.*	*Conditions attached to tenure.*
LONDON HOSPITAL, *continued.*	Buxton Scholarships. No. 2.	£20.	...	Competitive Exam. among Studs. in Subs. of Prel. Exam.	
	Hospital Medical Scholarship.	£20.	...	Competitive Examination in Clinical Medicine.	
	Hospital Surgical Scholarship.	£20.	...	Competitive Examination in Clinical Surgery.	
	Hospital Obstetric Scholarship.	£20.	...	Competitive Examination in Clinical Obstetrics.	
	Duckworth Nelson Prize.	£10.	...	Ditto, Practical Medicine and Surgery.	
	Hutchinson Prize.	£35.	...	For an Essay in Clinical Surgery.	Students of the Hospital who have not been registered Medical Students for more than ten years.
	Letheby Prize.	£30.	...	Competitive Examination in Chemistry.	
	1st and 2nd years' Scholarship.	£25.	...	Competitive Exam. in Anatomy, Physiology, and Chemistry.	
	1st year's Scholarship.	£20.	...	Competitive Examination in Anatomy and Physiology.	
	Minor Surgery Prizes. No. 1.	£15.	...	Zeal, Efficiency, and Knowledge of Minor Surgery.	
	" No. 2.	£15.	...	Ditto.	

	„ No. 3.	£10.	...	Ditto.
	„ No. 4.	£10.	...	Ditto.
	„ No. 5.	£5.	...	Ditto.
	„ No. 6.	£5.	...	Ditto.
	Practical Anatomy Prizes. No. 1.	£6.	...	Proficiency in Practical Anatomy.
	„ No. 2.	£4.	...	Ditto.
St. Mary's Hospital Medical School, Westbourne Ter., W. Dean:—George P. Field, Esq. Sub-Dean:—A. P. Luff, M.D.	Natural Science Scholarship. No. 1.	£105.	...	Competitive Examination among Students in Natural Science.
	„ No. 2.	£52 10s.	...	Ditto.
	„ No. 3.	£52 10s.	...	Ditto.
	„ No. 4.	£52 10s.	...	Ditto.
		£105.	...	Competitive Examination among Students from Epsom College, being sons of medical men.
		£52 10s.	...	Competitive Examination among University Students in Subjects of Preliminary Scientific Examination at London Univ.
		£52 10s.	...	Ditto.
		£20.	...	Competitive Examination among First-year Students.
		£25.	...	Competitive Examination among Second-year Students.
		£[illegible]0.	...	Competitive Examination among Third-year Students.
		£15 twice yearly.	...	Competitive Exam. among Third and Fourth-Year Students.

R

Institution.	Medical Scholarships, &c.	Amount or total value.	How long tenable.	How obtainable.	Conditions attached to tenure.
Middlesex Hospital Medical School, Cleveland Street, W.	Entrance Scholarship No. 1	£60 per annum	2 years	Open Competitive Examination	
	" No. 2	£40 per annum	2 years	Ditto	Course at Mdx. Hosp.
	1 Exhibition	£[illegible]		Competitive Examination among First year Students in Elementary Anatomy, Osteology and Physiology.	
	Broderip Scholarship No. 1	£40 per annum	2 years	Competitive Examination among Students in Clinical Subjects.	
	" No. 2	£25 per annum	2 years	Ditto.	
	Governors' Prize	£21		Competitive Examination among Third year Students in Clinical Subjects.	
	Hetley Prize	£20		Ditto	
St. Thomas's Hospital Medical School. Sec.: Geo. Rendle, M.R.C.S.	College Prizes	£[illegible]		Competitive Examination among First year Students.	
	" No. 1	£[illegible]		Ditto	
	" No. 2	£[illegible]		Competitive Examination among Second year Students.	
	" No. 3	£[illegible]		Ditto	
	" No. 1	£[illegible]		Competitive Examination among Third year Students.	
	" No. 2	£[illegible]		Ditto	
	" No. 3	£10			

	* Entrance Science Scholarship. No. 1.	£131 5s.	...	Competitive Exam. in Physics, Chemistry, Botany, Zoology, or Physiology.	Perpetual Course.
	Entrance Science Scholarship. No. 2.	£60.	...	Competitive Exam. in Physics, Chemistry, Botany, Zoology, or Physiology.	Ditto.
	Wm. Tite Scholarship.	£27 10s.	...	Competitive Examination among First-year Students.	
	College Prize. No. 7.	£20.	...	Ditto.	
	" No. 8.	£10.	...	Ditto.	
* If holder obtains a 1st class in his third winter.	Musgrove Scholarship.	£38 10s.	2 years.*	Competitive Examination among Second-year Students.	
	Peacock Scholarship.	£38 10s.	2 years.	Ditto.	
	College Prize. No. 9.	£20.	...	Ditto.	
	" No. 10.	£10.	...	Ditto.	
	" No. 11.	£20.	...	Competitive Examination among Third-year Students.	

* *Open Scholarships in Natural Science.*—As an inducement to the study of Natural Science before the commencement of the strictly Medical Course, two Scholarships, of the value of 125 Guineas (*i.e.*, a free admission) and £60 respectively, are awarded annually, after an examination in Physics, Chemistry, and either Botany, Zoology or Physiology, at the option of Candidates. The standard, so far as the subjects are the same, will be that of the Preliminary Scientific Examination for Honours of the University of London.

These Scholarships are open to all Students who have passed a recognized Preliminary Examination in Arts, and have not yet attended Lectures on Anatomy of the first year, without any condition as to their becoming Students of the Hospital, except in the case of successful Candidates, who must enter at once as "Perpetual" Pupils. Chemistry and Physics are compulsory subjects for this Examination, and Candidates must take up one of the other subjects. The Examination will be conducted by means of written papers and practical work, and will be held during the last week in September, 1891. The names of Competitors with Certificate of Preliminary Examination must be sent to the Secretary not later than September 17th

Hospital	Name of Scholarship	Amount or annual value	How long tenable	How obtainable	Conditions attached to tenure
[illegible]	[illegible]	£20		Competitive Examination among Third year Students	
	[illegible]	£10		Ditto	
	[illegible]			Competitive Examination among Fourth Year Students for Surgical Reports	
	[illegible] Prize	£10	1 year	Series of Preparations and Dissections	
	Treasurer's Gold Medal			For General Proficiency.	
University College Hospital	Entrance Exhibition No. 1	£100		Open Competitive Examination in Chemistry, Physics, Botany, and Zoology	Perpetual Course at Univ. Col.
	" No. 2	£60		Ditto	Ditto.
	" No. 3	£40		Ditto	Ditto.
	[illegible] Scholarship	£45 per annum	3 years	Theory and Practice of Surgery	
	[illegible] Scholarship	£55 per annum	2 years	Competitive Examination among Medical Students	
	Sharpey Physiological Scholarship	£100	3 years	Proficiency in Physiological Science.	
	Filliter Exhibition	£30	1 year	Competitive Exam. among Students in Pathological Anat.	
	[illegible] Prize	£10	..	Competitive Examination among	

				Students in Anatomy, Physiology, and Chemistry.	
	Erichsen Prize.	£10 10s. and instruments.	...	Practical Surgery.	
	Morris Bursary.	£16.	2 years.		
WESTMINSTER HOSP. MEDICAL SCHOOL. Dean:—Dr. Allchin.	2 Natural Sci. Entrance Scholarships (one each year).	£60 each.	2 years.	Competitive Exam. in subjects of Preliminary of London Univ.	Perpetual Course at Westminster Hosp.
	Guthrie Scholarship.	£60 per annum.	2 years.	Open Competitive Exam. among Candidates under 25 years of age in Latin, Mathematics, Experimental Physics, Chemistry, and French or German.	Perpetual Course at Westminster Hosp.
	Ent. Schship. No. 2.	£40.	2 years.	Ditto.	
	" Nos. 3 and 4.	£20.	2 years each.	Ditto.	
	" Nos. 5 and 6.	£10 per annum.	2 years each.	As above, save that Dental Students only can compete.	
	Rutherford Alcock.	£20 per annum.	2 years.	Open Competition in Chemistry and Experimental Physics.	
	Governors.	"	"		
	2 Senr. Scholarships.	£20 per annum.	2 years. each.	Competitive Exam. among Oxford and Cambridge Students in Anatomy and Physiology.	
	Treasurer's Prize.	£10 10s.	...	Competitive Exam. among First-year Students in Anatomy, Physiology, and Chemistry.	

Institution.	*Medical Scholarships, &c.*	*Annual or total value.*	*How long tenable.*	*How obtainable.*	*Conditions attached to tenure.*
Westminster Hospital, *continued.*	President's Prize.	£21.	...	Competitive Ex. among Second-year Students in Anatomy, Physiology and Histology.	
	Chadwick Prize.	£21 in books or instruments.	...	Competitive Ex. among Medical Students in Anatomy, Physiology, Histology, Medicine, Surgery, and Midwifery.	
	Bird Prize.	£14 with books or instruments.	...	Competitive Exam. in Medicine, Midwifery, Diseases of Women and Children, and Pathology.	
	2 Clinical Prizes, Medicine & Surgery.	£5 each in books or instruments.	...	Competitive Exam.	
Queen's College, Birmingham.	Sands Cox Prize.	£20.	...	Competitive Examination among Students who have completed their curriculum in Medicine, Surgery, and Midwifery.	
	Sydenham's Scholarship.	£10 10*s.* per annum.	3 years.	Award of Council to orphan sons of Medical Practitioners.	Good conduct and regl. attndnce. at Lectures.
	Queen's Scholarship.	£10 10*s.* per annum.	3 years.	Competitive Examination among sons of Medical Practitioners under 20 years of age in Arts Subjects and Chemistry and Osteology.	Good conduct and regl. attndnce. at Lectures.

	Open.	£10 10*s.* per annum.	3 years.	Similar subjects, but open to all Competitors.	
	Kigtely Scholarship.	£10.	...	Competitive Examination among Students in Midwifery and Diseases of Women.	
	Dental.	£7 17*s.* 6*d.*	2 years.	Similar subjects.	
BRISTOL MEDICAL SCHOOL. (Affiliated to Univ. Coll., Bristol.) E. Markham Skerritt, M.D.	Entrance Scholarship. No. 1.	£36 15*s.*	...	Competitive Examination among Medical Students in Subjects of General Education.	Perpetual Students.
	" No. 2.	£10 10*s.*		Ditto.	
	Clark Prize.	£15 15*s.*	...	Class Work of Third-yr. Stds.	
LEEDS—Yorkshire Coll. Medical Department (formerly Leeds Sch. of Medicine). Dean. — T. Scattergood.	Entrance Scholarship.	Total value, £63, being composition fees for lectures, &c.	Through curriculum.	Competitive Examination among Medical Students who have passed Preliminary Scientific Exam. at Lon. or Vict. Univ.	Whole medical curriculum to be taken at Yorkshire College and Leeds Infirmary.
	Infirmary Scholarship.	Total value, £42, being fees for Hospital attendance and Clinical Lectures.	Ditto.	Competitive Examination at beginning of curriculum.	Ditto.
	Hardwick Prize.	£10.	...	Competitive Exam. among Clinical Clerk Students of 2 years' standing in Clinical Medicine.	

Institution.	*Medical Scholarships, &c.*	*Annual or total value.*	*How long tenable.*	*How obtainable.*	*Conditions attached to tenure.*
Leeds (*continued*)—					
Leeds General Infirmary.	Entrance Scholship. The total value is a composition fee for Hospital Practice and Clinical instruction.	£42.		Open Competitive Examination in English, Latin, Mathematics, and a foreign language.	Whole medical curriculum to be taken at Yrkshre. Col.& Leeds Infirmary.
University College, Liverpool.	Holt Tutorial Scholarship. No. 1.	£100.	1 year.	Vote of Faculty to Senior Student of not less than 2 years' residence.	Teaching & Original Research.
	" No. 2.	£100.	1 year.		
	Lyon Jones Scholarship. No. 1.	£21 per annum.	2 years.	Open Competitive Exam. among Students in Arts Subjects.	Perpetual Course at Vict. Univ.
	" No. 2.	£21.	"	Competitive Examination among Third-year Students in Anatomy, Physiology, Chemistry, and Materia Medica.	
	Derby Exhibition.	£15.	1 year.	Competitive Examination among Third or Fourth-year Students in Clinical Subjects.	

CHISWICK PRESS: C. WHITTINGHAM AND CO., TOOKS COURT, CHANCERY LANE.

A SELECT LIST OF

WHITTAKER & CO.'S WORKS FOR THE STUDY OF MODERN LANGUAGES.

FRENCH.

WHITTAKER'S SERIES OF MODERN FRENCH AUTHORS.

WITH INTRODUCTION AND NOTES BY J. BOIELLE,

Senior French Master at Dulwich College; late Examiner in French to the Intermediate Examination Board, Ireland.

For Beginners.

LA BELLE NIVERNAISE. Histoire d'un vieux bateaux et de son équipage. By Alphonse Daudet. With Introduction, Notes, and Vocabulary, and Six Illustrations. *Third Edition, Revised.* 2*s.*

"The notes are apposite and well expressed."—*Journal of Education.*

For advanced Students.

BUG JARGAL. By Victor Hugo. With Life, Notes, &c. 3*s.*

"Intended as the book is for the use of the *Middle* Forms of Public Schools, the Editor has striven in the notes to elucidate points of Syntax as they occur, and to make the study of the book a help in a certain measure to the more advanced French composition which should be begun at this stage of the learner's work."—*Preface.*

"Well adapted for a shell, or lower fifth form."—*Journal of Education.*

URSULE MIROUËT. By Honoré de Balzac. With Introduction, Biographical Notice, and Notes. Cloth. 3*s.*

MODERN FRENCH COURSE.

By A. Barrère, Professor R.M.A., Woolwich.

JUNIOR GRADUATED FRENCH COURSE. Affording materials for Translation, Grammar, and Conversation. Being an Introduction to the Graduated French Course. 1*s.* 6*d.*

ELEMENTS OF FRENCH GRAMMAR AND First Steps in Idioms. With numerous Exercises and a Vocabulary. Being an Introduction to the Précis of Comparative French Grammar. Crown 8vo. 2*s.*

PRÉCIS OF COMPARATIVE FRENCH GRAMMAR and Idioms, and Guide to Examinations. *Third Edition Revised.* Cloth. 3*s.* 6*d.*

RÉCITS MILITAIRES. With Biographical Introductions and English Notes. Compiled by A. Barrère, Professor R.M.A., Woolwich. *Second Edition, Revised.* Crown 8vo. 3*s.*

"To make this book, which has been received with much favour, of still more practical utility to readers of French military works, a copious vocabulary of French military words has been appended."—*Preface to Second Edition.*

Prof. Barrère's books are in use at Uppingham School, Malvern College, Bedford Grammar School, R.M.A., Woolwich, &c., &c.

ELEMENTARY FRENCH READER. By John F. Davis, D.Lit., M.A., Assistant-Examiner in English in the University of London; and Ferdinand Thomas, B.A., B.Sc., Assistant Examiner in French in the University of London. With Vocabulary. Crown 8vo, cloth. 160 pp., 2*s.*

ARMY EXAMINATION PAPERS. French Questions set at the Preliminary Examinations for Sandhurst and Woolwich, from November, 1876, to June, 1890. With a comprehensive Vocabulary by J. F. Davis, D.Lit., M.A., Assistant Examiner in the University of London. Crown 8vo, 2*s.* 6*d.*

A GRADUATED FRENCH EXAMINATION Course. By Paul Barbier, Lecturer in French Language and Literature in the South Wales University College, and the Cardiff Technical School; Examiner to the Intermediate Education Board for Ireland, the Cambridge and Oxford Universities Syndicates, &c. Crown 8vo. 3*s.*

THE PUBLIC EXAMINATION FRENCH Reader. With a Vocabulary to every extract suitable for all Students who are preparing for a French Examination. By A. M. Bower, F.R.G.S., late Master in University College School, &c. Cloth. 3*s.* 6*d.*

BOSSUT'S FRENCH PHRASE BOOK. *New Edition.* 1*s.*

BOSSUT'S FRENCH WORD BOOK. *New Edition.* 1*s.*

DELILLE'S NEW GRADUATED FRENCH COURSE.

The Beginner's own French Book. 2*s.* **Key,** 2*s.*

Easy French Poetry for Beginners. 2*s.*

French Grammar. 3*s.* 6*d.* **Key,** 3*s.*

Repertoire des Prosateurs. 3*s.* 6*d.*

Modèles de Poesie. 3*s.* 6*d.*

Manuel Etymologique. 2*s.* 6*d.*

Synoptical Table of French Verbs. 6*d.*

WHITTAKER'S FRENCH SERIES.

For the use of Schools and Private Students. Edited by Professor A. Barrère, F. E. A. Gasc, and others. Each number with a literary Introduction and Arguments in English, footnotes explaining the more difficult passages, and translations of the idiomatic expressions into the corresponding English idioms. *Now Ready*, fcap. 8vo, sewed, each number, 6*d.*; limp cloth, 9*d.*

SCRIBE. **Le Verre D'Eau.** Barrère.

MOLIÈRE. **Le Bourgeois Gentilhomme.** Gasc.

MOLIÈRE. **L'Avare.** Gasc.

SOUVESTRE. **Sous la Tonnelle.** Desages.

MOLIÈRE. **Le Misanthrope.** Gasc.

GALLAND. **Ali Baba.** Clare.

CORNEILLE. **Le Cid.** Gasc.

LAMARTINE. **Jeanne D'Arc.** Barrère. (1*s.*)

PIRON. **La Metromanie.** Delbos. (1*s.*)

RACINE. **Andromaque.** Gasc.

RACINE. **Iphigénie.** Gasc.

MOLIERE. **Les Précieuses Ridicules.** Gasc.

RACINE. **Athalie.** Gasc.

RACINE. **Les Plaideurs.** Gasc.

OLLENDORFF'S (Dr. H. G.) Method of Learning French in Six Months. 12mo, 6*s.* 6*d.* Key, 8vo. 7*s.*

GERMAN.

WHITTAKER'S SERIES OF MODERN GERMAN AUTHORS.

First Series.—FOR BEGINNERS.

Edited, with a Grammatical Introduction, Notes, and a Vocabulary, by Professor F. Lange and Dr. H. Hager, Examiner in German at the London University.

HEY'S FABELN FUR KINDER. Illustrated by O. Speckter. Edited, with an Introduction, Grammatical Summary, Words, Notes, and a Vocabulary, by F. Lange, Ph.D., Professor. Cloth, 1*s.* 6*d.*

THE SAME. With a Phonetic Introduction, Phonetic Transcription of the Text. By F. Lange, Ph.D., Professor. Cloth, 2*s.*

Second Series.—FOR INTERMEDIATE STUDENTS.

Edited, with Biographical Introduction, Notes, and complete Vocabulary, by Professor F. Lange and Dr. H. Hager.

DOCTOR WESPE. Lustspiel in Fünf Aufzügen von Julius Roderich Benedix. Edited by Frans Lange, Ph.D., Professor. 2*s.* 6*d.*

Third Series.—FOR ADVANCED STUDENTS.

Edited, with a Critical Introduction and Notes, by Professor F. Lange, in co-operation with F. Storr, B.A., A. A. Macdonell, M.A., and H. Hager, Ph.D.

MEISTER MARTIN, der Kufner. Erzählung von E. T. A. Hoffmann. Edited by Professor F. Lange, Ph.D. Price 1*s.* 6*d.*

"An exceedingly well-written story of burgher life in the sixteenth century. Besides the interest of the plot, the pure and simple style and the faithful picture of middle-class mediæval life make the story admirably suited for use as an advanced reading book."—*Saturday Review.*

HANS LANGE. Schauspiel von Paul Heyse. Edited by A. A. Macdonell, M.A., Ph.D., Taylorian Teacher, University, Oxford. *Anthorized Edition.* Price 2*s.*

AUF WACHE. Novelle von B. Auerbach.—**DER GEFRORENE KUSS.** Novelle von O. Roquette. Edited by A. A. Macdonell, M.A. *Authorized Edition.* Price 2*s.*

Two novelettes of great literary merit. They are very successful pictures of various phases of German social life.

"The story is original, the interest is well sustained, and the easy every-day style makes it very suitable reading for students who wish to become familiar with colloquial German. The notes in lucidity and intelligence are much above the average."—*Saturday Review.*

DER BIBLIOTHEKAR. Lustspiel von G. von Moser. Edited by Professor F. Lange, Ph.D. *Authorized and Fourth Edition.* Price 2*s.*

EINE FRAGE. Idyll von Georg Ebers. Edited by F. Storr, B.A., Chief Master of Modern Subjects in Merchant Taylors' School. *Authorized Edition.* 2*s.*

DIE JOURNALISTEN. Lustspiel von Gustav Freytag. Edited by Professor F. Lange, Ph.D. *Authorized Edition.* Fourth revised Edition. 2*s.* 6*d.*

"If ever modern languages are to make good their claim to form a mental discipline and gymnastic, which may be advantageously substituted for classical training in the case of those whose formal studies end with school life, an editor of modern works must follow the lead Whitney has shown in his masterly compilation of a German-English Dictionary, *i.e.*, he must point out to the student the correspondences of the two languages, and make him acquainted with the gradual growth of word, meaning, and phrase, and with the practical side of comparative philology."—*Preface.*

ZOPF UND SCHWERT. Lustspiel von Karl Gutzkow. Edited by Professor F. Lange, Ph.D. 2*s.* 6*d.*

"The notes abound in useful information, giving the literal meaning and grammatical construction as well as suitable renderings of idiomatic phrases. The etymology of words is also traced out at length."—*Athenæum.*

GERMAN EPIC TALES. Die Nibelungen. Erzählung aus A. F. C. Vilmar's Deutscher National Literatur. Walther und Hildegund. Erzählung von Albert Richter. Edited by Karl Neuhaus, Ph.D. *Authorized Edition.* 2*s.* 6*d.*

EKKEHARD. Erzählung des zehnten Jahrhunderts, von Victor von Scheffel. Abridged Edition, with Introduction and Notes by Herman Hager, Ph.D., Lecturer in the German Language and Literature in the Owens College, Victoria University, Manchester. 3*s.*

FLUGEL'S COMPLETE DICTIONARY of the **German and English Languages.** *New Edition.* 2 vols. 8vo, £1 1*s.*

ABRIDGED EDITION, royal 18mo, 6*s.*

OLLENDORFF'S Method of Learning German in Six **Months.** Crown 8vo, 7*s.* Key, 8vo, 7*s.*

A COMPLETE GERMAN COURSE FOR USE IN PUBLIC SCHOOLS.

EDITED BY F. LANGE, PH.D.

Professor, Royal Military Academy, Woolwich; Examiner in German Language and Literature in the Victoria University, Manchester; and to the College of Preceptors.

GERMAN GRAMMAR. With especial reference to Phonology, Comparative Philology, English and German Correspondences, and idioms. In Three parts.

PART I.—ELEMENTARY ACCIDENCE AND SYNTAX. 2*s.*

PART II.—ACCIDENCE SUPPLEMENTED AND SYNTAX CONTINUED. 2*s.*

PART. III.—A CONCISE BUT COMPLETE SURVEY OF GERMAN GRAMMAR. 3*s.* 6*d.*

PROGRESSIVE GERMAN EXAMINATION Course. In Three Parts. Comprising the Elements of German Grammar, an Historical Sketch of the Teutonic Languages, English and German Correspondences, Materials for Translation, Dictation, Extempore Translation, Conversation, and complete Vocabularies.

1. Elementary Course. Cloth, 2*s*.
2. Intermediate Course. Cloth, 2*s*.
3. Advanced Course. *Second Revised Edition.* Cloth, 1*s*. 6*d*.

ELEMENTARY GERMAN READER. A Graduated Collection of Readings in Prose and Poetry. With English Notes and a Vocabulary. *Third Edition.* 1*s*. 6*d*.

ADVANCED GERMAN READER. A Graduated Collection of Readings in Prose and Poetry. With English Notes. By F. Lange, Ph.D., and J. F. Davis, M.A., D.Lit. 3*s*.

ITALIAN.

BARETTI'S DICTIONARY of the English and Italian Languages. New Edition, entirely rewritten. By G. Comelati and J. Davenport. 2 vols., 8vo, £1 1*s*.

GRAGLIA'S NEW POCKET DICTIONARY of the Italian and English Languages. With considerable Additions, and a Compendious Elementary Italian Grammar. 18mo, cloth, 4*s*. 6*d*.

OLLENDORFF'S Method of Learning Italian in Six Months. Crown 8vo, 7*s*. Key, 8vo, 7*s*.

SPANISH.

PONCE DE LEON'S SPANISH DICTIONARY. Containing the Terms and Phrases used in the applied Sciences, Fine Arts, Mechanics, Metallurgy, Agriculture, Navigation, Commerce, Engineering, &c., &c.

Vol. I. English-Spanish, £1 16*s*.
Vol. II. Spanish-English. *In the press.*

NEUMAN AND BARETTI'S DICTIONARY of the English and Spanish Languages. Revised. 2 vols., 8vo, £1 8*s*. Abridged, 18mo, 5*s*.

OLLENDORFF'S Method of Learning Spanish in Six Months. 8vo, 12*s*. Key, 8vo, 7*s*.

MESSRS. BELL'S EDUCATIONAL WORKS

FOR THE EXAMINATIONS OF 1892-93.

ENGLISH—Annotated Editions.

Notes on Shakespeare's King Lear—Merchant of Venice—Tempest—Julius Cæsar—Macbeth—Midsummer Night's Dream—Hamlet—Richard II.—Henry V. With Historical and Critical Introduction, Summary, Notes Etymological and Explanatory, Appendices on Prosody, Grammatical Peculiarities, &c. By T. Duff Barnett, B.A. (Lond.) *1s.* each.

Milton—Paradise Lost. Book I. and Book II. With Notes on the Analysis and on the Scriptural and Classical Allusions, a Glossary of Difficult Words, and Life of Milton. By C. P. Mason, B.A., F.C.P. Fifth Edition. *1s.* each.

Boswell's Life of Johnson. 1780—1784. Napier's Edition, Vols. III. and IV. *3s. 6d.* each.

Gray's Poetical Works. Edited by John Bradshaw, LL.D. *2s. 6d.*

Lamb's Essays of Elia. *1s.*

Sheridan's The Critique. *1s.*

Burke's Thoughts on the Present Discontents. *3s. 6d.*

LATIN—Annotated Editions.

Cæser—De Bello Gallico. Edited by George Long, M.A. *4s.*

Cæsar—De Bello Gallico. Book I. Edited by G. Long, M.A. With Vocabulary, *1s. 6d.*

Cæsar—De Bello Gallico. By Books I. to III. By George Long, M.A. *1s. 6d.*

Cæsar—De Bello Gallico. Books IV. and V. By George Long, M.A. *1s. 6d.*

Cicero—De Senectute. By George Long, M.A. *1s. 6d.*

Cicero—De Amicitia. By George Long, M.A. *1s. 6d.*

Cornelius Nepos. By J. F. Macmichael, M.A. *2s.*

Horace. Edited, with Notes, by A. J. Macleane, M.A. *3s. 6d.*

Horace—Odes, Carmen Seculare and Epodes. By A. J. Macleane, M.A. *2s.*

Horace—Odes. Book I. With Notes by A. J. Macleane, M.A., and Vocabulary. *1s. 6d.*

Horace—Satires, Epistles, and Art of Poetry. By A. J. Macleane, M.A. *2s.*

Juvenal—Sixteen Satires (Expurgated). By Herman Prior, M.A. *3s. 6d.*

Latin Unseen Papers—Prose and Verse. By T. Collins, M.A. *2s. 6d.*

Livy. Books I., II., III., IV., V. By J. Prendeville. *1s. 6d.* each.

Livy. Book XXI. and Book XXII. By Rev. L. D. Dowdall, M.A., B.D. Each, *3s. 6d.*

Lucretius. Text only. Edited by H. A. J. Munro, M.A. *2s.*

Ovid—Fasti. By Dr. Paley. *3s. 6d.*: or in 3 vols. *1s. 6d.* each.

Sallust—Catilina and Jugurtha. By G. Long, M.A., and J. G. Fraser, *3s. 6d.*; or in 2 Parts, each, *2s.*

Tacitus—Germania and Agricola. By the Rev. P. Frost, M.A. *2s. 6d.*

Terence. Edited by W. Wagner, Ph.D. *7s. 6d.*

Terence—Andria and Phormio. By W. Wagner, Ph.D. *1s. 6d.* each.

LATIN.—Annotated Editions (*continued*)—

Virgil—Bucolics, Georgics, and Æneid. Books I.—IV. By the Rev. J. G. Shepherd, D.C.L. Abridged from Professor Conington's Edition. 4*s.* 6*d.*

Virgil—Æneid. Books V. to XII. Abridged from Professor Conington's Edition by H. Nettleship and W. Wagner, Ph.D. 4*s.* 6*d.*

Virgil. Book I. Professor Conington's Edition, abridged, with Notes and Vocabulary. 1*s.* 6*d.*

Virgil. 12 vols. Professor Conington's Edition, abridged. Bucolics: Georgics, I. and II.; Georgics, III. and IV.; Æneid I. and II.; Æneid III. and IV.; Æneid V. and VI. (2*s.*), Æneid VII., VIII., IX., X., XI., XII. 1*s.* 6*d.* each.

GREEK—Annotated Editions.

Aristophanes. Edited by H. A. Holden, LL.D. **The Acharnians,** 2*s.* **The Knights,** 1*s.* 6*d.*

Aristophanes' Acharnians. Edited by F. A. Paley. M.A. 4*s.* 6*d.*

Æschylus—Choephoroe, Eumenides, Prometheus Vinctus, Septem Contra Thebas. By F. A. Paley, LL.D. 1*s.* 6*d.* each.

Euripides—Ion (2*s.*), **Bacchæ, Hecuba, Hercules Furens, Medea.** By F. A. Paley, LL.D. Each, 1*s.* 6*d.*

Greek Unseen Papers—Prose and Verse. By T. Collins, M.A. 3*s.*

Homer—Iliad. Books I. to VI. Edited by F. A. Paley, M.A., LL.D. 2*s.* 6*d.*

Plato—Apology of Socrates and Crito. By W. Wagner, Ph.D. 2*s.* 6*d.*

Sallust—Catilina. Edited by George Long, M.A. 2*s.*

Sophocles—Antigone, Electra, Œdipus Coloneus. By F. A. Paley, LL.D. Each 1*s.* 6*d.*

Sophocles—Philoctetes, Trachiniæ. By F. A. Paley, LL.D. 2*s.* 6*d.* each.

Thucydides. Book I. Edited by R. Shilleto, M.A. 6*s.* 6*d.* Book II. 5*s.* 6*d.*

Xenophon—Anabasis. Book I. By J. F. Macmichael, M.A. 1*s.* 6*d.*

Xenophon—Anabasis. Books II. and III. By J. F. Macmichael, M.A. 1*s.* 6*d.*

Xenophon—Anabasis. Books IV. and V. By J. F. Macmichael, M.A. 1*s.* 6*d.*

Xenophon—Cyropædia. Books I. and III. By G. M. Gorham, M.A. Each 1*s.* 6*d.*

Xenophon—Hellenica. Books I. and II. By the Rev. L. D. Dowdall, M.A., B.D. 2*s.* each.

FRENCH AND GERMAN.

Schiller—William Tell. Translated by Sir Theodore Martin, LL.D. 3*s.* 6*d.*

Schiller—Wallenstein. By Dr. A. Buchheim. 5*s.* Or the **Lager** and Piccolomini together, 2*s.* 6*d.* **Wallenstein's Tod,** 2*s.* 6*d.*

Goethe—Hermann und Dorothea. By E. Bell, M.A., and E. Wölfel. 1*s.* 6*d.*

Hauff's Caravan. Translated by Prof. S. Mendel. 1*s.*

Schiller's Poems. Translated by Sir E. A. Bowring, C.B. 3*s.* 6*d.*

FRENCH AND GERMAN—*continued.*

Voltaire—Charles XII. By L, Direy. 1*s.* 6*d.*

GOMBERT'S FRENCH DRAMA. Revised by F. E. A. Gasc. 6*d.* each.

Molière—Les Femmes Savantes, Les Fourberies de Scapin, Les Précieuses Ridicules.

Racine—Iphigénie, Britannicus, Phèdre, Esther, Athalie.

Corneille—Le Cid, Horace, Cinna, Polyeucte.

Concise Dictionary of the French and English Languages. Fourth Edition. Thoroughly revised, with New Supplements (42 pages). By F. E. A. Gasc. 10*s.* 6*d.*

Pocket Dictionary of the French and English Languages. By F. E. A. Gasc. Forty-Fifth Thousand, with Additions and Corrections. 2*s.* 6*d.*

German Prose Composition. By Dr. C. A. Buchheim, Professor of German Language and Literature in King's College, and Examiner in German to the London University. Fourteenth Edition, Revised. 4*s.* 6*d.*

KEY to 1st and 2nd Parts, 3*s.* To 3rd and 4th Parts, 4*s.*

MATHEMATICS.

Arithmetic. With Examination Papers and nearly 8,000 Examples. By C. Pendlebury, M.A., Senior Mathematical Master, St. Paul's School. Fifth Edition, with or without Answers. Crown 8vo., 4*s.* 6*d.* In Two Parts, 2*s.* 6*d.* each.

The EXAMPLES, in a Separate Volume, price 3*s.*

In use at Winchester, Wellington, Marlborough, Charterhouse, St. Paul's, Merchant Taylors', Christ's Hospital, Sherborne, Shrewsbury, &c., &c.

Examination Papers in Arithmetic. By the same Author. 2*s.* 6*d.*

KEY, for Tutors and Private Students only, 5*s.*

Arithmetic. By the Rev. C. Elsee, M.A., Mathematical Master at Rugby. Fourteenth Edition. 3*s.* 6*d.*

Algebra. By the Rev. C. Elsee, M.A. Eighth Edition. 4*s.*

Euclid. Books I-VI., and part of Book XI. By Horace Deighton, M.A., Head Master of Harrison College, Barbados. New Translation from the Greek Text, with numerous Riders and Chapters on Radical Axis, Poles and Polars, Transversals, Centres of Similitude, Harmonic Proportion, Plain Loci, &c. Second Edition, Revised, with Symbols and Abbreviations. Crown 8vo, 4*s.* 6*d.* Or in Parts: Book I., 1*s.*; Books I. and II., 1*s.* 6*d.*; Books I. to III., 2*s.* 6*d.*; Books III. and IV., 1*s.* 6*d.* Key (for Masters only), 4*s.* 6*d.*

Analytical Geometry for Schools. By Rev. T. G. Vyvyan, M.A. Fifth Edition. 4*s.* 6*d.*

Trigonometry, Introduction to Plane. By the Rev. T. G. Vyvyan, M.A. Third Edition. 3*s.* 6*d.*

Trigonometry, Examination Papers in. By G. H. Ward, M.A. 2*s.* 6*d.* Key, 5*s.*

Elementary Trigonometry. By J. M. Dyer, M.A., and Rev. R. H. Whitcombe, M.A. (Assistant Masters at Eion College). 4*s.* 6*d.*

Conics, The Elementary Geometry of. By C. Taylor, D.D., Master of St. John's College, Cambridge. Seventh Edition. 4*s.* 6*d.*

Conic Sections treated Geometrically. By W. H. Besant, D.Sc. Eighth Edition. 4*s.* 6*d.* Solutions to Examples, 4*s.* Enunciations and Figures, separately, 1*s.* 6*d.*

MATHEMATICS—*continued.*

Geometrical Optics, An Elementary Treatise on. By W. Steadman Aldis, M.A. Third Edition. 4*s.*

Astronomy, Introduction to Plane. By R. T. Main, M.A. Fifth Edition. 4*s.*

Solid Geometry, An Elementary Treatise on. By W. Steadman Aldis, M.A. Fourth Edition. Crown 8vo, 6*s.*

Hydrostatics, Elementary. By W. H. Besant, D.Sc., F.R.S. Fourteenth Edition. 4*s.* Solutions to the Examples, 4*s.*

Hydromechanics, A Treatise on. By W. H. Besant, M.A., D.Sc. Fifth Edition. Part I., Hydrostatics. 5*s.*

Elementary Dynamics, for the Use of Colleges and Schools. By William Garnett, M.A., D.C.L. Fifth Edition, revised. 6*s.*

Dynamics, A Treatise on. By W. H. Besant, D.Sc., F.R.S. 7*s.* 6*d.*

Heat. An Elementary Treatise. By W. Garnett, M.A., D.C.L.

The only authorized and complete "Webster."

WEBSTER'S INTERNATIONAL DICTIONARY.

An entirely New Edition, thoroughly Revised, considerably Enlarged, and Reset in New Type. Medium 4to, cloth, £1 11*s.* 6*d.*; half-calf, £2 2*s.*; half-russia, £2 5*s.*; calf, £2 8*s.* Also in 2 vols., cloth, £1 14*s.*

In addition to the Dictionary of Words, with their pronunciation, alternative spellings, etymology, and various meanings, illustrated by quotations and numerous woodcuts, there are several valuable appendices, comprising:—

A Pronouncing Gazetteer of the World; Vocabularies of Scripture, Greek, Latin, and English Proper Names; A Dictionary of the Noted Names of Fiction; A Brief History of the English Language; A Dictionary of Foreign Quotations, Words, Phrases, Proverbs, &c.; A Biographical Dictionary with 10,000 Names; A Classified Selection of Illustrations (filling 82 pages), &c., &c.

"We believe that, all things considered, this will be found to be the best existing English dictionary in one volume."—*Guardian.*

"We recommend the new Webster to every man of business, every father of a family, every teacher, and almost every student—to everybody, in fact, who is likely to be posed at an unfamiliar or half-understood word or phrase." —*St. James's Gazette.*

"A most ample, trustworthy, and cheap lexicon, not excelled for the purpose of general use by any other one-volume dictionary of the language."—*Daily Chronicle.*

"It i the most comprehensive and most useful of its kind."—*National Observer.*

Prospectus, with Specimen Pages, on application.

www.ingramcontent.com/pod-product-compliance
Lightning Source LLC
Chambersburg PA
CBHW071409050326
40689CB00010B/1802

* 9 7 8 1 1 4 2 8 1 3 1 5 4 *